# THE CANARY ISLANDS

# Landscapes of the Imagination

*Landscapes*

# THE CANARY ISLANDS
## A *Cultural History*

PETER STONE

Signal Books
*Oxford*

First published in 2014 by
Signal Books Limited
36 Minster Road
Oxford OX4 1LY
www.signalbooks.co.uk

A catalogue record for this book is available from the British Library

ISBN 978-1-908493-99-6 Paper

Cover Design: Devdan Sen
Production: Devdan Sen
Cover Images: Karol Kozlowski/shutterstock.com; Vcarceler/Wikimedia Commons; Cesar Gonzalez/Wikimedia Commons
Printed and bound in India by Imprint Digital Limited

# Contents

# Introduction

In 1963, aged 22, having already lived briefly amid the olive-lined hills of Andalusia, the delectable coves of the Costa Brava and the dusty table-lands of Castile, I set foot for the first time on Las Palmas de Gran Canaria to start a year's contract as a hotel receptionist.

I arrived by sea and took a taxi from the port along avenues lined with exotic shrubs and flowers and past squares filled with small dark green trees from whose foliage small brilliantly hued birds would rise squawking en masse. Above me a myriad of multicoloured houses clung impossibly to steep slopes and lined starkly volcanic cliff-tops. Palm trees were every-where. The air was balmy. Birds sang. The temperature was around 25°C.

A transient hotel guest from London needed me as a translator on one of my free mornings to help him settle matters at a modest property he and his wife were thinking of buying in Maspalomas, down at the island's extreme southern tip. We drove along a narrow road that curved round the south-east shoreline past dusty gorges, gritty forbidding crags and—as I recall—one shockingly surrealistic orange-grey mound of vol-canic earth that resembled a melted blancmange. We paused at a roadside shack for coffee and then continued on past palm and prickly pear oases and grey-black beaches lapped by a cobalt sea.

After an hour and a half we finally reached our destination: a light-house, a huge expanse of sand dunes, some wandering camels and an all but deserted beach called Playa del Inglés. The air was salty, the breeze warm and relaxing and the silence almost total. As we sat together in the simple stone-built house overlooking the dunes, sipping dirt cheap *cuba libres* and indulging in a halting three-way conversation with the prop-erty's owner, none of us remotely imagined the monster international resort this area would become. (For sure the owner would have charged a good deal more if he had.)

Summer was off season—more visitors came for the mild winters—and the hotel was hardly overloaded with guests. One colourful fiesta evening, however, four young English musicians checked in wearing suits with strange collarless jackets. They were all about the same age as me and their apparent leader, whose name featured on the register as Richard

Starkey, glanced back at the raucous activities going on in the square outside and was excited yet cautious about joining in. "Hey, they won't beat us up or anything if we go out there, will they?" he asked in strong Liverpudlian tones, his face generously open and friendly. I assured him they would not and when he realized I was English he shook my hand and exhorted the others to follow suit. Only one, coolly quiet, did so while the other two eyed me edgily. It was a month or so before I saw their photos by chance in a magazine and realized they were The Beatles, and that Ringo and George had shaken my hand while John and Paul, perhaps already aware of the colossal fame that was still to come, remained sensibly aloof.

My working hours easily allowed free time for the odd swim. A twenty-minute bus ride north along the narrow sprawl of the lower town brought me to Las Canteras beach, which faced west on a narrow isthmus. Further on was the bare, dusty, circular headland of La Isleta. On the eastern side of the isthmus stood the busy port and the adjoining smaller beach of Alcaravaneras. But Las Canteras held the palm. It was a gentle curve of golden sand backed by a hotel and café-lined promenade and washed clean twice a day by the tidal Atlantic, protected from rough seas by a mile-long offshore reef. In its clear waters swimmers would come face to face with hordes of tiny, brightly coloured multi-shaped fish never seen in the Mediterranean It made me suddenly realize how far south I was. Bronzed girls, long dark hair slicked down their backs as they emerged from the waters, sauntered along to bask on the sands or on adjoining rocks alongside fat pink German tourists reading two-day-old editions of *Die Zeit*.

In other free hours I sometimes taught English to Alfonso, a bald, bespectacled forty-something freelance journalist from Madrid, who had decided to move to the island to escape the stress of the Spanish capital. All he wanted to do was to converse about anything that entered his mind while driving round the island. So with him I managed to see the black canyons and peaks of the central Cruz de Tejeda and the stark seaside cliffs known as the *Dedo de Dios* (Finger of God) near Puerto de las Nieves with its jet black shingle beach on the north-west coast near Agaete. All the time we chatted about London, the British class system, the mysteries of cricket and suchlike. "You mean the game goes on for five days?" he asked incredulously when I described test matches with Australia, India and Pakistan.

One of the most memorable drives took us to the rum-producing town of Arucas, whose botanical gardens, known as the Jardín de la Marquesa or Jardín de las Hespérides, had been owned by the family of the Marqués de Arucas since 1880. The mansion at their centre, white and elegant, was set a dark sea of green, a rich carpet-like expanse of banana plantations. The gardens did not open to the public until over two decades after my departure from the island, however, so while I could read about their 200-year-old Dragon tree, colourful araucarias and jacarandas and 500 species of exotic plants and trees, I was tantalized by the fact that I could not see them. Even so, the imagined scene was evocative enough. Gran Canaria, along with other islands in the archipelago, has long claimed to be the real site of the mythical Garden of the Hesperides, whose golden apples were said to give eternal life. The Hesperides themselves were Grecian nymphs who tended the apples, the source of the sunset's golden light.

By the end of the year I was so intoxicated with the island that I wanted to live there forever. Destiny and curiosity subsequently drew me to a hundred other places but my heart always held a special place for this strange, wild island. Over the years I have returned time and time again, not just to Gran Canaria but to the other six different islands. I have switched allegiances: sometimes I favoured the moonscape of Lanzarote, other times the lush *caldera*-centred La Palma, both of which I explored on several occasions. For a while my favoured location was Valle del Rey in La Gomera, where friends had set up house and I passed a couple of happy winters, from there hopping across regularly to neighbouring Tenerife to climb (or, rather. ride by cable car) the 3,718-metre Mount Teide or saunter around the lovely capital Santa Cruz. Last of my island visits was to El Hierro a tiny volcanic gem with nothing but the wide Atlantic between it and the Americas.

## AROUND THE ISLANDS

This essentially African archipelago (Spanish only by virtue of conquest and the language spoken) is an endless source of romantic legends, from the Elysian Fields to the Isles of the Blest or the Greeks' Fortunate Isles. In all there are eleven islands: Tenerife, La Gomera, Gran Canaria, Fuerteventura, Lanzarote, La Palma, El Hierro, Graciosa, Alegranza, Monte Claro, and Lobos. Graciosa has a tiny community of approximately 700 people

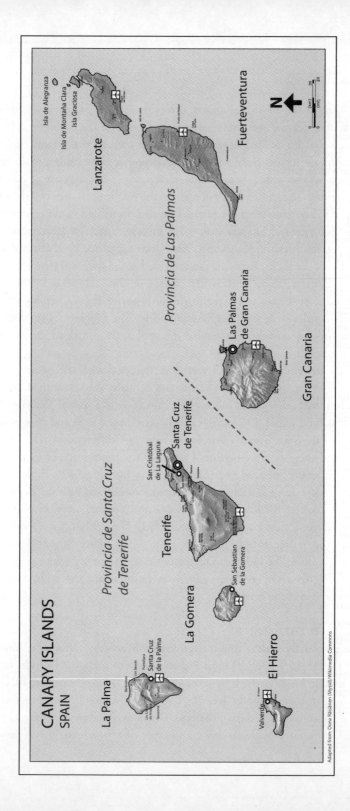

CANARY ISLANDS
SPAIN

La Palma

Provincia de Santa Cruz
de Tenerife

Santa Cruz
de la Palma

Provincia de Santa Cruz
de Tenerife

La Gomera

El Hierro

Valverde

San Sebastián
de la Gomera

Tenerife

San Cristóbal
de la Laguna

Santa Cruz
de Tenerife

Gran Canaria

Las Palmas
de Gran Canaria

Provincia de Las Palmas

Lanzarote

Isla de Alegranza
Isla de Montaña Clara
Isla Graciosa

Fuerteventura

N

who live permanently on the island, but the last three—all located (like Graciosa) offshore from Lanzarote—are uninhabited.

The islands are sometimes confused with Madeira, the Azores and Cape Verde, the territories comprising Macaronesia. There are other evocative references. Plato (in *Timaeus and Critias*) conjures up a land the size of Libya and Asia combined—just past the Pillars of Hercules—which sank without trace. This was Atlantis, the lost "Happy Continent" that basked in a perennial spring-like climate. Ovid, Homer, Plutarch, Pindar and Virgil all produced their versions of this dream paradise in brief or glowingly imaginative terms. Pliny the Elder, (who died when Vesuvius erupted in 79 AD) was the first historian to refer to the Canaries by name when he included them in his vast *Naturalis Historia* which had been commissioned by the Roman Emperor Titus. The work survives today as an invaluable chronicle of that era and his Nivaria has been identified as Tenerife.

There are various theories as to how the archipelago was formed. One is that a tremendous succession of earth- and sea-quakes plunged Plato's imaginary continent to the bottom of the ocean, leaving the seven highest peaks above the surface water level. Only here did life survive and resume its natural course. The theory of a possible Atlantidian submersion in the Miocene Age was also put forward as recently as the early twentieth century by the French geologist Pierre Termier, though his view is outside the mainstream. The general consensus by scientists and geologists today is that quite the reverse happened, and that the islands were cataclysmically formed around 30-40 million BC when a moving plate produced cracks in the seabed and floods of lava poured through. Admittedly, a huge seismic explosion did rock westerly El Hierro 50,000 years ago despatching massive portions of that tiny island into the depths, but that was a minor hiccup compared with what seems to have occurred when the islands were born. The gap remaining after this gigantic exodus of land is El Hierro's impressive amphitheatre-like Valle del Golfo.

The first person to put the islands, literally, on the map was the first-century Alexandrian astronomer, mathematician and geographer Ptolemy. Miraculously, considering the means at his disposal, he produced a fair depiction of the then known world with the Mediterranean at its centre and the Canaries, or Fortunate Isles, at its Atlantic-bordering extremity. He believed the zero meridian passed through the extreme western end of El

Hierro, and that the wild headland on which the Orchilla lighthouse now perches was the end of the world. (In 1884 it was officially confirmed that the meridian in fact passes through Greenwich in London.) Ptolemy accurately located the archipelago as being just off the north-western coast of Africa but instead of depicting seven different-shaped and different-sized Atlantic islands extending horizontally away from the continent he drew six small round-shaped islets equidistant from each other in a line stretching from north to south. This minor quibble apart, the mere fact that they had been identified by a cartographer in that comparative age of darkness, and had been included with some degree of accuracy in a map of that time, was a real breakthrough. A beam of light had at last fallen on them.

Though all volcanic in origin, each island is uniquely different. Lanzarote, nearest to Africa, is hauntingly and colourfully lunar in appearance. At its heart the region known as Malpais still shows the ravages of a six-year period of great eighteenth-century eruptions. The island has pools of green water, orange sand dunes, mauve-black cliffs and gleaming white villages, the most beautiful in all the archipelago. Its late much-lamented native artist-architect César Manrique did more to preserve and promote the essential Canarian character and atmosphere than any other creative soul in the archipelago.

Fuerteventura, its southerly neighbour, is the oldest and second largest island, yet one of the least populated (its capital Puerto del Rosario has a modest 20,000 inhabitants.) Shaped roughly like a sperm whale, it resembles a vast sand dune that has strayed out into the ocean from the Sahara. I once flew over it on my way from Tunisia to London and could see nothing below but a colossal expanse of muted yellow scarred by occasional shadowy ochre clefts and fringed by the deep blue, white flecked, ever moving Atlantic. Arid hillocks, dunes, waves and sea breezes predominate, and those drawn to it today tend to be yachtsmen, wind- or kite-surfers and lovers of peace and quiet. In the past artists and odd literary geniuses like Miguel de Unamuno made brief recuperative stays here.

Gran Canaria is the third largest and by far the most heavily populated island. On a map it looks like a hand grenade with the capital Las Palmas in the north-east representing the pin. The city is the biggest and most cosmopolitan in the archipelago and also boasts one of the best urban beaches in the world: calm-watered, reef-protected Las Canteras. Though

The spectacular landscape of Fuerteventura (Hansueli Krapf/Wikimedia Commons)

the south coast is marred by the sprawling mass tourist resort of Playa del Inglés—whose adjoining overdeveloped sand dune area of Maspalomas is unrecognizable since my first visit—most of the mountainous inland and northern areas remain fairly unspoilt. The island's most notable literary son is Perez Galdós (who as a social commentator of his times became for Madrid—where he moved as a young man—what Dickens was for London). His house museum is located in the capital's traditional quarter of La Vegueta.

Moving west we come to Tenerife, large, triangular-shaped and rising conically from the sea, with Spain's highest mountain, Teide, at its centre. Falling away on either side of this monumental peak are two landscapes so dramatically different it is as if the island has been severed and had two totally different pieces of land attached to it. To the north the landscape is green and fertile with lush banana plantations, wild black coastal cliffs and volcanic soot-hued beaches. To the south lies a wild, barren semi-desert with scrub tufted plains, dried up *arroyos* and long grey-ochre beaches bordered by orderly mass-market resorts like Playa de las Americas with its golden sands imported from the Sahara. The beautiful flower-filled capital Santa Cruz rivals Las Palmas as the Canaries' most cosmopolitan city, with wide avenues and intricate old district that are a delight to explore at leisure.

La Gomera, like some satellite appendage to Tenerife, is just a short ferry ride from its Big Brother. Circular-shaped and mountainous from end to end, the island has long been popular with both nature enthusiasts and hikers. Its magnificent Garajonay National Park is a UNESCO World Heritage site, cut by deep ravines filled with *laurasilva* (laurel rain forests) and subject to constant weather changes, from bright sunshine to swirling treacherous mists. (Most of the park is mercifully still intact in spite of a disastrous forest fire in the summer of 2012.) A strikingly steep coastline features some extraordinary natural phenomena such as Los Órganos, a surrealistic version of Northern Ireland's Giant's Causeway, while its uncompromisingly rugged terrain, notably difficult for communication, helped give birth to the island's unique whistling language, *el silbo*. Its diminutive capital, San Sebastián, entry point for ferries on the east coast of the island, rises above a sheltered harbour in an amphitheatre-like array of multi-coloured houses.

Diamond-shaped La Palma, the most north-westerly of the islands and fifth largest in size, continues the lushness of northern Tenerife, though here the greenery is ubiquitous, transforming the entire island into a latter-day Garden of Eden. The tiny east coast capital of Santa Cruz de la Palma, which reached its trading heyday in the seventeenth century, is a historic gem filled with elegant period houses with traditional wooden balconies. Crisscrossed by narrow lanes, it sprawls downhill along a former lava flow surrounded by rich farmland. At the island's centre is the Caldera de Taburiente, a crater-shaped national park overlooked by the 2,400-metreRoque de los Muchachos peak and filled with towering Canary pines and junipers. (It was an almost impregnable retreat for the *benahoare* inhabitants when the first *conquistadores* arrived.) High up in these mountains is the northern hemisphere's most sophisticated observatory, home to the famed trio of Isaac Newton Telescopes which constantly monitor outer space.

The smallest and most westerly of all the Canaries is the rocky islet of El Hierro, known as the Meridian Island until the nineteenth century when the longitude zero (now at Greenwich) ran through it. Dotted with caves and an amazing number of volcanoes considering its size (a mere twenty kilometres from end to end) it has been declared a Biosphere Reserve by UNESCO. Three major landslides in the past 30,000 years transformed its appearance, especially in the north where the El Golfo depression looks as if a giant has taken a great bite out of the island. It is still highly vulnerable to seismic activities and those in the summer of 2011 were so strong that a total evacuation of the inhabitants was considered at one stage. On this occasion a volcano six metres underwater had erupted and its lava eventually emerged to form a tiny new island. Fortunately no persons or buildings were harmed.

Today each of these islands has its own distinct identity and is proud of both its individual and common heritage. Exactly where the very first settlers to this mystical, ocean-surrounded world came from was a puzzle for centuries. Now, thanks to DNA checks and carbon dating processes, it is generally agreed that their original homes were on a similar latitude in the neighbouring continent of Africa and that they left them to head west around 200 BC.

Before them there was a thirty million-year void. Only the odd primordial reptilian species, like the now virtually extinct El Hierro Giant Lizard, lived amid the lava-streaked slopes and rocky fissures. Volcanic disruptions, seismic upheavals, Atlantic storms and balmy weather all went unseen by man during that unimaginably long period on this wild and windy archipelago at the edge of the known world.

cဢ

he Virgin of Candelaria with Guanche worshippers, eighteenth-century painting, Icod de los Vinos, Tenerife (Wikimedia Commons)

*Part One*

# FROM GUANCHES TO CONQUISTADORES

Mencey Bencomo (Koppchen/Wikimedia Commons)

## *Chapter One*

# NATIVE CANARIANS

When, during those early days as a Canary Island traveller, I briefly worked as a hotel receptionist in Las Palmas I would regularly, at mealtimes in the basement staff *cantina*, find myself facing a sixteen-year-old kitchen apprentice called Raul who had dirty blonde, wild hair, a pale complexion, jutting jaw and semi-crouched, compact build. His apparently paradoxical Nordic features in these latitudes made little sense to me then. I even thought he might have some Viking blood in him. He was certainly aggressive enough. Clearly a magnificent career awaited him in the army, which he was intent on joining when he reached eighteen.

It was only later, after reading more of the history of the islands, that I deduced that he might have descended from the original Guanche inhabitants, members of a tall, fair, blue-eyed race known as the Mechta-el-Arbi who are said to have come from Mauretania (the old North African kingdom that extended from modern-day Morocco to western Algeria and was ruled in its heyday by the erudite historian King Juba II). Their tribal blood had apparently mingled with that of past northern invaders, but their language and inscriptions featured many Berber words and terms. It is not particularly unusual today to see Canary Islanders with such features as Raul's though past darker hued visitors, from early Phoenicians, Carthaginians and Greeks to latter-day Italians, Portuguese and Spaniards, have all clearly left their mark. The *conquistadores* effectively wiped out the Guanche male population in the fifteenth century but did spare many of the females, so offshoots like this pugnacious young kitchen worker might easily pop up among the rich *pot-pourri* of features seen the length and breadth of the archipelago, from Arrecife to Valverde, today.

The Guanches are still something of a mystery. In the nineteenth century a welter of theories appeared, many of them differing in their views of exactly where these native Canarians came from. British ethnologist James Cowles Prichard (also a psychiatrist who administered several London asylums) believed strongly in a Berber influence but also saw a link with the early Spanish Iberians and even the Pyrenean Basques, whom he called the "Atlantic races". Alexander von Humboldt, Prussian geographer and naturalist *par excellence*, believed they were of Central European descent. The Wagnerian scribe Franz von Löer claimed they were Goths and Vandals fleeing to more welcoming climes in the twilight years of their brief period of destructive glory. He even suggested that the name *Guanche* was a derivation of *wandches* or vandals (though it is widely accepted today that the real meaning (from *gwanchinet*) is "son of Tenerife" since that was the first island they settled in. His contemporary Gustav Kossinna thought they came from even further north, perhaps from Celtic regions or Scandinavia. The early twentieth-century American anthropologist Ernest E. Hooton was one of the first to put forward the more accepted view that, with their low foreheads, prominent cheekbones, sunken nostrils and jutting jaws (as evidenced by skulls found on the islands), they were descendants of Cro-Magnon men from the last Ice Age who gradually migrated south.

Whatever their origin, these newcomers rapidly established themselves throughout the whole archipelago. For centuries the Tenerife Guanches and their other island compatriots lived in splendid isolation, cocooned in the seclusion of their individual ocean-surrounded locations, with scarcely any outside contact and making minimal "civilized" progress compared with the rest of the world. Their cross section of historically factual or invented names seems designed to confuse. Lanzarote was known alternatively as Tyterogatra or Tikanaren, and might have been one of Pliny's two semi-imaginary "Purple Isles"; Fuerteventura was Erbane or Maxorata or Pliny's other "Purple Isle"; Gran Canaria was Canaria or Tamaran; Tenerife was Cheche or Achineche or Ninguaria. La Gomera was Gomera or Capraria; La Palma was Benahoare or Junonia Major or Pluvaria; El Hierro was Ezero or Hero or Plivaria.

This time warp existence was rudely interrupted when the first Castilian *conquistadores* landed in the fifteenth century. The future colonizers were dumbfounded to find the islanders still living mainly in Stone Age conditions in caves, unaware of the existence of metals. Also, though surrounded by ocean, they appeared to have no knowledge of how to navigate or sail. What sea fishing they did was from the shore. So how did they get there in the first place? Were they brought to the islands by sailors or traders? Perhaps they were landlubbers who had been forcibly exiled here from their inland North African farms and settlements for reasons unknown by Roman overlords. Maybe they originated from the Canarii tribes of the Atlas Mountains—an alternative explanation for the islands' name, though it is commonly accepted today that it originates from the Latin *canes*, in honour of the large dogs encountered by early Mauretanian explorers on Gran Canaria. They certainly brought their own animals with them: goats, sheep, pigs and dogs. They also brought wheat and barley which they planted and cultivated.

Though the Spaniards viewed the native Canarians as undeveloped primitives, they admired them for their morality, bravery and intelligence. Not that this halted the usual Hispanic expansionist policy of ruthlessly exterminating all opposition. The combined effect of wars and enforced slave labour—and European-introduced illnesses against which the Guanches had no resistance—led to the devastation, barely a century later, of these innately peaceful people who loved sports and tests of strength and only resorted to violence when threatened. Then they became truly formidable, even when confronted with superior weapons. Their main arms were bludgeon-like, leather-wrapped stones known as *teniques* and polished sharp-edged rocks which they threw with deadly accuracy. They also used wooden spears known as *binots*, but all these weapons were eventually outclassed by the forged steel lances and swords and early flintlock guns of their opponents.

As we move further into the Atlantic and away from mainland Africa, the island landscapes change from bleached lunar-cum-desert to lushly verdant subtropical and we find slight differences in their culture and settlements as well. Though they were colonized essentially by the same people different names evolved for the dwellers on each island. *Guanche*—as already mentioned—was the name given specifically to the *tinerfeños*, or locals of Tenerife. Inhabitants of Gran Canaria were simply called *canarios*, while in El Hierro they were known as *bimbaches*, in La Palma as *benahoritas*, in La Gomera as *gomeros* and in both Lanzarote and Fuerteventura as *majoreros*.

The Guanches of Tenerife were the strongest and most influential of the island races. They were originally ruled by a single governor, or *mencey*, called Tinerfe the Great. On his death the island was divided into nine separate mini-kingdoms (*menceyatos*), each with its own leader. Most *menceys* ruled in a strictly authoritarian fashion though Bencomo, the benevolent lord of Taoro who was also known as *Quevehi*, was a more tolerant leader who saw himself as "first among equals" rather than a supreme ruler whose order must be obeyed without question. His capital was located in the lushly verdant Arautava (today's Orotava) Valley, a paradisiacal setting for a comparatively democratic system which formed the political heart of the island during the Spanish invasion. Benevolent with his people, he was also a ruthless warrior leader who—against all odds—won the first battle against the *conquistadores* at Acentejo in 1494 (of which more later). Another *mencey*, Beneharo, epitomized the Guanches' attitude of total defiance against outside authority. He was known as the *El Rey Loco* (the Crazy King) by the Spaniards after he and many of his warriors jumped to their deaths from the cliffs of Anaga rather than surrender to the victorious invaders.

## INDIGENOUS SOCIETY

The Guanche social scale was patriarchal and clearly delineated not just in Tenerife but throughout all the islands, with the wealthiest, unsurprisingly, at the top. Below the ruling *mencey* (*guanarteme* in Gran Canaria) in order of authority and importance came the *achimencey*, or noble, and below him the *guañamené* (high priest) and *chaurero* (magistrate). The military were divided into *sigoñes* (captains) and *chichiciquitzos* (warriors) and the plebeian population into *achicaxna* (agricultural workers) and *achiclaxmais* (artisans and fishermen). Bottom of the hierarchy were the embalmers, in spite of the specialist skills required for this unique art.

Though male-dominated, Guanche society throughout the islands also placed great importance in the role of women. In some cases the rights of inheritance—and even responsibility for the transfer of authority—were actually passed down by females. Some acted as symbols of power for the island rulers, like the daughter of the King of Gran Canaria, who represented the island on its surrender to the victorious Spanish forces. The women of the easterly islands—Lanzarote and Fuerteventura—were considered the most gentle and submissive (even to the extent of being offered as "gifts" for the night to visiting guests) in marked contrast with the "Amazons" of La Palma and belligerent female warriors of Tenerife who fought back aggressively against the invaders. Such was their love of freedom and independence that, like the men, they often preferred to commit suicide than submit to a foreign yoke. On the other hand, when times were particularly difficult, such as when the population looked like outgrowing the resources at its disposal, they were clearly regarded as the inferior sex. Then female babies, apart from the first-born, would be dispassionately and ruthlessly "culled" in systematic acts of infanticide.

As a romantic antidote to the alternately aggressive and victimized face of the Guanche woman—perhaps with those hospitable easterly island females in mind—is provided by the chronicler Victoriano de las Torres in his engaging, self-translated 1962 guide *Carnet Guanche*: "[The women] had very thin long hair they combed naturally. Their waist [was] genteel and well-shaped; fresh their mouth, showing the wonderful treasure of their very white pearls. And at the back of their eyes, as the quietness of a lake, the contrasted blue of the Atlantic was reflected: sweet, dreaming [*sic*] looking; showing alive their intense and faithful loves."

Women produced much of the islanders' primitive art, especially the handle-less oval and circular clay vessels called *gánigos* often featuring solar symbols added with a pointed stick. They were also responsible for sowing crops (as a sign of fertility) after the men had tilled the soil with crude ploughs made from goats' horns, and for gathering plants and wild fruits and harvesting the Guanche staples of barley and wheat. The men in turn made tools and weapons by means of cutting stones and mills. But their day-to-day role, at which they excelled, was shepherding the islands' multitudes of goats and sheep. Some of the cattle, known as *guanil*, were allowed to graze freely but the pigs were kept in corrals (*goros*). Whether they were marked or unmarked, the animals were all individually known to, and recognized by, the herdsmen: an ability the early Spanish arrivals noted with astonishment and admiration.

The livestock also provided the means for fabricating the Guanches' clothing. Their rough leather or pigskin garments included *xercos* (sandals), *hiurmas* (sleeves to protect the arms), *guaycas* (leggings) and *ahicos* (shirts). They used the animals' hides to make these items, curing and tanning them with stone- or bone-made tools, though their favourite implement was the sharp-edged *tabona* knife made from razor-sharp shards of dark volcanic glass (obsidian).

Though they only had access to very basic materials, the native Canarians managed to sport a modestly varied wardrobe. Juan Abreu Galindo, an Andalucian Franciscan friar who wrote a key account of their culture called (in translation) *The History of the Discovery and Conquest of the Canary Islands* while residing in La Palma in 1632, makes these observations on the standard attire worn by the *lanzaroteños* (Lanzarote inhabitants):

> Their shoes were of goats' skins, the hairy side outward, and they also wore bonnets made of goats' skins, having three large feathers stuck in the front; the women wore the same, with a fillet of leather, dyed red with the bark of some shrubs. The above-mentioned cloak they called Tamarco, and the hood Guapil: shoes they called Mahil. The King of the island wore a diadem or crown like a bishop's mitre, made of goat's leather and adorned with seashells.

On female Gomeran outfits he additionally comments: "The woman's petticoat was made of goat skins, dyed and curiously painted. The red dye they extracted from the tree which they called *Taginaste,* and the blue dye from a herb they called Pastil: all between the petticoat and head dress was laid bare. When the men had any quarrel which was to be decided by combat they paid aside their cloaks tied a bandage about their waists and bound their foreheads with a sort of turban."

The Guanches' unsophisticated diet was also based on their livestock and crops. They drank goat's milk and ate goat's cheese and butter (which they also used as a healing agent for wounds). The staple *gofio*—still a standard feature on all Canary menus today—was made from flour ground from roasted grain or barley (*ahoren*).Rich animal fat (*amulán*) and meat-based (goat, sheep or even dog) dishes such as *tamazanona* were set aside for holidays and feast days. Tiny infants could enjoy the added luxury of *aguaman,* a pudding made from fern roots dipped in lard. (This delicacy has, for some reason, not survived to modern times.)

The Guanches celebrated a variety of esoteric ceremonies. The most eerily melodramatic of these, the rain ritual, took place when there were sustained periods of drought, crops withered and they were in real danger of starving. In their desperation they stopped all forms of entertainment such as singing and dancing, took their livestock to selected spots on high ground—separating baby goats and sheep from their parents—and cried and yelled in conjunction with the squeals and bleats of the poor disoriented, temporarily orphaned animals. Clearly they were aiming at eliciting pity from the gods and hoped that they would oblige with some life-saving downpours. Some of the locations where these heartfelt pleas took place still bear the name *baladero* (from the Spanish *balar*, meaning to bleat.)

The opposite of this plaintive outpouring was the dancing and feasting that traditionally greeted the New Year. As the Guanches used a lunar calendar this took place not in January but at the end of April or beginning of May when newborn livestock was frolicking on the hillsides and the fertile valleys were in full bloom. But even these joyous revels were surpassed by the harvest festival (or *beñasmen*), which took place annually in mid-summer. Then all wars and petty conflicts between different *menceyatos* and tribes would be (temporarily) cancelled and feasting and dancing were the order of the day. Wealth was redistributed (again, temporarily) as the *menceys* ensured that for once even the poorest Guanches received a generous quota of food and drink. The populace wore their best and most lavish finery and decorated their villages with flowers and plants. All the islanders loved sporting activities and exhibitions of strength and agility, and in addition to running, jumping, spear-throwing/avoiding competitions there were exhibitions of hand-to-hand combat that included energetic bouts of Canary wrestling, similar in style to feats performed in ancient Rome and Greece. *Lucha canaria* is still popular today and can be seen as various *fiestas* throughout the islands.

Though the Guanches had few musical instruments other than conch shells, sticks that they clapped together and small pebbles that reverberated in a clay vessel, they did love music and one of their favourite dances, the *Tajaraste*, survives to this day and can be seen regularly in folklore shows at, among other places, the Asociación Cultural Tajarastein Santa Cruz de Tenerife. A more sophisticated version of the dance, brought back by Spanish *conquistadores* and Genoese traders, became briefly fashionable in Europe in the sixteenth century.

Charmed by this hedonistic side of their nature, Juan Abreu Galindo reports:

> They were of a humane, social and cheerful disposition, very fond of singing and dancing. Their music was vocal, accompanied with a noise they made by clapping their hands and beating with their feet. They were very nimble and took great delight in leaping and jumping which were their principle diversions: two men took a staff or pole, which they held by the ends, and lifted as high above their heads as they could reach,

keeping it parallel with the ground, and he who could leap over it was accounted to very dexterous. Some of them were so expert at this exercise, that they could at three jumps leap over three poles placed in that manner behind each other.

(He was writing specifically about the inhabitants of Lanzarote and Fuerteventura on this occasion, but similar sporting activities were common throughout the whole archipelago.)

When a *mencey* or *guanarteme* died, the election of his successor was decided by the local council in another key Guanche ceremony. The role did not pass automatically from father to son but might be from brother to brother depending on the personal qualities of the candidate-elect. The highlight of the ritual, once the new *mencey* had been chosen, was when he kissed the bone belonging to the dynasty's oldest ancestor which had been traditionally kept wrapped in fine skins and brought out from its place of storage especially for this momentous event. Only when this bone had been kissed was the chosen one officially recognized by the council as their new leader. Each member would then pronounce the words: "I swear by the bone of he who made you great."

Dwellings or *auchones* were where the families lived together with their livestock. Some consisted of circular-shaped huts with stone walls and thatched roofs. The majority of inhabitants, however, lived in caves and grottoes close to water and pasturelands (one such popular and densely inhabited area was Anaga in the north of Tenerife.) The higher up the cave was situated the greater the status or importance of its occupants. Community spirit was strong and meetings regularly took place in the *tagoror*, a kind of senate where participants sat in a circular array of stone seats to discuss justice, morality or religion and social and political affairs in general. The location was chosen for its proximity to sacred rocks and trees with medicinal qualities such as the dragon tree. On arriving to govern the meeting the *mencey* carried a symbolic carved wooden sceptre and his approach would be announced by the mournful one-note hoot of a conch shell horn, or *añepa*.

## FAITH AND DEATH

The Guanche religion had a strict hierarchy of priests and other spiritual figures. The top rung was occupied by the high priest, followed by the *faykan* (or religious guardian figure) and the *maguada* and *maguadez* (male and female assistant priests). Below them came the *kankus*, who observed the cult of the goddess mother; the *samarines*, who worshipped their ancestors; and the *iboibos*, who were dedicated to studying the afterlife.

Before their post-colonial Christian conversion the Guanches' supreme deity was the sun god *Magec* (hence the frequent geometric depictions of the sun on their pottery). They also worshipped other gods such as *Acahaman*, or the Heavens, and *Achguayaxerax*, the Sustainer of Heaven and Earth, and revered *Achmayex Achguayaxerax Acoron Achaman*, a Mother Goddess whom the *conquistadores* associated with the Virgin Mary.

The native Canarians also believed strongly in the Devil, regarding him with fear and respect. For the *tinerfeños* he was *Guayota* (the Ominous One) who lived high up in Echyde (the 3,700-metre Mount Teide). Anyone careless enough to roam its high slopes at night risked encountering him in the guise of a large solitary dog that was both fierce and dangerous. Mount Teide also provides evidence of their alternative polytheistic religions, and tiny effigies and offerings aimed at appeasing the spirits of natural forces have been found in high altitude rock clefts and caves. Subtle or explicit sexual figures formed part of the family unit's veneration of health and fertility, and specimens and remains of these have also been found throughout the Canaries. The most striking icon of this kind is

The Idolo de Tara (RémiStosskopf/Wikimedia Commons)

Gran Canaria's surreal russet-gold Idolo de Tara, a tiny (27-centimetre high), partially preserved terracotta figure with a miniscule head, stunted arms and exaggeratedly bulbous crossed legs, which today occupies a key place in Las Palmas' archaeological museum.

Perhaps their obsession with death and the afterlife inspired the Guanches to achieve such remarkable skill in embalming corpses (see p.62). The process, which has many links with Ancient Egyptian methods, was carried out over a period of several weeks. First, the body was thoroughly washed. Then the internal organs were removed and a liquefied mixture of animal lard, herbs, rock dust and pine bark was introduced into the corpse via the mouth to preserve it. Then the body was put out to dry in the sun in order to complete the mummifying process. Once this was accomplished the mummy (or *xaco*) was covered in tightly wrapped skins painted in a manner that would make later identification of the corpse possible. The skins were then sewn tight and the mummy was placed on raised wooden boards in a cave which was recognized as the family tomb. The whole process took place in conjunction with an official mourning period and once the mummy had been placed in the cave, offerings in the form of clay vessels and ornaments, limpet shells and spears were placed beside it. A leader—*mencey* or *guanarteme*—would be buried with his sceptre (*añepa*). (Today, removed from their original cave locations, mummies are on view in different archaeological museums throughout the archipelago.)

The islanders were as fearless of death as they were fascinated by it. Whether defiantly asserting their right to be free when faced with intolerable enemy oppression, making a traditional gesture of total obedience to a new ruler in the form of self-sacrifice or even trying—as would-be mediators between the living and the dead—to make contact with their predecessors, the Guanche never hesitated to give up his, or her, own life: often spectacularly, by jumping from high cliffs on to the rocks below, or sometimes passively as in the case of the captive King of La Palma who starved himself to death on a vessel carrying him back as a prisoner of the *conquistadores* rather than surrender to Spanish rule (see p.XXX). It is fairly certain the *tinerfeños* had their own unique vision of an afterlife—long before missionaries tried to indoctrinate them with a Christian version—in which the good souls went to the fertile and lovely Aguere Valley, where the city of La Laguna stands today, and the bad ended up on Teide mountain in the company of Echeyde, the Evil One.

Considering the generally cohesive form of social life that linked all the islands, punishments for crimes were surprisingly varied. In Fuerteventura, according to Juan de Abreu Galindo, if one Guanche took the life of another the sentence depended on how the attack was carried out. If the killer entered by the victim's door and made his presence clearly visible—thus supposedly giving the person ample time to defend himself before the assault—he went unpunished. If the attacker came upon the victim without warning, however, and caught him (or her) unawares the crime was deemed unpardonable and the murderer's execution would be ordered by the chief. This sentence was carried out on the seashore where the killer would have his brains dashed out by a large round stone as he lay with his head on another flatter stone. Murderers were also executed in Gran Canaria, depending on the circumstances, but on most of the other islands there was no death penalty. On Tenerife murderers were exiled after having all their worldly possessions seized by the *menceyato*. Robbers on all the islands were usually imprisoned, but El Hierro alone had a unique way of dealing with such offenders. After the first robbery the thief would have one eye removed. After a second offence the other eye would go. This was a deterrent strong enough to ensure that very few robberies occurred on the tiny island.

## THE GUANCHE LEGACY

According to a dedicated group of twentieth-century European investigative anthropologists (Wolfel, Fischer, Fusté, Rösing and Schwidetzsky), a surprisingly large number of Guanche descendants are still evident today in spite of early Hispanic attempts to eliminate them and the fact that today virtually the whole population has Castilian names (though some direct *mencey* and *guanarteme* descendants still have surnames like Doramas and Bencomo). This knowledgeable quintet of researchers explored the subject in some depth and Wolfel concluded in 1930 that as many as two-thirds of the archipelago's population could have at least partially descended from the original native Canarians. Isla Schwidetzsky came up with the most detailed figures, and Nicole Maca-Meyer echoed her findings in 2003.

Both of them concluded that signs of the Guanche legacy are most prevalent in La Gomera where the native *gomeros* display the largest number of Cro-Magnon-cum-Mediterranean features. Their heritage includes an atmospheric sanctuary in the heart of the richly wooded National Park of Garajonay (a UNESCO World Heritage site named after the Romeo and Juliet-style lovers Gara and Jonay who committed suicide when their parents forbade the match).

Nearby El Hierro's *bimbache* inhabitants, in contrast, constitute the lowest number of native Canary descendants, though this tiny westerly outpost is a positive microcosm of their life and times. The name, incidentally, has nothing to do with iron (the direct Spanish translation) as there is none to be found there, but could in fact be a corruption of the word *hero* which in the local language means "milk" (traditionally produced in abundance by local goats). The island contains numerous *petroglifos*, or chiselled stone engravings, such as the *Letreros* of El Julan, and the well-preserved remains of an ancient *tagoror*. Burial sites have also been found in hillside clefts together with human remains, votive offerings, domestic utensils and containers made of clay and wood.

The percentage of identifiable Guanche descendants on the other five islands comes somewhere between these two, and further traces of the

The Belmaco Cave (Zyance/Wikimedia Commons)

native Canarian legacy can be found in all of them. La Palma's *benahorita* inhabitants left behind a variety of etchings and artefacts in the island's Belmaco Cave which once served as a palace for the Mazo kings. It is now a museum displaying ornaments made from shells and bones, and has a wide range of ceramic bowls and plates. At La Zarza, Garafía and Caldera de Taburiente visitors can also see their rock carvings.

The most complete collection of Guanche artefacts and finds is contained in Santa Cruz de Tenerife's Museo de la Naturaleza y el Hombre, a striking ochre-façaded neoclassical building designed by the city's most revered architect Manuel de Oráa, and originally the home to the island's Civil Hospital. One of the finest museums not only in the archipelago but the whole of Spain, it also incorporates an important archaeological section. The highlight is the San Andrés mummy, covered in strips of goatskin and laid out on a wooden board, the embalmed body of a man in late youth (25-30) found in a cave near the small village of that name.

Elsewhere on the island a key place of Guanche worship was the Cave of Achbinico at Güimar where a statue of the Virgin de la Candelaria—

The Güimar "pyramids" (Wikimedia Commons)

originally left by early Christian missionaries at the nearby cave-palace of Chinguaro before being moved here—was venerated by the Guanches as if it were one of their own deities. Guïmar, incidentally, is the home of some deftly layered stone-built structures which the Norwegian ethnographer Thor Heyerdahl—famed for his 8,000-kilometre *Kontiki* raft trip from South America to the Tuomoto Islands in French Polynesia in 1947—believed dated from Guanche times. Other researchers, however, have estimated their construction period at no later than the nineteenth century. They are pretty modest fare: step terraces that resemble smaller versions of Mexican, Peruvian and Mesopotamian pyramids, but nonetheless fascinating.

Gran Canaria's most important cave-palaces, where the *guanartemes* lived and ruled, were at Galdar and Telde. The latter is now home of the Cuatro Puertas museum, which contains exhibits demonstrating the area's religious importance and its traditional low-key style contrasts strongly with the Barranco de Fataga's decidedly modern Mundo Aborigen open-air museum, a self-conscious theme park-style reconstruction of a native Canarian village, complete with life-size model figures (from farmers to executioners) re-enacting various facets of day-to-day life in the Guanche-*canario* world.

Further east, the *majoreros* of Lanzarote are believed to be responsible for the intricately carved symbols on the island's unearthed Zonzama stone, though in comparison with the other islands there is surprisingly little else to suggest that the native Canarians ever lived here. It is believed that their cave dwellings and crafts were largely destroyed by the apocalyptic series of eighteenth-century eruptions. Fuerteventura's *majoreros* in turn left a variety of tombs and religious symbols on Tindaya Mountain in the centre. In a past existence the island was divided into two *majorero* kingdoms: Maxorata (in the north) and Jandia (in the south), partially separated by a long low stone wall.

In spite of the Spanish conquest, the Castilian language does not dominate everything on the islands. Many of the geographical regions and villages have distinctly non-Spanish names like Tacoronte, Chimche and Adeje: all native Canary words phonetically reproduced from the spoken tongue used when the Guanches were living on the islands (there was no written version). Its pronunciation was guttural and the Berber origins were strongly evident. Accents varied, but the basic language was the same from Lanzarote to El Hierro. Even today *guanchismos* linger on in rural pockets: shepherds, for example, still often use words like *axa* (goat) and *haña* (sheep).

Though their lifestyle was rustic and simple in the extreme, the Guanches did also have a sound practical knowledge of the sciences. They used mathematics for counting livestock, geometric figures on ceramic ornaments, and formed a lunar calendar from their knowledge of astronomy which also helped with their calculations of harvesting according the phases of the moon. Therapeutic knowledge of plants and herbs helped them cure the ailments of human beings and animals and a basic understanding of geology helped them develop a mining industry. They understood the nutritional value of foods and devised different techniques for tilling and ploughing the earth.

It took most of the fifteenth century for the Castilian invaders to completely subdue the native Canarians, starting with Lanzarote and Fuerteventura, where they encountered relatively little resistance, and continuing with El Hierro and La Gomera, where they also had a fairly easy time of it. Defiant La Palma was a harder nut to crack, however, and in Gran Canaria the inhabitants fought back with a ferocity that surprised the Spaniards. But the greatest shock of all for the Hispanic invaders came in Tenerife, where the primitively equipped locals roundly defeated the better equipped and more numerous force of *conquistadores* in the ravine of Acentejo in 1494, leaving barely one in every five of the invaders alive. Two years later the Spaniards re-assembled an army of heavily armed and well-trained soldiers and horsemen and won their revenge in a fierce battle at Aguere. The Guanche warriors fought as bravely as before but this time found themselves on foot facing the enemy's cavalry on an open plain. They did not stand a chance. Their fate, along with that of the whole Guanche nation, was sealed.

The defeated native Canarians now found themselves part of a totally new society. To add injury to the insult of no longer being in charge of their own land many of them succumbed to an epidemic (brought from Europe and nicknamed the "Spanish Drowsiness") against which their bodies had no resistance. Survivors were either sold into slavery or accepted conversion to the Christian faith and, after being baptized, were allowed to live on in the islands, though they now had to forsake their native tongue and learn Spanish. The spirit of independence lived on till the bitter end, though, and in the more rugged islands many diehards fled to the mountains and fought a determined but ultimately doomed guerrilla offensive for several more decades. But by the middle of the sixteenth century their glorious days of innocence and independence were over. A whole new phase in the islands' history had begun.

## Chapter Two
# EARLY VISITORS

Though the Guanches were the Canary archipelago's first human inhabitants, a host of other visitors briefly came and went during the long stay of those blonde-haired Berber descendants. Among the earliest were the Phoenicians who arrived on the islands in search of the rich red dye they needed for colouring their ceremonial robes and garments. A vital ingredient for this dye, available in local abundance, was shellfish, though sometimes lichens (mixed with goat's urine) were used as an alternative.

The same highly valued dye also attracted the Romans nearly a thousand years later and the modest remains of one of their dye factories can still be seen on the tiny Isla de Lobos, between Lanzarote and Fuerteventura. The whole archipelago was referred to as the "Purple Isles" by the Roman soldier and naturalist Pliny the Elder, who succinctly describes the process by which the dye was actually made from shellfish:

> The vein of the mollusc is extracted and about a sextarius (7lbs) of salt is added to each 100 pounds of material. It should be soaked for three days for the fresher the extract, the more powerful the dye, then boiled in a leaden vessel. Next, five hundred pounds of dry stuff, diluted with an amphora (8 gallons) of water, are subjected to an even and moderate heat by placing the vessels in a flue connecting with a distant furnace. Meanwhile the flesh adheres to the veins and a test is made on about the tenth day by steeping a well-washed fleece in the liquefied contents of one of the vessels. The liquid is then heated till the colour answers to expectations. A frankly red colour is inferior to one with a tinge of black. The wool drinks in the dye for five hours and after carding is dipped again and again until all the colour is absorbed.

Though there is no doubt that the Phoenicians and Romans definitely spent time on the islands, a question mark hangs over the presence of some of the other visitors who purportedly came during those in-between decades. Take for example the Carthaginian sailor-king Hanno the Navigator, who ambitiously led an expedition down the west coast of Africa around 500 BC. He is believed by some to have attempted a landfall in the archipelago en route and his simple eighteen-line, diary-like "Periplus" (which means simply "Journey" and was translated into English in 1912 by the historian Wilfred H. Schiff) recounts how he sailed past the Pillars of Hercules (the gap between today's Gibraltar and Tangier) into the open Atlantic with sixty ships known as *pentekontas* and 30,000 men and women, a figure regarded by some historians as a gross exaggeration. (According to Gallic researchers J. Meirat and J.-G.Demerliac in their 1983 opus *Hannon et l'empire punique,* 5,000 may be nearer the mark.) He then went along the West African coast and after a couple of days founded a city above a wide plain and called it Thymiaterion. Continuing south he next discovered Cerne, a tiny islet less than two kilometres across and which may have been Arguin just off the Mauretanian coast. But by Hanno's calculations the islet lay the same distance from the Pillars of Hercules as the latter was from Carthage, so an alternative location for Cerne could well have been Mogador, just offshore from Essaouira in Morocco and only about 400 kilometres from Lanzarote, the nearest Canary Island.

Hanno left some of his men to form a tiny settlement on the islet, sailed across a river called Chretes and "after a day" sighted three much larger islands. One of them was very mountainous and the locals he encountered when trying to land there were dressed in animal skins and threw stones at him and his men. Though he mentions travelling across a "bay" (the same one in which he claims Cerne was located) he might conceivably have been sailing *away* from the African mainland into the Atlantic and actually reached Tenerife. His account of the island's scenery and belligerent attitude of the natives, who subsequently proved on occasions to be the Spaniards' most aggressive foes, certainly supports this theory. No other islands or islets close to the African mainland fit this description.

Deterred by the hostile reception he received on landing, he and his men returned to their ship and sailed back to Cerne. From there he continued his exploration of the African coast, sailing as far south as Senegal where the humidity, intense heat and loud howls and nocturnal drumbeats emanating from the mainland jungle combined with diminishing provisions eventually compelled him and his frightened companions to return home. The epic journey still lives on in people's minds today and such is Hanno's fame that he has a crater on the moon named after him and even a 2008 song by Al Stewart called "Sparks of Ancient Light" commemorating his astounding journey.

After the Phoenicians, Carthaginians and early Romans came explorers from Mauretania (present day Morocco and Western Algeria) who are said to have given the islands their name. On landing in Lanzarote in the first century BC the Mauretanians encountered a large pack of dogs (clearly the ancestors of today's indigenous breed, the *verdino* or *dogo canario,* a mastiff-style mutt) and decided to call the archipelago the Canaries or Canarias (from the Latin *canes,* or dogs). They took two puppies of this breed back to their scholar-king Juba II who had planned and authorized the expedition.

*Dogo canario* ( Canecorsodog/Wikimedia Commons)

Probably the most surprising early visitor (unless this is merely a case of Irish blarney) was St. Brendan, who founded the Clonfert monastery in County Kerry and was prone to taking incredibly daring voyages every now and then into the Atlantic. It is quite possible that he landed in the archipelago some time during the sixth century AD as in his biographical *Navigatio sancti Brendani abbatis* (usually simply called the *Navigatio*) he records a visit, at the end of a long sea journey with adventurous fellow monks in a large wattle- and oak-built coracle or *currach,* to the lushly idyllic *Terra Repromissionis Sanctorum* or Promised Land—which some researchers have taken to be Tenerife. (Others more fancifully claim it is a mythical isle called San Borondón, also known as St. Brendan's Isle, which lies in the midst of the Sargasso Sea, but appears and disappears at will in the mists. Amazingly enough, this fairy tale creation is clearly marked in a location due west of El Hierro—L'Isle de Fer—on an otherwise accurate seventeenth-century French map of West Africa and the Atlantic by Guillaume de l'Isle of the Académie Royale de la France. There have also been reported "sightings" of the phantom island over the centuries and even

Mythical San Borondón (private collection)

Columbus is said to have believed in its existence, but at the end of the day it remains the stuff of legends.)

It is more likely to have been in Tenerife than in the fantasy world of San Borondón that Brendan reportedly landed in 512 AD and held a mass with a dozen or so monks, one of whom, somewhat beside himself, described the isle as an eternally sunny, thickly wooded place filled with singing birds, where night was unknown, the fruit was rich and fresh water was abundant. And if it was indeed Tenerife, he could well have been the very first priest to preach the Christian faith here, a pioneer missionary paving the way for the Franciscans and Mallorcans who came several centuries later. The material evidence may be thin but it is a thought-provoking possibility.

St. Brendan's other epic voyage, across the North Atlantic to Newfoundland, is far more famously documented. Yet, one might think, if he could get that far from Ireland in such unforgiving seas and weather, then coming down to the sunny Canaries would have been relatively easy. What is more, his exotic description of the apparently subtropical *Terra Re–*

*promissionis* hardly matches any island in those sub-Arctic latitudes. The adventurer-researcher Tim Severin built a boat in 1976 similar to the one Brendan used and followed the Irish saint's northerly route via the Faroes, Iceland and Greenland to prove that this journey was possible in such a vessel. He wrote a book about it called *The Brendan Voyage*. It is a pity he did not undertake any similar ocean trip to the Canaries to test out the likelihood of the Kerry saint having taken that route.

There is also talk of other Nordic victors. Viking explorers may well have reconnoitred the islands around the eighth century AD but that again is debatable. Some theorists have even suggested that Norsemen colonized the islands early on and that the Guanches are descended from them and not from Berbers, though the islanders' documented ineptitude at sailing and navigation rather undermines that idea. Wild Nordics are far more likely to have dropped in for one of their usual raping and pillaging incursions, and any Viking-like features that may be discerned in some present-day inhabitants are possibly due to one of those visits.

The archipelago also received a couple of confirmed visits by peace-observing Arabs during that era. The most famous of these was Ibn Farrukh (or Ben Farrouckh) a Muslim captain and navigator from Granada during the period when it formed part of the Umayyad caliphate. He landed in 999 AD on Gran Canaria at an easterly spot he himself later named as Gando and together with his men made the difficult crossing of the island—by all accounts its peaks, gorges and plains were then also covered with dense woodlands—till he reached the Guanche capital, Agaldar (today's Gáldar), in the far north-west. There he paid a hospitable call on a local king named Guanarigato. What they discussed is not recorded but it is fascinating to speculate what they must have made of each other. Did they both explore their past heritage and conclude their ancestors both originally came from the same part of the African continent. Did they compare life in their respective worlds?

A couple of decades later another expedition of North Africans landed on Lanzarote and named it, together with all the other islands, Al-Kaledat, which means eternity in Arabic. Little is known of where they went and whom they saw. Presumably they too shared words and thoughts with Guanche chiefs and perhaps did a little trading. As with Ibn Farrukh's visit there were no reports of any conflicts.

## THE EUROPEANS ARRIVE

The first long-term outside influence to affect the Canaries came from Italy, from the great Ligurian port of Genoa which by the fourteenth century had peaked in its knowledge of marine skills. The city possessed the most adept navigators in Europe as well as remarkably advanced compasses, astrolabes and other refined nautical equipment. Its ships had already established strong trading links with Africa and the East, so now was the time to start looking west. With this new horizon in mind the Vivaldi brothers, Vandino and Ugolino, a colourful buccaneer duo if ever there was one, left Genoa in 1291 and sailed past the Pillars of Hercules into the open Atlantic. Their quest, as with more successful expeditions that followed, was to find a new route to India and China. Possibly, instead of continuing westwards they headed south, by accident or design, to take the long route around Africa. We will never know which direction they took or what they encountered as they were never seen again.

In 1312 another Genoese called Lanzarotto Malocello, a member of one of the city's noblest families, arrived off the coast of the volcanic isle then known as Tytheroygatra, the closest place in the archipelago to the African coast. He and his crew were exhausted and almost devoid of provisions after failing in their mission to locate the Vivaldis or even ascertain what might have happened to them. Instead of continuing their search, Malocello and his men decided instead to rest awhile on the island. This intended short breathing space turned into a twenty-year sojourn during which he built a fortress near Teguise. His arrival and stay completely changed the Western World's knowledge of, and interest in, the Canaries. (Such was Malocello's subsequent fame that even as late as the Second World War a destroyer was named after him.) Surprisingly little, however, is known of his activities during those two decades. The most accepted account is that he tried to set himself up as a ruler of the Guanches and was eventually expelled by them.

What happened after Malocello's departure is not clear either. Some even say he never left but actually died in Teguise at the hands of Guanche inhabitants from both this island and neighbouring Fuerteventura. Others report that he returned to Genoa and in 1336 tried to assemble an expedition under the auspices of Alfonso IV of Portugal that would have seen him comfortably re-installed in his Teguise castle. There is no confirmation that this ever took place though there are tales of uncovered documents that falsely reported such an expedition. The most valid proof of his original stay is a *portalan* map made in 1339 by the Mallorcan cartographer Angelino Dulcert on which the island is marked by a Genoese shield bearing the name *Insula de Lanzarotus Marocelos*. The map, which was far more accurate and realistic than earlier "imagined" attempts to depict the archipelago, also includes Fuerteventura and the Isla de Lobos. Whatever the facts and the fantasies that surround him Lanzarotto opened the route up for future Spanish colonizers. (The Norman knight Jean de Béthencourt, in the employ of Castile, reputedly lodged in his castle during the start of Spain's 1402 invasion: see Chapter 3.)

The island was subsequently renamed Lanzarote in Malocello's honour and the 700th anniversary of his landing was celebrated with talks and symposiums arranged in April 2012 by the capital Arrecife's town council. Reactions among islanders to these events were far from enthusiastic, however, particularly on the internet where local bloggers asked indignantly what all the fuss was about. They wanted to know why a mercenary opportunist, who had no other interests than his own at heart and never did a single thing to support or help the Guanche population during his two-decade stay, had come to be regarded as a hero. Similar commemorative events were held in Genoa to a muted but more positive reception, and three months later a septuagenarian sailor from the Ligurian capital, Giorgio Blondette, followed up with his own private celebration of the occasion by successfully retracing Lanzarotto's route in his yacht.

Other Italians, from Florence and Pisa as well as Genoa, also visited the Canary archipelago in the following years. Some travelled on behalf of their country, others acted as captains and navigators for the Portuguese, who increasingly saw the archipelago as an ideal base for their own ambitions of territorial expansion. One of the most important of these "coalition" trips was made in 1341 when two galleons sailed from Lisbon under the captaincy of the Genovese Nicoloso da Recco and Florentine Angiolino del Tegghia de Corbizzi. Da Recco wrote a detailed account of the visit and related how the expedition brought back four of the local "savages" to Lisbon. The latter had innocently swum out to his ship to greet him only to find themselves taken prisoner. Once on board they impressed the crew with their gentle ways and good manners and made a similar impression back in the Portuguese capital where they were displayed to the populace. It is said they were persuaded to adopt the Christian faith and returned later with missionaries to help convert some of their Guanche compatriots.

Da Recco's report of this adventure was read and subsequently amplified in a vivid account by the Renaissance poet Giovanni Boccaccio. Of the locals and the landscape, he wrote (according to Herbert Wendt in his *It Began in Babel*):

> They were rocky, uncultivated isles, but rich in goats and other animals and inhabited by naked men and women who looked like savages but were governed by leaders who wore goatskin garb stained with saffron and red dyes. From far off these skins seemed very fine and delicate, carefully sewn together with the intestines of animals. They have a king to whom they show great respect and obedience. Their language is gentle but can be as animated and hasty as that of an Italian.

But before Boccaccio had even begun to write these words the famed Tuscan scholar and poet Francesco Petrarca (better known as Petrarch) had already beaten him to the draw. The first writer since Pliny the Elder to mention the "Fortunate Isles", Petrarch wrote an account of a 1346 Portuguese incursion to the Canaries after apparently receiving "insider information" from his close friend Pope Clement IV. It was only then that Boccaccio, who idolized Petrarch, followed suit, turning his attention to geography as a medium for expanding the country's vision and conception of the world. Though the subsequent creator of the classic *Decameron* never actually visited any of the islands, his passion for writing about them was fierce. Boccaccio was also fascinated by marine charts and enjoyed trying to make sense out of their multiple contradictions through the ages. The full title of his island book was *Della Canaria e delle altre isole oltre Ispania nell'oceano nuovamente ritrovate* (*Of Canaria and Other Islands Recently Discovered in the Oceans beyond Spain*) and his account of the Portuguese King Alfonso's expedition is the only version to survive today.

The research of these two Italian literary giants was also inspired by a need to escape the problems Europe was experiencing during this period, from severe economic recession to the devastating effects of the Black Death which claimed millions of victims. The depleted coffers of Italy and Spain and other European countries desperately needed refilling and for Italy in particular, according to Toby Lester in *The American Scholar*, there

Boccaccio (Project Gutenburg/Wikimedia Commons)

was a strong urge to revive the learning, power and geographical reach of Rome's glorious past.

Just before Boccaccio's travel opus appeared a papal bull (a formal written proclamation or charter and sealed authenticated by a *bulla*, the attached round lead seal) had been issued by Pope Clement VI in 1344 controversially granting a Castilian-French noble, Luis de la Cerda, sovereignty over the Canary Islands and title of "Prince of Fortuna". An ambassador to the papal court in Avignon, Cerda won this favour by promoting the idea of converting the islanders to Christianity, but during the time this short-lived privilege lasted (Cerda died just four years later) both Castile and Portugal raised strong objections to his appointment. Not unlike a certain Surrey-based Governor of Menorca who never left England to exert his power locally during Britain's eighteenth-century rule of that Mediterranean island, Cerda did all his administrative work from his French home base and never once set foot anywhere on the Canaries during his period of authority. A second bull the following year put forward the idea of a Cerda-led crusade and tried to persuade the Spanish kings to support him on this mission. Cerda met with two point of opposition. Alfonso XI felt the islands should be governed by Spain, while his Portuguese counterpart Alfonso IV protested that his country had discovered the islands first and that Portugal should be the ruler. Both bowed to the pope's decision but their joint stalling ensured that no such mission set off before Cerda's unexpectedly early death.

Inspired by a further bull issued by the above Pope Clement in 1351 and possibly encouraged by Lanzarotto's pioneering, if far from religiously-inspired, stay, Franciscan-organized expeditions from Mallorca now began to arrive in the Canaries with the idea of Christianizing the islands. They were initially unsuccessful, but the Mallorcans had brought some natives back from some of these earlier trips and the latter, having learnt both the Catalan language and something of the Christian religion, now regularly returned alongside the Balearic missionaries and together with them attempted more successfully to convert some of their own island compatriots to the faith, as had those earlier Lisbon captives. They set up missions in many of the islands and left paintings and various statues of the Virgin Mary which the Guanches started to worship as if they were their own goddesses.

Christian conversions apart, the canny Mallorcans next devoted themselves to their real forte of making money. Balearic merchants began visiting the Canaries on a purely commercial basis, their objective being to capture locals they could sell as slaves, or to negotiate over newly sought-after commodities like the lichens or dragon's blood resin used for making dyes like those treasured by the Phoenicians and Romans, and whose value had now shot up hugely. With remarkably ecological insight, the Mallorcans also brought many trees to be planted, thus beginning the transformation of some of the island's more barren areas into densely wooded landscapes.

Two of the most important business trips were arranged in 1342 by Roger de Robenach, a deputy of the Mallorcan King Jaime III, on the instructions of a private merchant consortium. Their respective captains were Francesc Duvalers and Domenech Gual and they made no bones about the fact that their main objective was capturing natives to sell as slaves. Both visits proved highly lucrative.

The Mallorcans became more ambitious. An audacious mission four years later, aimed at following the West African coast all the way to Senegal in search of gold (to the legendary "Riu d'Or", Africa's equivalent of El Dorado), may have also seen its captain Jaume Ferrer make landfall on one of the Canary Islands to rest up and replenish stores. A map created in 1375 by the noted Jewish-Mallorcan cartographer Abraham Cresques and known as the *Catalan Atlas* (the original can be found in the Bibliothèque Nationale in Paris) depicts an Aragonese flag on the islands inscribed with the name "Jacme Ferrer". There are echoes of Hanno's earlier visit to the same regions here, and though there is less documentation of the voyage it is far more likely that Ferrer did stop off, as by now the islands were better known to the western world and had more harbour and provision facilities. What became of him and his crew once they sailed south of Cabo Bojador on the Moroccan mainland, at that time regarded as a "point of no return", is anyone's guess. Like the Vivaldi brothers half a century before, they were never seen again.

Ferrer's memory is celebrated in his home town of Palma de Mallorca, where he has a statue in his honour in the Plaça de Drassanes and a street named after him.

Other visits during this era to the islands have been recorded by the twentieth-century chronicler-historian Rumeu de Armas in works such as *Piraterías y ataques navales contra las Islas Canarias*. Foremost among them is his account of a 1352 expedition planned by Joan Doria and Jaume Segarra, both Mallorcan merchants with the by-now familiar blend of acquisitive and religious aims. Christian conversions were the main priority on this occasion for among their missionary complement were a dozen converted Guanches who had been brought back to the Balearics on previous expeditions and were now ready and willing to help their compatriots at home to see the light. This crusade was regarded as particularly important as the pope himself had created the autonomous "Diocese of Fortuna" in its honour and named a Carmelite friar, Bernardo Gil, its first bishop. Its captain, Arnau Roger, a veteran of many previous Canary trips, was in turn instructed to claim the islands for Peter IV and establish himself as a feudatory chief.

As it became more involved with the Canaries Mallorca also increasingly saw itself as a sort of fourteenth-century marine police force acting on behalf of the Crown of Aragon, and in 1366 an expedition led by Joan de Mora set sail for the archipelago with instructions from King Pedro IV to patrol the islands in search of possible hostile interlopers. Mora managed to chase off several would-be corsair invaders and was deemed successful in this enterprise and well rewarded.

In the next couple of decades several more crusades took place, although after Pope Clement's intervening death the Church began to lose interest in the Canaries. The last of these was a 1386 sortie from the Balearic capital sponsored by Peter IV of Aragon and Pope Urban VI and carried out by a religious order known as the Pauperes Heremite. Thirteen of the Franciscan priests who set up mission on arrival were reportedly murdered during an uprising by the inhabitants five years later.

While that particular story was probably true, some of the tales relating to other late fourteenth-century expeditions may need to be taken with a pinch of salt, even if they do make stimulating reading. One such saga recounts how all the members of a 1360 Mallorcan-Catalan expedition were—apparently on a whim—killed by Gran Canarians who had treated them as guests for several years. Another, in contrast, tells of a Galician-led 1372 landing in La Gomera where the Europeans, after engaging in battle with the locals and suffering many losses, found that their lives were spared and that they were allowed to return safely home. For romantics the most popular tale is of a Bizcayan sailor Martín Ruiz de Avendaño who in 1377 had a love affair with a Lanzarote queen called Fayna who bore him a daughter called Ico. How the king, her husband, felt about this is not recorded, but Ruiz somehow avoided punishment. His offspring eventually married the island's next king Guanarame and after his death saw her own son Guardafia accede to the throne in spite the attempts of an islanders' court to prove she was not of noble lineage. (She was found innocent after surviving a gruelling local "ordeal by fire" trial which involved her being sealed in a smoking hut.)

The islanders' idiosyncrasies, unpredictable actions apart, also included celestial superstitions. Both Christian and Islamic worlds observed with interest their obsession with the heavens. Another papal bull in 1369 noted that the Guanches worshipped the sun and moon and in 1377 the Arab historian Ibn Jaldún remarked that they regarded the rising sun as a kind of God. (His observation, incidentally, roughly coincided with the time of the Hegira, in the Arab Year 622, when Mohammed and his followers emigrated from Mecca to Medina and launched the Muslim era.)

As the expeditions increased so did the quality and accuracy of the maps depicting the islands. Domenico and Francesco Pizzigano's *portolan* of 1367 included El Hierro and La Gomera for the first time and Abraham Cresques' above-mentioned *Catalan Atlas* actually named ten islands, including the smaller Graciosa, Alegranza, Lobos and Roque alongside the familiar and larger Lanzarote, Fuerteventura, Gran Canaria, Tenerife, La Gomera and El Hierro. Unaccountably, though, it omitted La Palma, which basked invisibly between La Gomera and El Hierro, ignored by Cresque and sleepily unaware of the days of glory that awaited its capital Santa Cruz de La Palma four centuries later.

Throughout all the struggles for domination of the islands in the fourteenth and fifteenth centuries Portugal was Spain's keenest and most powerful enemy. The rivalry began in earnest in the 1370s, three decades after the Italian-captained expedition had brought the first native Canarians back to Lisbon. As the two countries struggled for domination of the lucrative slave-taking business a series of petty trade wars and actual battles broke out. Pedro I of Castile (the infamous Pedro the Cruel) had just been assassinated, severing links with Navarre and even England, placing Spain in a more fragmented and vulnerable position and encouraging Portugal to take advantage of the situation and strike out at what it now perceived as a weakened foe.

As time went on Lisbon's interest in ruling territories in this strategic corner of the Atlantic increased. The country's ambitious king, Henry the Navigator, now concentrated on wrestling on a mainly diplomatic level with Spain over the occupation of the Canaries, though the occasions when did he resort to force tended to have calamitous results. His full-scale military attempt to take Gran Canaria in 1402 was a resounding failure, immediately followed (to add insult to injury) by Jean de Béthencourt's more successful incursions on behalf of the Kingdom of Castile, who gradually took over control of the islands as Mallorca's star faded (see Chapter 3).

Henry did briefly achieve papal recognition to his right to claim the islands but the Catholic Church's allegiance changed shortly afterwards and the archipelago officially came under Spanish rule. In the end he had to settle instead for Madeira and the Azores and their adjacent satellite islets—nota bad alternative by any means. In one way, moreover, he had an easier time of it since those equally coveted islands were uninhabited

Henry the Navigator
(National Museum of Art, Lisbon/Wikimedia Commons)

when the Portuguese finally took over and his armies were never faced with the costly sequence of guerrilla skirmishes and pitched battles that the Spanish experienced with the Guanches in Gran Canaria and Tenerife.

As Henry ruminated and planned in his great Sagres School of Navigation at the south-western tip of the Iberian Peninsula his territorial interests grew wider. (The school, alas, no longer exists, having been destroyed in the great 1755 Lisbon earthquake). After colonizing Madeira and the Azores he pressed his captains to explore the west coast of Africa. He also ordered his fleets to go far out into the Atlantic and beyond with innovative caravels that measured a mere 55 to 69 feet in length, used a triangular lateen sail and were smaller, faster and lighter than any used before. Columbus later used one such ship on his epic pioneer trip to the Americas. The country's own new age of discovery was about to begin, as was Spain's.

It took Castile practically the whole of the fifteenth century to finally assert its sovereignty over the Canary Islands. But this long, hard struggle would prove to be worth it in the end.

## Chapter Three
# THE CONQUEST BEGINS

The invasion of the Canaries began in earnest in 1402. It was spearheaded not by Spaniards but by two Frenchman, Jean de Béthencourt and Gadifer de la Salle. Béthencourt was a nobleman with a long and distinguished lineage, highly respected in his home town of Grainville-la-Teinturière in Normandy. Outwardly, he seemed to be living a life of aristocratic ease, yet he had plenty of motives for getting out of France. One was his penchant for adventure. In his earlier days he had raided corsair bases on North Africa's Barbary Coast and even carried out pirate attacks against English ships (a trial on charges of piracy was imminent in an English court). Another reason was the need to escape from his personal entanglements (mainly legal and financial). He was by nature extravagant and had accumulated numerous debts. In his eyes the Canaries offered opportunities to make money, perhaps by exporting the much-sought-after orchil lichen to textile-producing companies for dyeing purposes. And yet another motive could have been to curry favour with the French court. The prestige in carrying off such a mission successfully would be great.

To fund the expedition he sold all his properties. In exchange for his Granville-la-Teinturière and Béthencourt chateaux, he borrowed a large sum from his cousin Robin de Braquemont, who was an influential Castilian courtier and a *jefe de guardia* of the Antipope Benedict XIII. He had originally received these possessions in a dowry after marrying the wealthy Jeanne de Feyel in 1392, but relations between them had generally been acrimonious, suggesting that he had only entered the liaison as a business arrangement. They never had children, though he did father at least one offspring from extramarital affairs.

Once the die was cast Béthencourt met up with Gadifer in La Rochelle in April 1402 and convinced this equally adventurous fellow Norman to join him as second in command (at his own expense). Together they assembled a crew of eighty fighting men—a rough and ready band of Gascons and Normans with purely mercenary ambitions that were not entirely discouraged by the expedition's leaders themselves since profits

Jean de Béthencourt
(Wiki05/ Wikimedia Commons)

from trade, spoils and slavery were still regarded as entirely acceptable.

The expedition was accompanied by two translators, baptized Lanzarote natives who had taken on the Christian names of Isabel and Alfonso plus two Franciscan monks, Pierre Bontier and Jean le Verrier, whose dual roles were as chaplains and chroniclers and whose main objective was on arrival to "convert the heathens". Their later account of the whole enterprise appeared as *Le Canarien*, a detailed, diary-like tome which can be viewed today both in Rouen's Municipal Library (in medieval French) and in the British Museum in London (in English).

Gadifer, ten years older than the forty-something Béthencourt, was a silver-haired, Chaucerian-style "genteel knight", a gentleman of the French king's court and a *mayordomo* in the Gascon province of Bigorre. He cut a dashing Quixote-like figure, idealistic and perhaps a trifle naïve, quite different in character from the more calculating and pragmatic Béthencourt. His narrative of the expedition and its consequences as retold by the two friar-chroniclers le Verrier and Bontier was aimed at the lofty and romantic world of French princes, while Béthencourt's more down-to-earth version of the same events was intended primarily for the more practical eyes of the Castilian court who funded the expedition and expected results in terms of both religious conversions and financial profit.

After several weeks they set sail south and eventually docked at Puerto de Santa María in Cádiz province for refitting and gathering provisions. There 27 members of the force mutinied. They had been impatient with the delay and dubious at the future outcome of the trip when Béthencourt was urgently called away to Seville to (successfully) refute charges brought against him by Genoese merchants who had accused him of misappropriating their ship. Neither shocked nor vindictive on his return, rather than punishing the offending crew members he simply sent them back to France.

Not willing to risk enlisting any new recruits in Cádiz, Béthencourt sailed on further south into the open Atlantic with his now reduced force of 53 fighting men. After eight days they sighted three small satellite islands just north of Lanzarote. Sudden squalls forced them into temporarily anchor on La Graciosa, the largest and closest of these islets to the main island. There Béthencourt set up a "council of war" to discuss tactics to adopt after landing on Lanzarote.

The islanders, however, presented no problems when Béthencourt,

Gadifer and their followers set foot there the following day. Guardafia, the local king and a hearty giant of a man, was warmly amenable and treated the visitors like old friends. His relationship with Béthencourt and Gadifer was more of an alliance than an act of subservience to new overlords. They recognized him as king and promised to protect the island from pirate invasions; he in turn encouraged them to build a fort at the south coast bay of Rubicón, which was to be eventually recognized as a bishopric by Spain and the Vatican (see p.177).

Béthencourt and Gadifer de la Salle were delighted to have found such a solid and comfortable niche in the island, and the commander sailed back to Europe to consolidate his claim on Lanzarote with Spain.

## BETRAYAL

But every Eden has its serpent. This one was a coldly capable young knight called Bertin de Berneval who had been authorized by Béthencourt to hold the fort under Gadifer's orders in his absence. Berneval was highly regarded by his superiors. Yet they, strangely, seem to have overlooked his attempts en route to whip up discord between the Gascons and Normans who formed the crew. Worse, they failed to realize the sheer intensity of his ambitions. For Berneval proved ruthless in his quest for power and had no qualms about treating the local indigenous inhabitants like chattel to achieve his aims. Though he apparently respected Béthencourt he regarded Gadifer with jealousy and contempt.

When Gadifer decided to take a few men to the nearby barren Isla de Lobos to hunt seals whose skins would provide the material for much needed shoes for the mostly barefooted contingent, Berneval seized his chance and in just a few days managed to undo all the good that his leaders had so far achieved. First, he invited the king and various high-ranking Guanches to dine with him. Then, when they were at their most relaxed and unsuspecting, his men seized them and locked them up. The adroit and formidable Guardafia managed to overcome his guards and break free together with a few of his followers but over twenty Lanzarote natives were taken to a Spanish ship called the *Tajamar* which had just anchored off shore, and were in turn imprisoned by its unscrupulous captain, Fernando de Ordoñez, who aimed later to sell them as slaves.

Gadifer, meanwhile, quite unaware of these events, sent a boat back to the Rubicón to collect desperately needed provisions as there was no

Expedition of Gadifer de la Salle and Jean de Béthencourt to Lanzarote in 1402
(Piopio/Wikimedia Commons)

water or food on the Isla de Lobos. Berneval ignored their request, gave abundant supplies stored in the fort to the visiting Spaniards and even seized or destroyed much of Gadifer's personal property, apparently out of pure vindictiveness. As an added insult he encouraged the sailors to violate the French women staying there.

Gadifer's view is recorded in *Le Canarien* by the two friar-chroniclers as follows: "So now you can see and know the great disloyalty of Bertin Berneval, who committed three chief treasons: one was against Gadifer, their captain, whom he left on a desert island to die of hunger and also deprived of men, food and munitions; the second, under the cloak of good faith he welcomed the king of the island of Lancelot [Lanzarote] who had been reassured by him and by us all, and captured him and his people and sold them to Spaniards to carry into slavery; the third, when he was through with his own sworn companions he left them behind for which reason they died" (most of them shipwrecked trying to escape to North Africa: see below).

According to the historian Jennifer R. Goodman in her *Chivalry and Exploration 1298-1630*, after one of his most infamous acts (when he handed over the Poitevin women staying in the fort to be raped by the aforementioned Spanish sailors) Berneval mocked Gadifer—from a safe distance—about his age: "I want Gadifer to know that if he were as young as I am I'd go to kill him, but since he isn't I'll control myself. But if he continues giving me more trouble I'll arrange for him to be drowned at the Island of Wolves: that way he can go fishing for seals." (English version by Peter Stone from Alejandro Cioranescu's Spanish translation of *Le Canarien*).

It was left to the chaplains and two *escuderos* at the Rubicón fort to plead with the Spanish captain of the *Tajamar* to send provisions to their beleaguered leader, who, together with his group of ten men, was close to dying of hunger and thirst on Lobos after eight days without food or fresh water. He and his men had survived by drinking dew caught in a cloth. The captain somewhat reluctantly obliged and sent the provisions, although the crossing ("the most horrible strait of sea that anyone knows") was not easy. In a further attempt to prevent Gadifer getting any help from Lanzarote itself Berneval had removed the oars from longboats moored near the fort.

Probably aware by now that he had gone too far, Berneval made good his escape from Lanzarote with the Spanish ship. He evidently aimed to forestall any revelation of his actions by putting a false account of the situation to both Béthencourt and the Castilian kings.

As a parting stroke to his brief reign of terror, when requested by the chaplains to release the now captive native translator Isabel as she was their only means of mediating and communicating with the islanders, he had her thrown overboard. She would have drowned had the chaplains and their colleagues not rowed frantically to save her.

Berneval ended up imprisoned in Cádiz for his treachery. His lies were exposed by one Courtille, Gadifer's trumpeter, who had accompanied him on his retreat and had no wish to see him go scot free. What prompted Berneval's brief descent into depravity was not clear. Perhaps the sudden access to power in such a strange, new and isolated location went to his head.

Of the French who remained on the island, many were now stricken with remorse that they had been party to Berneval's actions and, fearing reprisals (not from the natives but from their own leader), a dozen of them even tried to get away by boat to Algiers. Ten of them died in a shipwreck during a storm off the Barbary Coast and the remaining two were captured and enslaved. "Advise yourselves as best you can for you're not coming with me," were Berneval's last encouraging words to them.

So Gadifer, having left an island full of friendly locals, returned to a distinctly hostile reception. As a result of Berneval's deeds, attacks on the French occupants had become common and some had been fatal. Distrust and disillusion dominated the indigenous view of the invaders. "How will you protect us when you betray each other?" asked a native spokesman. "It seems you do not possess such a strong and good faith as you would have us believe."

Taking advantage of this reversed situation a local rival to the king, called Ache, tried to befriend and outwardly support Gadifer, whose aid he needed in ousting Guardafia and making himself regent. Together they contrived to capture the king and several of his close followers and put them in irons.

Ache enjoyed a brief period of power before Guardafia made another spectacular escape (mere chains, it seemed, were not enough to hold him). Ache's ultimate aim, predictably, had been to get rid of Gadifer as well, but this ambition proved still-born. Turning the tables once more, the king seized Ache, and had him stoned to death and his body cremated. For the hitherto benign Gadifer this was too much. Suddenly transformed into a cold and unsparing oppressor, he responded in kind. He ordered his men to capture a random Guanche, have him decapitated and his head stuck on a high hilltop post for all to see. The once peaceful French occupants suddenly found themselves openly at war with the native inhabitants, many of whom took refuge in some of the island's many caves, emerging only to launch occasional guerrilla raids on their oppressors.

Béthencourt, meanwhile, still in Europe, had become a subject of the court of Castile after a fruitful meeting with a highly impressed Enrique III, and on hearing of this insurgency sent a ship with 44 soldiers and substantial provisions to help combat the rebellious islanders. During the course of this visit Gadifer received another blow, though it was some time before he heard of it. His own ship, accompanying Béthencourt's small fleet as it sailed up the Guadalquivir, sprang a leak and sank, causing many more his treasured possessions to be lost forever in the deep estuary mud. Though the circumstances were suspicious, no one discovered how or why this occurred.

## GADIFER'S EXPEDITION

Blissfully unaware of the Guadalquivir mishap at this stage, Gadifer found time to plan and carry out visits other islands. His first expedition was to Fuerteventura, also known then as Erbania or Irbane. This proved largely uneventful, with little trouble from the locals although Béthencourt had already established a claim there on the growing of the dye-producing orchil lichen. He went on to Gran Canaria where the reception was mixed. The friendlier islanders brought him gifts such as dragon's blood, much appreciated for its medicinal qualities, while the more warlike of the inhabitants either fought among themselves or intimidated Gadifer and his crew to such an extent they were forced to leave. Another incentive to abandon the island, at least until they could return with more men, came when they found out that thirteen Franciscan priests who had earlier arrived and lived peacefully among the Guanches for seven years had been summarily executed by their hosts on realizing the missionaries had been sending letters back to Europe warning that islanders were not to be trusted.

Gadifer went on to briefly reconnoitre Tenerife and then La Gomera where he and his men spent around three weeks. At the end of this period they captured four women and a child, an act that so incensed the Gomerans that they attacked the crew and forced them to sail before they had even had time even to take on a supply of drinking water.

The small expedition headed now for La Palma but a fierce storm swept them off course to the westerly islet of El Hierro. There the friendly but depleted population (many of whom had been captured and spirited away by pirates in the preceding decades) allowed them a more peaceful stay of 22 days. The island was simply but glowingly described by one of the trip's chroniclers: "excellent water, a rich abundance of quails and frequent rain". Evidently greener then than the stark rocky backwater to be seen today, this tiny Eden is also said to have been home to hawks, larks and parrot-sized birds with pheasant-like feathers as well as lizards as big as cats that were strikingly ugly but quite inoffensive.

Shortly after Gadifer and his crew had sailed back east and dropped anchor in Lanzarote, Béthencourt made his own grand return from Europe to a tumultuous welcome. The valiant but pragmatic Guardafia offered to be baptized, together with his people. Peace and harmony were at last restored, though now with Béthencourt instead of Guardafia as the island's acknowledged "king".

After a subsequent trip back to Europe Béthencourt returned with artisans and farmers who settled and worked on both the easterly islands. Fuerteventura had now assumed as important a role as Lanzarote for the colonizers and in 1404 Béthencourt founded the town of Betancuria in the centre of the island to protect it both from aggressive local natives and Berber pirates from North Africa and to officially establish a capital to his domains. He also built the Richeroche fort close to the capital and shortly afterwards Gadifer built another fort called Valtarhais.

It is interesting to imagine how Fuerteventura was in those times. With so few people occupying such a vast area (it is the second largest of the Canaries after Tenerife), the sense of space would have been immense. The sprawling, whale-shaped island with its strange, other-world aura boasted a mere 340 inhabitants and even this tiny number was split into two mini-kingdoms separated by a rough stone wall that crossed the entire island. On the northern side were the Maxorata and on the southern side the Handia (occupying the area now known as Jandia). The two factions were bitter enemies, which was unfortunate for them as united they might well have defeated Béthencourt and Gadifer's relatively modest forces.

Not that it went easily for the Normans at first. There were several pitched battles during one of which the Richeroche fort was destroyed and Béthencourt's men were forced to retreat to Lanzarote. Eventually, after a series of defeats and weakened by interminable Maxorata-Handia conflicts, the Fuerteventurans succumbed, accepted Christian rule and followed Guardafia's example, offering themselves to be baptized and encouraging their followers to do the same.

The Canarian anthropologist Luis D. Cuscoy, who, in addition to being a leading authority on the Guanche era and founder of the Museo Arqueológico de Tenerife, was an accomplished poet, essayist and novelist, recounts in his colourful historical work *Entre el volcán y la caracola* how the two reconciled Fuerteventuran kings, after being baptized and changing their original names of Guize and Ayoze to Luis and Alfonso respectively, sat down to a sumptuous dinner with the elegantly clad Béthencourt. There, for the first time in their lives, they heard the melodic wail of flutes, played by Norman musicians. Accustomed only to the whistling of the wind and sifting hiss of ocean swells they were mesmerized by this delicately haunting new sound. When the music had finished they approached the king and one of them (which one is not recorded) said: "Sire, if you had come to us earlier, dressed as you are now and with the music you have just allowed us to hear, you would have conquered the island much sooner as there would have been no need to fight. And if you wished, you could conquer many other countries simply by dressing as you are dressed now and bringing with you the men who are playing these marvellous instruments."

Like El Hierro at the far western end of the archipelago, Fuerteventura appears to have been more fertile then than it is today. Barley grew in abundance and there were lush valleys and rich forests which Gadifer's men had encountered with delight on their first expedition. When Béthencourt introduced his northern artisans and farmers to work and develop the land they were pleased with the opportunity to start a new life in this perennially warm paradise.

Seeking now to widen his expanding Christian mini-kingdom beyond the islands Béthencourt made a brief trip to Cabo Bojador on the African mainland where after some brief skirmishes with Berbers he decided to retreat, taking on board—instead of the usual hostages—some camels. He

Camels in Lanzarote (Frank Vincentz/Wikimedia Commons)

transported them back to the surprised *lanzaroteños* who had apparently never set eyes on such creatures before and wondered why he had brought them. In fact the astute Béthencourt had envisaged their use as beasts of burden working in the often water-deprived countryside. Today you can see their haughty descendants loping condescendingly up and down the orange-black volcanic slopes of Fire Mountain with tourists precariously seated in wooden chairs on their backs en route for, or precariously returning from, the ash-covered summit.

Next he followed Gadifer's example by setting off on his own tour of the other islands. His first port of call was Gran Canaria where he met the island's king, Artamy. His aim was, at least outwardly, peaceful and his approach cautious for he had heard many tales of the warlike nature of the island's 10,000 inhabitants. But some of his over-confident followers had other ideas. While Béthencourt was still engaged in relaxed negotiations with the king a group of 42 ambitious soldiers, led by his deputy Jean de Courteois and convinced of their military superiority (in prowess if not numbers), decided to engage Gran Canarian warriors in battle at Arguineguin on the island's south coast. They lost twenty men, among them Jean de Courteois himself and Gadifer's bastard son, Hannibal. Small though the number may sound it represented the biggest strategic error the Normans had yet made.

Shaken and exhausted, the survivors fled the island with a jaundiced Béthencourt, who, having broken off his discussions with the island king in order to rejoin his men, was saddened by his losses and dismayed at seeing his diplomatic moves and long-term plans for Gran Canaria suddenly come to nought.

The expedition headed westwards to La Palma, the second most mountainous island in the archipelago. Here the terrain aided the local warriors in further inevitable skirmishes, though none of these proved as destructive as the sobering experience in Gran Canaria, and the Normans suffered far fewer losses than the islanders. Nevertheless they failed to control the whole island and decided to leave.

Their next destination was El Hierro where Béthencourt changed his tactics and for the first time acted with an unexpected harshness. The local *bambiches* put up virtually no resistance to his expedition and for their pains, having been promised peace, were treacherously deceived. Béthencourt took seventy inhabitants hostage and sold many of them as slaves.

The gently persuasive pragmatist of yesterday was gone. Perhaps he had been hardened by recent experiences, or was trying the placate followers who thought him too soft. More likely, he was simply trying to advance and amplify the power and authority of both himself and his followers. He next indulged in some ingratiating nepotism, installing many friends and relatives he had brought with him from France on the island, handing out properties and land seized from the ousted *bambiches* to around 26 Norman and Gascon families.

Back in Lanzarote he made similar provision for other French families as well as for a fair number of locals. All were given their own homesteads and land to cultivate and the newer arrivals were exempted from paying taxes for two years but had to pay Béthencourt one-fifth of the profit from everything the land produced. There was one taboo. Absolutely no one was allowed to have any dealings with the orchil trade apart from Béthencourt himself. The Norman ruler now made his base the Valle de Tarajal fortress in Fuerteventura, which had been built by Gadifer during his absence in Spain.

In view of his success in converting the inhabitants of both the easternmost islands to Christianity, Béthencourt raised his sights and sought recognition of this new bastion of Catholicism from Rome. He accordingly planned a visit to see the pope himself with the aim of appointing a bishop as the islands' ecclesiastical leader.

It might seem that now was the right time for him and his fellow Norman Gadifer to enjoy the fruits of their successful enterprise after all they had gone through together, but alas the two were barely on speaking terms. Gadifer had expected Béthencourt to bequeath other islands to his authority and the latter had responded that these were all now the rightful property of Castile.

Both returned to Spain to try and settle their material differences in lawsuits but in the end Gadifer received nothing and retired disgruntled to his native France. He must have felt the gods were against him ever since he arrived in the archipelago. His setbacks had been threefold. The first had occurred when Berneval briefly assumed power and not only left him abandoned and in danger of dying with his handful of men on the Isla de Lobos but also took or destroyed many of his possessions and left him facing a fiercely rebellious local population when he did get back to terra firma to assume control again; the second when Gadifer's own ship had sunk with many more valued possessions on board in the Guadalquivir when Béthencourt was travelling alongside it on his way from the Cádiz coast to Seville to secure recognition from Castile for his achievements; and the third when his son Hannibal had died during the abortive battle with Gran Canaria islanders at Arguenguin. Being denied his right to own as well as govern the islands after all he had endured was, in his eyes, the last straw. For him it was a bitterly disappointing end to an enterprise that had started so harmoniously.

With Gadifer no longer on the island Béthencourt appointed his young nephew Maciot to govern Lanzarote, Fuerteventura and El Hierro and set off for Seville on the first leg of his journey to Rome. From there he continued to Valladolid where King Enrique III received him warmly, made him an honoured guest at his palace for two weeks and persuaded him to recount all the exploits and successes he had achieved in such a short time and with such—relatively—little bloodshed. Béthencourt then continued across Europe by land, laden with regal gifts, riding a mule (also a present from the king) and accompanied by a modest retinue of ten men. Enrique had agreed to write ahead to the pope requesting a bishop for the islands on his behalf. Béthencourt's welcome when he finally arrived, road weary, in Rome, was equally warm.

The pope was highly impressed with his work for the Church and appointed a Spanish bishop, Alberto de las Casas, to be the religious leader of the islands. He even discussed the possibility of exploring the African coast in depth with an aim to making future conversions there. Béthencourt next went on to visit Florence, where he was again impressively feted, and then eventually headed, tired and content, northwards to Paris and his home town of Grainville-la-Teinturière to visit the wife he had not set eyes on for many years. Though the welcome he received was warmer than those in the past he and his aging wife still did not have the closest of relationships. She died not long after his return and he, after more military action, eventually became ill and passed away in his home village, never managing to set eyes on the Canaries again. (Grainville-la-Teinturière is now twinned with Teguise and Betancuria.)

The historian José de Viera y Clavijo said of Béthencourt: "In addition to his noble features, highflown thoughts and impetuous yet firm and resolute boldness, Jean de Béthencourt was capable of chivalrous action. His character epitomized the two key traits of his century: valour and piety."

This somewhat over-glowing assessment was tempered in reality by the fact that the highly practical and business-minded Béthencourt had often acted selfishly and opportunistically (notably in El Hierro) and had no qualms about feathering his own nest at Gadifer's expense. It was left to the latter, his erstwhile friend and colleague, to demonstrate the true knightly virtues of—in the words of Jennifer R. Goodman—"daring, loyalty and generosity". Gadifer did not waste away in melancholic solitude during his final years, mourning the loss of what might have been. He spent them on active duty in the service of the Duke of Orléans, a brave and noble knight to the end.

But it is Jean de Béthencourt who is remembered today and who left the most lasting legacy. He was a seminal influence in developing the eastern islands and the feudal system set up by him lasted until the nineteenth century, even after the Castilians had completely taken over. His name, with all its possible variations (Betancort, Betencour, Betencort, Betancuria), lives on and is commonly found throughout the archipelago. It now recalls an era of relative innocence and chivalry which disappeared when a powerful and uncompromising Castile ruthlessly conquered the rest of the peninsula.

## ISLANDS FOR SALE

Sadly, the Béthencourt name came to be regarded by the islanders with considerably less esteem before the Castilians arrived. When Jean de Béthencourt left the islands for good, he installed his nephew Maciot in his place as Governor of Lanzarote, Fuerfeventura and El Hierro. It was one of his rare errors of judgement. The eager youngster began his tenure as a benevolent and just leader but later succumbed—like the notorious Berneval—to greed and ambition.

Extortion, expropriation of private property and selling native Canarians into slavery soon became the order of the day. Thanks to the excesses of Maciot's rule further rebellions broke out and for a brief period the natives came close to reassuming their former domination of the island. By 1414 Maciot's "exactions and tyranny" had reached such a level that the Spanish Queen Catherine felt compelled to send three caravelles under the captaincy of Pedro Barba de Campos, Lord of Castro Forte, to bring him under control. The result was hardly what she had in mind. The wily and manipulative Maciot managed to cede the islands to Barba and then sail to Madeira where he sold them—along with the as yet unconquered Tenerife and Gran Canaria—to King Henry (the Navigator) of Portugal.

The wheeling and dealing accelerated as Maciot went on to grant the islands to the Duke of Niebla, while Barba sold them to Fernando Perez of Seville who in turn tried to sell them back (apparently for a second time) to the self-same Duke of Niebla. The latter then sold them to Guillermo de las Casas who sold them to his son-in-law Fernan Peraza (the Elder). And here the merry-go-round mercifully ended. The islands stayed under the ownership of Peraza and his family, including children Guillén and Inés and their offspring, until 1477.

While all these labyrinthine transactions were taking place, Béthencourt, back in France, was still legally deemed to be the islands' only real owner and he accordingly left them in his will to his brother Reynaud, apparently to patch up differences the two had had in the past. But Reynaud never saw, nor was allowed to assume possession of, the islands.

Maciot's private life was as colourful as his business transactions. In 1415 he had a relationship with Guardafia's daughter Teguise and had at least two known children, Rodrigo and Inés Margarida, by her. When his shady dealings caught up with him later he and his family were imprisoned in El Hierro, from where they later escaped and fled to Portugal. After more dubious activities—including a last-ditch attempt to sell Lanzarote once more to the Portuguese regent—he died in Madeira. The final days of Béthencourt rule had ended in ignominious confusion.

Largely as a result of Maciot's intrigues there were constant tussles between Portugal and Spain over the rightful ownership of the archipelago. A 1479 treaty at Alcaçova signed by Alfonso V of Portugal and Ferdinand and Isabella of Spain finally settled matters by confirming that the Canaries were Spanish territory and that Portugal, in turn, was the legal owner of Madeira, the Azores and Cabo Verde.

Throughout all this wrangling Tenerife and Gran Canaria still remained largely under the control of the native Canarians, who had perhaps enjoyed watching from afar their would-be rulers' self-defeating squabbles. But the Guanches' days of independence were numbered. The Norman invasion was over, having only partly achieved its aims. Spain's merciless conquest of the rest of the archipelago was about to begin.

Torre del Conde, La Gomera
(Diego Delso/Wikimedia Commons)

## *Chapter Four*
# UNDER THE CASTILIAN FLAG

After Maciot's disastrous tenure as governor of half the archipelago an avaricious band of *señoríos* (feudal lords) took over, extending their tentacles of power throughout the islands. The neo-Borgian Peraza family coalesced into the single most influential of these and exerted a firm grip on their four strongholds: La Gomera, Lanzarote, Fuerteventura and El Hierro. But by the late fifteenth century change had begun. The archipelago gradually came under the direct control of Spain's *realengo* system which appointed regional governors directly responsible to the Catholic monarchs Ferdinand and Isabella. Arbitrary decisions based on individual whims or personal tastes were now being superseded by a uniform and harsh code of conduct in which the crown came foremost but the Inquisition would soon play a powerful role as well. On the cusp of New World domination, the first Hispanic mini-colonies were born.

### JUAN REJÓN, THE ISLANDS' FIRST *CONQUISTADOR*
In 1478, just one year before the Alcaçova treaty (see Chapter 3), an Aragonese captain called Juan Rejón was appointed Castile's official pioneer *conquistador* to the islands. He sailed from Puerto de Santa María with a fleet of three ships and an army of 600 mainly Andalusian soldiers to Lanzarote where he convened with the Bishop of Rubicón, Juan de Frias, before continuing on to Las Isletas in Gran Canaria.

The island was at that time divided by its native *Canario* inhabitants into the *guanartematos* (kingdoms) of Galdar and Telde which, respectively, covered the north-western and south-eastern regions. Rejón and his men camped in a palm grove close to the centrally located Guiniguada gulley. After swiftly fortifying the area they engaged in an early battle with native islanders led by Doramas, the legendary *guanarteme* (chief) of Galdar.

The *Canarios* lost spectacularly and their casualties totalled around 300 men. Fearless in conventional hand-to-hand warfare between foot soldiers, they were thrown into panic and disarray at seeing horses in battle for the first time and most of their losses were caused by cavalry charges. The Spaniards suffered only slight casualties and after this victory assumed control of the north-west of the island.

The indigenous Canarians were hardly pushovers, though. Their warriors, like many of those of the other islands, were noted for their exceptional strength and agility. None more so than a wrestler called Ardogama whom the Spaniards managed to take prisoner and send back to Spain after the Guiniguada battle to show the Catholic kings just what they were up against. Ardogama had incurred serious wounds during the battle, and the Spaniards, impressed by the way he had fought, refrained from killing him and instead cared for him until he was well again. He reciprocated by allowing himself to be baptized and converted to Christianity.

Juan de Abreu Galindo relates how later, when Ardogama was staying in Seville at the house of a noted priest, a visiting peasant from La Mancha who also fancied himself as a wrestler challenged the converted Canarian to a bout. Ardogama responded that the fight was on only if the man could prevent him from raising a glass of wine to his lips without a single drop being spilt. The Manchegan agreed to this condition but though he tried with all his might, using both hands, to stop Ardogama drinking from the full glass, he failed. Wisely, he decided not to go ahead with the wrestling match.

In spite of the Castilians' first flush of military success at Guiniguada strong differences of opinion arose among the invaders. Relations between Rejón and a certain Bermúdez, his accompanying dean, became strained to near breaking point. But other priorities came first. After the battle Rejón realized that his small contingent was badly in need of reinforcements. He accordingly went for support to Lanzarote, which was still under the feudal rule of Diego de Herrera, a prominent member of the Peraza family. This intractable governor, who had barely tolerated Rejón's presence before when he had met with the Bishop of Rubicón, not only refused to help him but actually had him and his small entourage ejected from the island.

On his return to Gran Canaria, Rejón found that Bermúdez and Pedro de Algaba, his replacement in his absence, had been conspiring against him. They arrested him on a variety of contrived charges, put him in chains and sent him back to Spain as a prisoner. There the charges were dismissed by the Castilian court and Rejón was allowed to return to the islands with a fresh supply of provisions and munitions. While he had been in Spain Bermúdez's and Algaba's forces had been defeated by the Guanches under Doramas at Moya, where the wily *guanarteme* had chosen a battle site at which the Spanish found it difficult to use their cavalry.

Taking advantage of the demoralized atmosphere and his own vindication by the Spanish crown, Rejón assumed he now had *carte blanche* to make his own laws as governor. He arrested the would-be usurper Algaba on a counter charge of treason and after a brief trial had him executed on the site that is now Las Palmas' Plaza de San Antonio Abad. Bermúdez was in turn exiled to Lanzarote. With his rivals removed, the future looked promising again for Rejón until his force of 500 soldiers and 400 horsemen suffered a heavy defeat at the hands of the Guanches in Tirajana in 1479 where the rugged terrain favoured their guerrilla-style warfare.

It was time for Rejón to reflect. Over a year had passed since his arrival and though he controlled most of the northern part of Gran Canaria the rest still remained unconquered. He had made no further headway against the Canarians since the initial Guiniguada battle. His one great achievement, however, had been to found the city of Las Palmas and for this he is largely remembered on the island today. The historic Vegueta quarter stands on the very spot where he first landed and his name can be found on plaques there and throughout the capital.

The Spanish monarchs suddenly decided to recall him to the peninsula and to appoint Pedro de Vera as new island governor. Apart from being disappointed by Rejón's failure to conquer the whole island they felt he needed to explain the excessively savage nature of some of his actions, in particular his execution of Algaba. He was exonerated once again at his trial in Spain and allocated other duties in the peninsula. After a few months, the crown gave him another chance and allowed him to return with a new expedition whose aim was to conquer La Palma and Tenerife.

But this time fate dealt Rejón a bad hand. Before he was able to reach either of those two islands he found himself swept off course by strong winds to La Gomera, which was still partially under native control but mainly in the hands of another leading member of the Peraza clan, Hernán (the Younger), who—like de Herrera in Lanzarote—was one of Rejón's deadliest enemies. He was a man described by the German historian and anthropologist D. J. Wölfel as being "without a conscience, proud and brutal".

Though Rejón had the weight of the Spanish crown behind him the intransigent Peraza was both unimpressed by this fact and outraged his presence, even accidentally, in his domain. He brought a well-armed force to the spot where Rejón was attempting to land and as the latter was disembarking ordered his men to seize and arrest him. When Rejón vigorously resisted, one of Peraza's men thrust a lance into his body. Rejón died in the arms of his wife, who was accompanying him on the expedition, and was buried in San Sebastian parish church.

Now it was Peraza's turn to face the Catholic monarchs and explain his actions. Either his pleas were highly persuasive or he had influential friends in high places (probably the latter) but in the end he was exonerated. There were, however, two conditions for his release. One, that he agreed to a marriage of convenience to a lady of the court called Beatriz de Bobadilla with whom King Fernando was said to be in love (this ploy was, of course, stage managed by Queen Isabella herself); the other, that he bring his own troops to Gran Canaria and help conquer the island, thus finishing the work that Rejón had intended to accomplish before dealing with La Palma and Tenerife.

## THE PERAZA CLAN

The Perazas warrant a close look. Their half-century-long *señorío* domination of the archipelago effectively began in 1440 when Fernán Peraza the Elder married Inés the daughter of Guillén de las Casas, who had in turn inherited the islands twelve years after the conniving Maciot de Béthencourt passed their ownership on to the Conde de Niebla, Enrique Pérez de Guzmán y de Castilla, in 1418. (The latter, an elegant military figure, was later drowned during one of many sieges of the Moorish-held peninsula of Jebel al Tariq—today's Gibraltar.)

Peraza the Elder had a daughter, also named Inés, and a son, Guillén. The latter achieved lasting posthumous fame after he was killed by a rock hurled by a native *Benahoritan* during a Spanish attack on the Aceró kingdom inside the fertile crater valley of Taburiente in La Palma. He was the first Castilian commander to be lost in a Canary Island battle and his death inspired a heartfelt *endecha* (tragic poem or song). Written and dedicated to his memory by an anonymous author, this was the very first poetic work to appear in Canarian literature. Its text is brief enough to quote in full:

*Llorad, las damas, si Díos os vala.*
*Guillén Peraza quedó en La Palma*
*La flor marchita de su cara.*
*No eres palma ni retama,*
*Eres ciprés de triste rama,*
*Eres desdicha, desdicha mala,*
*Tus campos rompan tristes volcanes,*
*No vean placeres, sino pesares,*
*Obran tus flores los arenales.*
*Guillén Peraza, Guillén Peraza,*
*¿dó está tu escudo? Dó está tu lanza?*
*Todo lo acaba la maladranza!*

The estimable George Glas' highly florid eighteenth-century translation of this reads as follows:

O pour forth, ye damsels, your plaint
For God's sake, ye damsels, lament
For Guillén Peraza the Brave
At Palma is left in the grave
The flow'r on his cheek brightly shone
That flow'r now is blasted and gone.

Let dire volcanoes now destroy
Thy fields, that lately filled with joy;
Let no glad prospect met our eyes,
On every side let sorrows rife!
Let all the flow'rs that graced thy lands
Be buried under burning sands.
Alas! Peraza is no more!
Peraza's loss we all deplore!
O! where now is thy trusty shield!
O! where the lance thy arm did wield!
A fore lamented enterprise
Cut short thy schemes, and closed thine eyes.

Guillén's brother-in-law, Diego de Herrera, the man who turned down Rejón's plea for reinforcements, was a nobleman from Seville. He had married Guillén's sister Inés Peraza and become the "lord" of Lanzarote in 1444. Over the next couple of decades he ruled the island with uncompromising harshness and made a partially successful expedition to Gran Canaria as a result of which the *guanartemes* of Telde and Gáldar initially agreed to be his vassals only to rise against him shortly afterwards. He also attempted to establish a Spanish base in Tenerife, where he suffered two resounding defeats at the hands of the Guanche leader Imobach de Taoro. He died of a serious but undocumented illness in 1485 in Fuerteventura and was buried in the San Buenaventura Monastery.

De Herrera fathered five children: Sancho de Herrera, who, after his demise and in conjunction with sisters María de Ayala and Constanza de Sarmiento, inherited Lanzarote and Fuerteventura; black sheep of the family Pedro García de Herrera, who inherited nothing; and, most famous and formidable of them all, our hero Hernán Peraza (the Younger) who inherited La Gomera and El Hierro in 1485, launched a reign of oppression against the islands' inhabitants and was responsible, as we have just seen, for Juan Rejón's violent end.

Four years after this infamous act, Hernán received his own grizzly comeuppance. Lovelessly espoused to Beatriz de Bobadilla in the marriage of convenience mentioned earlier, he indulged in a secret affair with a beautiful Gomeran called Iballa. Her fellow native islanders got wind of this and Iballa's jealous admirer Hautacuperche, urged on by the island's spiritual native leader Hupolupo, persuaded her to arrange a tryst in the Guahedun cave—one of their habitual meeting places. There he and his colleagues planned to seize and murder the hated governor.

Hernán Peraza's end was poetically just: as sudden and brutal as his treatment of the Gomerans and Rejón had been. According to Juan de Abreu Galindo, Iballa had a change of heart when she was face to face with her lover. She regretted her involvement in this plan and told Peraza to escape as his life was in danger. She made him disguise himself by wearing female clothing but when he heard the sound of enemies approaching he threw these garments off proclaiming "If I'm to be taken or killed it shall not be in a woman's dress." As he stepped determinedly out of the cave brandishing his sword, Hautacuperche, who was poised in readiness on a ledge above, plunged a sharply pointed dart attached to the

Statue of Hautacuperche, La Gomera
(Pediant/Wikimedia Commons)

end of a long wooden pole down into his neck, piercing the armour and killing him instantly. (The hapless squire and page who habitually accompanied Peraza on these trysts were also mercilessly slaughtered by Hautacuperche's accomplices, sad to relate.)

There were no *endechas* for this Peraza. Instead, the populace rose in outrage when it heard of the relationship and saw only one common enemy—the unwelcome, overbearing *señorial* intruders. Beatriz, humiliated and furious, found herself forced to hide for her own safety in a tower, the Torre del Conde, built by Peraza, desperately awaiting help from Gran Canaria.

## PEDRO DE VERA

Her saviour was the chillingly efficient Pedro de Vera, who landed on the island promising pardons for those who had retreated to the Garajonay heights on learning of his arrival but now wished to come down and surrender. He then proceeded to hang or sell into slavery anyone—men, women and children alike—who was foolish enough to commit such a trusting act. (There are advance echoes here of the Extremaduran *conquistador* Pizarro's even more treacherous and brutal treatment of the Incas and their trusting king Atahualpa during his conquest of Peru.)

A symbol ironically commemorating de Vera's inhumane cruelty is the "Cuatro Caminos" (Four Ways) cross which stands on a ridge known as the Risco de la Hila. The cross's name refers to the dismembering execution technique by which a prisoner's arms and legs are tied to four separate horses, each of which is then encouraged to gallop off in a different direction.

It was left to Pedro de Vera to eventually conquer Gran Canaria, where so many others had failed, this time largely thanks to increased military aid provided by Diego de Herrera. At the Battle of Arucas in 1481 he decisively defeated the forces led by Doramas (Juan Rejón's former opponent at Guiniguada). The chronicler Juan de Abreu colourfully relates how, after already having killed a Córdoban champion Juan de Hoces whom the Castilians had put forward as their most accomplished warrior after a challenge from Doramas to engage in single man to man combat, the valiant Guanche chief engaged in a similar contest with the Castilian general himself, only to lose ignominiously when a foot soldier attacked him from behind and Pedro de Vera was able to take advantage of the distraction and plunge a lance into Doramas' chest.

According to Abreu, the Guanche chief converted to Christianity before dying though most sources claim he was defiant and unbending till the end, contemptuous of the fact that de Vera had only managed to best him through treachery. To seal this victory for the Spaniards, and as a stark warning to other rebels, de Vera arranged for Doramas' decapitated head to be placed on a pole at the entrance to the town of Las Palmas.

## DORAMAS: A *CANARIO* LEGEND

Doramas was the last charismatic Gran Canaria chief to fall and his passing marked the end of an era. Today, in towns throughout the island, a multitude of streets and squares are named after him, as is one of Las Palmas' most beautiful parks, a lovely urban oasis of subtropical plants, *drago* trees, twinkling fountains and evocative sculptures located in the heart of the city.

His name was a corruption of Durar Ammas, which means roughly "mountains in between" and referred to his exceptionally wide nostrils.

He was of medium height and broad-shouldered, and had risen to the heights of leadership thanks to his limitless ambition and fearless agility in combat. Over the years he led many rebellious uprisings against the Spanish invaders, defeating Pedro de Algaba's forces at the Cuesta de Tenoya and destroying Diego de Herrera's Torre de Gando fort in reprisal for the Castilians' continuous cattle rustling.

Though he in fact came from a very modest background he referred to himself as a *guayre* (noble), a term ridiculed by "higher-class" *Canarios*, in particular one Bentagoche of Telde who, after beating him in combat, asked the young Doramas, as he lay pinioned on the ground, who he thought he was now. *Doramas, achic Doramas, achiscana* ("Doramas, son of Doramas, *atrasquilado*, or "shorn", plebeian) was his rueful reply, admitting that his short hair confirmed his low status on the Guanche social scale. Bentagoche, satisfied, returned Doramas his weapons and they became firm allies.

According to the historian Martín de Cubas, Doramas' great love was a nobleman's daughter called Abenohara, who disrupted the island's class conventions by ardently reciprocating his attentions. Her parents, Maninidra and Tenesor Semidán (Bentagoche's sister-in-law and brother), removed her to a fort on a wild secluded islet called Roque de Gando for her safety and protection, but the tactic proved useless as Doramas had no difficulty in swimming across the straits to spend amorous nights with her. It seems he was eventually accepted into the Semidáns' circle, however, for when Bentagoche died and Tenesor took over as *guanarteme* he appointed Doramas as *Guayre* of Galdar and Captain of Gran Canaria, two of the highest positions on the island.

Back now to the Battle of Arucas. After Doramas' death Tenesor and Maninidra were taken prisoner as they hid in a cave. The remaining native survivors fled to the most mountainous and inaccessible corners of the islands. De Vera spared the lives of Tenesor and several other Canarians and sent them to Spain—less from mercy than with a view to enhancing his personal prestige as a conqueror. Tenesor was presented to the Catholic monarchs, baptized and given the Christian name of Fernando Guanarteme. From then on he sided with the Castilians and helped them in their conquest of the island. As a reward for this collaboration Spain granted him his own lands and freedom. His remains are in a hermitage in Plaza San Cristóbal in the Tenerife town of La Laguna.

Not all the Guanches gave up so peacefully or—in the eyes of harsher judges—so cravenly as this pragmatic prince. Doramas would undoubtedly have turned in his grave had he known of Tenesor Semidán's actions. Many Gran Canarian rebels, such as the guerrilla leader Tasarte, also despised the very suggestion of surrender and were defiant to the end, preferring to die leaping from high cliffs to surrendering to invaders. Opposition slowly petered out, however. Mountainous Ansite was the last Guanche bastion to fall and by 1487 the whole island was officially recognized as Spanish territory.

### COLUMBUS AND BEATRIZ DE BOBADILLA

In 1492 a forty something global seafarer from Genoa, whose commemorative statues today extend throughout Iberian ports from Barcelona to Lisbon, tarried a while in Gran Canaria before continuing the voyage that led to his eventual discovery of the Americas. Silver haired, no longer in the flush of youth, yet on the very threshold of international fame, Christopher Columbus dropped anchor first in the Bahía de Gando and then at what is now Puerto de la Luz in Las Palmas. When he eventually set sail

Casa de Colón, Las Palmas (sailko/Wikimedia Commons)

westwards on that first historic voyage, he noted in his diary that as he passed Tenerife he saw a violent eruption from the 12,000-foot Teide's volcanic peak. Whether or not he thought it augured well, he did not say.

During subsequent Gran Canaria visits Columbus stayed at a house now known as Casa de Colón in the street of the same name (Calle Colón, 1, in the Vegueta district of Las Palmas). Dating from the end of the fifteenth century, the building belonged to the first governor of the island. Today visitors can see the plaque commemorating the fact that, just before that first epic Atlantic voyage, Columbus offered prayers at the San Antonio Abad hermitage. Clearly they were answered.

He also landed several times in La Gomera on subsequent trips to stock up with water and provisions. Another reason for calling there was to see Peraza's widow, Beatriz de Bobadilla, whom Columbus had met at the Spanish court and with whom he is said to have had intimate relations. The two alleged lovers also had a common interest in the slave trading business—one of the reasons the countess was not popular on the island. Another reason, as we shall see, was her uncontrollably tyrannical nature.

Beatriz de Bobadilla y Ossorio was a unique figure of her age: a woman of "character" who stood out in a predominantly male-dominated world. In portraits she appears self-contained, quasi-demure, distantly captivating. Yet clearly there is more. *Fogosa y bella* ("fiery and beautiful") is Las Palmas journalist Alejandro Zabaleta's succinct assessment. The modern Canary-born historian Antonio Rumeu de Armas goes further with his assessment that she was "passionate and hard, prone to unpremeditated reactions when the impulse of violence seized her". He further adds that she was "a tender sensitive woman who fell in love easily, and was capable of volcanic amorous passions, of a dazzling beauty which is still very much a topic of discussion today". He concludes: "In her private life she fell out with all her relations. In governing the region her iron hand dealt equally harshly with all levels of society, from the powerful to the humble, but was especially bloodthirsty when it came to dealing with the local natives." The eighteenth-century historian Viera y Clavijo in turn writes of "a strange woman, with all the graces and weaknesses of her sex, she also displayed the cruelty and perseverance of a vicious male."

Clearly Beatriz inspired more incendiary comments than did most of her contemporaries, male or female. Her love of power (she had ruled La

Gomera in her son's name since becoming a widow in 1488) was intense. So was her love of men. Three notable suitors stand out above the rest. The first was a Master of the distinguished Calatrava Order called Rodrigo Tellés Girón. Next came Fernando, King of Castile. And third was Columbus, who on his second visit to La Gomera is said to have become hopelessly captivated by the "jade green" eyes of La Bobadilla over dinner one evening.

Experts differ in their opinions as to whether this last relationship really existed or was simply a lavish invention. The self-exiled Romanian-born linguist and historian Alejandro Cioranescu, who made Tenerife his new home after escaping from the Ceausescu dictatorship, confirmed his belief in the liaison in his *Colón y Canarias* (1957). (Cioranescu was also responsible for the Spanish translation, from its original medieval French, of *Le Canarien*: see Chapter 3). His view, however, was questioned by two other heavyweight chroniclers: Rumeu de Armas, one of the most thorough researchers of Beatriz' life and times, and who, in the course of his lengthy exchange of correspondence on the subject with the distinguished essayist and philologist María Rosa Alonso (who died in Puerto de la Cruz in 2011 at the ripe old age of 101), expressed the belief that much of the story was the fruit of an over-heated imagination. Most Canarians prefer to believe the tale is true, though, as it adds to the romantic appeal of the islands. One thing is sure: as a strong, independent woman well ahead of her time, Beatriz attracted more attention than any other female of this era—with the exception of Queen Isabella herself. But in the end her cruel side got the better of her and she overstepped the mark by committing two particularly brutal acts.

The first occurred when her decision to marry the recently-widowed Alonso Fernández de Lugo attracted outspoken criticism from a Gomeran subject called Nuñez de Castañedawho thought her actions unseemly in view of her own "state of widowhood". She ordered him to come to visit her and explain himself. When he admitted having criticized her she had him hanged from a beam in her house, after which she had the corpse taken to his own house and "hanged again on a palm tree before his own gate".

The second was when, while absent in Tenerife with de Lugo, she received anonymous letters stating that Hernán Muñoz, whom she had left in charge of La Gomera, was plotting against her to assume control of the island. She returned in fury and in spite of receiving his strenuous denials ordered him to be hanged without a trial or any vestige of truth being proved and returned to Tenerife while the sentence was being carried out.

The grieving widows of both men went to Spain to lodge bitter complaints against Beatriz to the queen and the latter summoned her to Medina del Campo in Castile where she was then residing. La Bobadilla, thinking herself above reproach, and against the warnings of her new husband, decided to go—anxious to revisit both her homeland and the town where she was born. She was received warmly by the royals and well feted. Yet shortly after her arrival in Spain the servants discovered her dead one morning in her bed. No explanation for this was ever found or given. The era's most wilful and tempestuous lady was gone. The year was 1501. She was just 39.

Beatriz de Bobadilla
(http://www.guanches.org/enciclopedia/images/f/f9/Beatriz_de_Bovadilla.JPG)

## Alonso Fernández de Lugo and the Battles of Acentejo

Alonso Fernández de Lugo, now a widower again, returned to Tenerife, alone, sad and disappointed after his days of recent glory. For it was he who had conquered the two last two major islands for Spain. To follow his formidable achievements we have to retrace our steps once more to 1492, when, just as Columbus was beginning his courtship of Beatriz, de Lugo had just been given the title of *adelantado* (military governor of a frontier province) and the green light from the Spanish crown to conquer La Palma and Tenerife.

In La Palma he had come up against considerable opposition before finally achieving victory, defeating the native *Benahoritas* in the rugged heights of Aceró and capturing and imprisoning the island's last native

Awara chief Tanausú in the process. After promising him peace and safe conduct de Lugo went back on his word and put him in chains. The defiant-to-the-end Tanausú succumbed to a hunger strike on board the ship in which he was being transported back to Spain where he was due to be presented to the court. His final single word *vacaguaré* (meaning, simply, "I want to die") expressed a traditional islander's wish to honour his country rather than submit to outsiders.

In 1494 de Lugo headed for Tenerife. He managed to make peace deals with some of the *menceys* such as Añaterve of Guïmar, but not with the *guanarteme* brothers Tinguaro and Bencomo of Taoro, and it was against their combined forces of 3,300 men that he launched the first of his two battles. The outcome came as a complete shock to the Spaniards. Confronted by fierce but primitively equipped warriors bearing wooden spears and wielding rocks they were roundly defeated, even though they were equipped with full armour, guns and cavalry.

The explanation for this debacle was simple. The Spaniards had chosen, or found themselves lured into, a rugged, rock-strewn gulley called Acentejo, more suited to guerrilla warfare, at which the Guanches were masters. Here de Lugo's horsemen, guns and armour proved useless. His forces were harried, hemmed in and rendered virtually impotent. Around a thousand Spaniards perished that day, the greatest military loss their country had suffered up till then. De Lugo himself narrowly escaped death after being seriously injured by a hurled rock that hit him in the face and left him scarred for life. He only survived when his fellow soldiers ushered him to safety, exchanging then vivid red cape he wore to identify himself as the army's *adelantado* for the garb of a common soldier.

This was the Guanches' finest hour. Their army, which had launched a brilliantly tactical two-pronged attack on the Spaniards, was exultant as its warriors seized the Castilian standard and hundreds of swords as trophies. The whole island celebrated. Today one of the highlights of any visit to Santa Cruz is the large mural in the city's municipal park colourfully depicting the *Matanza de Acentejo* (the Acentejo slaughter).

The Guanches thought they had now seen the last of their would-be oppressors but it was, alas, their own swansong. They had underestimated their enemies' determination to avenge hurt pride, their innate instinct to win at all costs and above all their burning lust for power. Alfonso de Lugo soon returned with a stronger army, ready and eager for the fray.

Alfonso Fernández de Lugo by Manuel González Méndez (Parliament of the Canary Islands, Santa Cruz de Tenerife)

The first new engagement took place at Aguere near La Laguna, in November 1494. Though still greatly outnumbered by the Guanches, who were now under three *menceyes*—Tinguaro, Bencomo and Acaymo of Tacoronte—and had over 6,000 men compared with the Castilians' 1,200 soldiers, 70 knights and 600 Guanche allies, this time the Spaniards managed to select the battle site: a vast plain.

De Lugo's forces had built a strongly fortified garrison at Santa Cruz on their arrival from Spain as a contingency measure, a bolthole to escape to should they suffer another defeat, but they need not have worried. Their well-trained infantry and cavalry quickly gained the upper hand, inflicting terrible losses on the primitively equipped Guanches who, as always, only wore goat- or sheep-skin coats for protection, bore neither shields nor armour and whose only weapons—apart from rocks—were *banots* (wooden lances with fire-hardened tips). Such weaponry offered little challenge to the Spaniards' crossbows, arquebuses and pikes which could now be used to full effect in open country.

As before at Guiniguada in Gran Canaria, it was the Spanish cavalry that created the real havoc. Historian-essayist-philosopher supreme Miguel de Unamuno (who spent three months in Fuerteventura during the Civil War before exiling himself further afield to Paris) compared the slaughter here with that inflicted by Hernán Cortés a few decades later in Mexico, where the mere sight of horses spread terror among the Aztecs. In disarray, the Guanches lost up to 2,000 warriors on the Aguere plain that day, while the Spanish casualties barely totalled sixty.

The Guanche retreat was massive and all three of their *menceyes* were badly injured. They first headed for Tacoronte but were cut off by the cavalry and instead switched their goal to the higher San Roque peak where the horses could not reach them. Here one of the three leaders met his end. Most sources claim it was Tinguaro though a minority of researchers, including Francisco de Luca, believe it may have been his brother Bencomo. The body was so disfigured, however, that it was difficult to tell later whose of the two it really was. The *mencey* (let us assume was Tinguaro) had managed to fend off a number of horsemen until an infamous Castilian soldier of Canary descent called Martín Buendía ran him through with his pike as he fell helpless on the ground, vainly entreating the soldier not to kill him as he was a Tenerife prince. Some Spanish soldiers around him are even said to have echoed his plea but the

*Matanza de Acentejo* (© Sandra Cohen-Rose and Colin Rose)

implacable Buendía showed no mercy.

The other brother, perhaps Bencomo, died of wounds suffered on the battlefield only two days later but the third *mencey*, Acaymo, seems to have escaped a violent end, though historians disagree as to what happened to him. Some say he converted to Christianity and served under the Castilians, while others believe he was sold into slavery.

Barely a month later, the second Battle of Acentejo, where around 6,000 Guanches suffered a similar defeat on similar terrain, rang their death knoll. After this final humiliation Bencomo's young son, Bentor, chief of the nation, jumped off a high cliff at Tigaiga. His brief reign and his people's days of glory were over. All the archipelago was now in Spanish hands, and barring a few scattered skirmishes with guerrilla diehards in the high regions there were no further battles. To commemorate this final resounding battle the site was called La Victoria de Acentejo, and the town named after it still features the hermitage built by de Lugo. He subsequently founded the city of San Cristóbal de La Laguna—now known simply as La Laguna—and made it capital of the island (a role it kept until the nineteenth century when that privilege was transferred to Santa Cruz de Tenerife.)

Now unopposed, the Spaniards were free to concentrate on developing their new colony, trading with the Americas and Europe, building their magnificent cathedrals, palaces, mansions and plazas, unaware that a new series of predators would harry them in the coming years almost as fiercely as they had preyed upon the brave but hapless Guanches, whose unique way of life they had destroyed forever.

*Part Two*

CORSAIRS AND CATACLYSMS

Lorenzo A. Castro, *A Sea Fight with Barbary Corsairs*, 1680s
(Google Art project/Wikimedia Commons)

*Chapter Five*

# ISLANDS UNDER SIEGE

## HUGUENOT AND BERBER INCURSIONS

After the victories over the Guanches a wide variety of immigrants, mainly Spanish, came to settle in the islands. They ranged from nobles and aristocrats to simple artisans and they transformed the whole archipelago into a complete new Spanish-speaking colonial outpost. Builders and architects created Catholic monuments and churches, while expert military technicians (many of them from Italy) set up sophisticated defences and fortifications. Businesses boomed as go-ahead merchants arrived from various corners of Europe, taking full advantage of the vast opportunities to be gleaned from starting their operations here.

By the beginning of the sixteenth century the Canary Islands suddenly found themselves enjoying a burgeoning trade with Europe, Africa and the Americas. Among their main exports the islanders had uncovered a particularly lucrative source of income from the abundant local sugar cane. This industry had been launched at the end of the previous century (the first mill was built in 1484) and as the economy boomed so a new and unwelcome series of rapacious visitors appeared. Some were corsairs, acting on behalf of their countries, others were pirates acting simply for themselves. All had one sole objective: booty.

These raids were of a different nature from the ones they had known before. The original Spaniards, Italians and Barbary Coast buccaneers had arrived principally in search of slaves who could be sold both in Europe and in the market places of North African cities. The new invaders were more ambitious, better prepared and most impressively equipped. Some of them boasted fleets the size of small navies.

This initial wave of highly organized plunderers was formed, once more, by Frenchman, many of them Huguenots who, enraged by the St. Bartholomew's Day Massacre of their followers in Paris and in other cities throughout France by Catholics in 1572, had a religious as well as mercenary reason for targeting Spanish ships and territories.

Among the first of them to attack the islands was Jean Fleury (known to the Spanish as Juan Florín) who during the 1520s had boarded and seized barques heading for the Americas and West Indies. When he became aware of the trade explosion in the Canaries he switched his attention there, launching a series of highly effective raids over a five-year period. Eventually he was captured by a fleet of Basque ships, taken to Seville, judged there, found guilty of piracy and hanged at Mombeltrán castle in Ávila province.

His fate did not deter others. Next came the formidable François Leclerc (nicknamed *Pata de Palo,* or Peg Leg), who sacked and burned Santa Cruz de la Palma in 1553. His ships were huge galleons up to sixty metres long captured from the Spanish, French and Dutch navies and armed with up to 35 powerful cannons. They had sizeable quarters as well and resembled floating garrisons.

He was followed by Jacques de Sores (known as "The Exterminating Angel" after his 1555 destruction of Havana) and Durand de Ville-gaingnong, a dashing soldier of fortune. Both carried out further assaults on La Palma's capital. De Sores was the most fanatical of the Catholic-hating Huguenot invaders. He achieved lasting notoriety when he seized forty Jesuits and their pacific leader Padre Acevedo who were caring for the wounded of the *Santiago,* a ship en route from Portugal to Brazil, which the pirates had just attacked. After torturing the missionaries de Sores threw their chained and weighted bodies into the sea to drown just off shore from the La Palma town of Tazacorte. According to Rumeu de Armas, the crew of the *Santiago* had offered the Jesuits weapons so they could defend themselves, but Padre Acevedo had bravely and selflessly refused, saying "Our duty is to aid the injured and dying, either by curing them or consoling them in their final moments." (Hopefully his luckless acolytes agreed with this sentiment.)

La Palma was now an Atlantic Shangri-La for searchers of get-rich-quick pickings. The Gallic buccaneers had specifically selected Santa Cruz since that small coastal city's unexpected trade boom had even outstripped that of the larger island capitals, transforming it almost overnight into the most prosperous port in the whole archipelago. Already it was exporting great quantities of Malvasia wine, honey, beeswax, the moss-like orchil and, above all, sugar to the Americas, the Iberian Peninsula and other European destinations. German and English merchants were among the many foreign businessmen who moved in to control exports on the island.

Dynamic entrepreneurs included the Weizers, who from 1513 ran an estate controlling the waters of the Tazacorte Valley, and Thomas Malliard who from 1515 managed a sugar refinery at Río de los Sauces in liaison with Genoese merchant Francesco de Spinola. In return the island imported items it desperately lacked, such as cloth from English hosiers like Nicholas Thorne of Bristol, according to the historian Javier Méndez.

After these successive sackings the city was compelled to reinforce its defences. Almost impregnable bastions like the Castillo de Santa Catalina were built, devised and supervised by expert Italian engineers led by the Cremona-born Leonardi Torriani. The port of Santa Cruz de la Palma was now the third most important after Seville and Antwerp in the Kingdom of the Austrias or *Casa de Austria* which was ruled by the penultimate Spanish Habsburg King Carlos I (known, in his other guises, as the Holy Roman Emperor and Archduke of Austria Charles V). His territories not only extended from the Netherlands to Naples, Sicily and Sardinia, but also embraced Mexico and the Philippines, making Spain the largest power in Europe. In the early sixteenth century the city's wealth drew immigrants from Portugal, Italy and Northern Europe as well as Spaniards from different regions throughout the peninsula. The native *Benahoritas*, though defeated, assimilated into the new way of life as governed by Spain and still made up nearly half the island's population.

The other islands were equally harried by invaders. Jean Capdeville from the Pyrenean province of Béarn, another Huguenot, sacked San Sebastián de Gomera in 1571, while Lanzarote and Fuerteventura drew the unwelcome attentions of Barbary Coast corsairs and their Ottoman allies from further east. In 1568 the North African pirate Calafat and his 600 men sacked Lanzarote and took 200 prisoners. Two years later Dogalí (known as *El Turquillo*, the "Little Turk") attacked the island, razing Arrecife and abducting many more inhabitants to sell as slaves. In the coming years Lanzarote suffered similar violent incursions from Morato Arráez, Tabac Arráez and Solimán who took turns in destroying the capital Teguise.

The latter duo, acting together in a 1618 raid, performed the most savage pirate assault on the archipelago so far. Their army of 4,000 men arrived in a fleet of 36 ships and seized 900 captives, many of whom had hidden in the vast Cuevas Verdes near Haria and had thought themselves safe until they were betrayed by a treacherous local. However, as the eighteenth-century poet and chronicler Ignacio López de Ayala tells us in his well documented *Historia de Gibraltar*, the corsairs soon received their just desserts. While they were attempting to return with their booty to Algeria a Spanish fleet under the command of a Basque admiral, Miguel de Vidazabal, and aided by other vessels from the Dutch navy, cut them off at the Straits of Gibraltar, boarded the ships and released the prisoners. What had incensed Spain most during this particular incursion was that the pirates had decapitated the statue of the Virgen de Guadalupe after stealing it from the parish church of Teguise. The Turks received no quarter. Those who were not killed found themselves sold into slavery in the market places of Algeciras and Málaga.

## "El Draque"

The English, too, had been eyeing the islands enviously for some time. In the midst of these Turkish raids, pirates under Robert Devereux, the Duke of Essex, attacked Lanzarote in 1596, only to be effectively repulsed. Barely a year earlier, Sir Francis Drake, under direct orders from Elizabeth I, had suffered a similar setback while besieging Gran Canaria, where the newly fortified capital of Las Palmas had strongly resisted his raid and sent him packing.

After their success against such a famous foe the Canarians were understandably jubilant and Rumeu de Armas reports that they celebrated in makeshift party style: "The governor sent new order to the communal granary, taking out the sponge cake that had been kept there, together with the wine that was given by the bishop and any food the officer could find transported in wagons and on tops of camels to the Bays of Santa Catalina and Santa Ana so they could refresh the troops." Drake then switched his attack to Argueneguin in the south but had no better luck there and withdrew shamefaced from the island.

These ineffective assaults came as a surprise in view of the charismatic Drake's many other victories which included his famed sacking of Cádiz in 1587, when, in his own words, he "singed Felipe II's beard". (For years after, *gaditano,* Cádiz-born, children are said to have been warned by their parents when they misbehaved: "Be careful, or *El Draque* will get you.") Yet the Canaries were clearly proving a harder nut to crack—and not just Gran Canaria. Drake suffered similar failures at La Gomera and La Palma in 1585, where San Miguel fort's imposing cannons had won the day.

Nevertheless, Drake was the most famous international figure to appear on the scene so far. Spain's illustrious sixteenth-century poet and playwright Lope de Vega chronicled the corsair knight's Canary failures and subsequent death in Panamá in his 1598 epic poem *La Dragontea*. Lope relates Drake's great Gran Canaria assault, which begins boldly:

> ... and now the avaricious and powerful English fleet appear on the scene
> already judging themselves victors of the day.
>
> They rush towards the Canaries in the rosy dawn, eager for the fray,
> As if their foe would turn its face away from such fierce arrogance...
> But it ends disastrously as the invaders encounter the stiff Spanish opposition on landing:
>
> They [the Spanish] were arquebusiers and pikemen and skilled horsemen. And they killed forty Englishmen in the first wave, while the rest fearfully withdrew.
>
> Drake, alert to their bold courage and the intricate passageways of the dangerous port, turned tail and ran, deciding the game wasn't worth the candle.

(Free translation by Peter Stone)

Lope was quite restrained in his assessment of the English losses as other, more floridly patriotic writers of the time, such as Cabrera de Córdoba, put their number as ten times higher.

Sir Francis had learned the pirating trade from his older second cousin John Hawkins who accompanied him on the failed Las Palmas attack. Hawkins was another corsair under Elizabeth's orders who also had a keen business eye. With the help of Canary associates Pedro Soler and Pedro da Ponte he had managed to get contracts from them to seize Guinean slaves from Portuguese vessels and transport them across the Atlantic sell them in the West Indies. Both these seafaring relatives were allocated a further dubious place of honour in *Templo Militante,* another series of epic poems written by the seventeenth-century Las Palmas-born author Bartolomé Cairasco de Figueroa who lived through many of the city's sieges.

## PIETER VAN DER DOES AND THE SIEGE OF LAS PALMAS

Interest in the islands was spreading like wildfire. All Europe was now conscious of their economic and strategic importance, especially Las Palmas, which had now taken over from Santa Cruz de la Palma as the most prosperous city and become the political, legal and ecclesiastical capital of the archipelago. In the course of organizing fleets to the Indies, it was the main port for carrying out business transactions with America. Free trade was prohibited and in 1589 the political and military command for all seven islands was brought under the central control of the captain general of Gran Canaria, Don Luis de la Cueva y Benavides, who was also named president of the *audiencia* (court or assizes) created six decades earlier.

In 1599 the city experienced its largest and most terrifying attack so far when the Dutch vice admiral Pieter van der Does arrived with a monumental flotilla of 74 ships and around 9,000 men, well over double the city's population. Born in Leiden, van der Does was a superintendent in the Dutch fleet which had witnessed the Armada's ignominious defeat in 1588. He was a seasoned tactician and had participated in the sieges of Geertruidenberg and Groningen, where he had been badly wounded.

Van der Does was initially authorized to blockade the coast of mainland Spain and its possessions by the new Protestant authorities in his homeland, which until then had been known as the Spanish Netherlands. The Protestants had led the revolt against the Habsburg King Felipe II's Catholic rule to form an independent Dutch Republic (also known as the Republic of the Seven United Provinces) in 1581 under William of Orange's leadership, sowing the seeds for Holland's later growth as a world power.

The Dutch admiral's fleet was split into three groups, one led by himself and the others by commandeers Jan Gerbrantsz and Cornelis Geleyntsz van Vlissingen. On his way south along the Spanish and Portuguese Atlantic seaboards his forces had failed to make even a dent on the heavily defended ports of La Coruña and Cádiz as they had been prewarned and were well prepared, but on his arrival in the Canaries he found less resistance. Las Palmas was not yet accustomed to repelling large scale attacks by sea.

Pieter van der Does showed no mercy. He sacked and destroyed much of the city. Yet he failed to achieve a total victory. In spite of being outnumbered and outgunned the inhabitants simply refused to surrender and

*Ataque de la flota y tropas del almirante holandés Pieter van Der Does a Las Palmas de Gran Canaria* (1599) (Pepelopex/WikimediaCommons)

during the course of the attack his army suffered total losses of 1,400 men, according to the island's young modern chronicler German Santana Perez.

After then trying ineffectually to conquer the interior of the island van der Does withdrew and moved on to attack La Gomera instead. José de Viera y Clavijo records that most reports of the alleged destruction suffered by that island's capital San Sebastián were exaggerated and that the Dutch, after again suffering substantial losses, only managed to burn down the town's Santiago hermitage and steal the city's archives, artillery and parish church bell. Here, as in Gran Canaria, the ferocity and determination of the island's defenders had surprised them.

After sending Gerbrantsz's fleet back to Holland van der Does consoled himself by invading and taking the Portuguese-owned island of São Tomé just off the central West African coast. The lucrative spoils he obtained there included artillery and sugar but he was destined never to enjoy the benefits or the credit for this success. He contracted malaria shortly after the attack and—still only in his late thirties—perished alongside 1,800 of his men.

AFTER THE ARMADA

This wave of French, English and Dutch attacks had materialized thanks to two major incentives. One was the already mentioned strategic location and booming economy of the Canaries. Another was Spain's plunge in prestige since its disastrous Armada attack on the British Isles in 1588. No longer the all conquering colonizer, it now appeared to be more vulnerable and less able to defend itself. The loss of over a third of its ships and their crews in that fateful enterprise was a crippling blow.

Felipe I's once-glorious fleet had suffered particularly badly due to the viciously premature autumn storms that had lashed them as, in their desperate haste to escape the English fleet, they had tried to get round Scotland and return past western Ireland to Spain. "I sent the Armada against men, not God's winds and waves," said the heartbroken Spanish king on receiving news of the debacle. (He also referred to the winds that had undone him as "Protestant".) In many cases longitude errors on the part of the ill-equipped Spanish navigators had brought the beleaguered fleet too close to the wild shores where the helpless wooden-hulled galleons had broken apart on concealed rocks and sunk.

Inspired by this victory, a new group of distinguished English pirates and freebooters set their sights on the Canaries. The brave but suicidal action of an intractable admiral Sir Richard Grenville may also have fired their imagination. It happened like this. In the summer of 1591 Grenville and fellow commander Lord Thomas Howard were sailing with their six ships of the line just off the Azores, north of the Canaries, waiting to attack the odd Spanish vessel carrying treasures back from the Americas, when they saw a fleet of 53 enemy galleons approaching. Howard, with Grenville's blessing, was compelled to withdraw with five of the ships as they were "out of gear" and half the crews ill.

Lone wolf Grenville—an English David against a host of Spanish Goliaths (even individually, their ships were bigger)—decided to attack the enemy with his regally prized warship, *Revenge*. Grenville was, by all accounts, an obdurate and impossible man, but the inevitable Thermopylae-style finale of this battle gave him lasting fame as a heroic English figure. Unbending to the end, totally surrounded, his ship in tatters after the multiple assaults of the Spanish galleons, he defiantly gave one last order: to blow up *Revenge* rather than surrender. The exhausted crew (the few who were left, that is) had by now had more than enough, though, and gave themselves up as prisoners. Grenville died from the battle wounds he had received two days later on board one of the Spanish ships.

Alfred Lord Tennyson immortalized (and, of course, highly romanticized) the event in his stirring narrative poem "The Revenge":

> But never for a moment ceased the fight of the one and the fifty-three
> Ship after ship, the whole night long, their high-built galleons came,
> Ship after ship the whole night long, with their battle-thunder and flame;
> Ship after ship, the whole night long, drew back with her dead and her shame.
> For some were sunk and many were shatter'd, and so could fight us no more–
> God of battles, was there ever a battle like this in the world before?

## WARS BETWEEN ENGLAND AND SPAIN

Just two years after Grenville's melodramatic swansong, William Harper attacked Lanzarote, first badly damaging a Portuguese ship in Arrecife harbour and then going on to destroy San Marcial del Rubicón church in the south of the island. That same year George Clifford, Duke of Cumberland, attacked Teguise's Santa Barbara Castle and stole bells and cannons from the church.

They were followed in 1595 by the multifaceted courtier, royal favourite, explorer, poet, privateer, Virginia colonizer and pioneer tobacco-smoker, Sir Walter Raleigh, who launched assaults on Tenerife and Fuerteventura, both of which met with little success.

A six-year-long Anglo-Spanish War, one of several, began half a century later. By now Spain was in full economic decline and battles over commercial rivalries were taking place in the West Indies and Spanish Netherlands as well as in Spain. The English were no longer concerned merely with pirate raids. They wanted to add the Canary Islands to their list of colonial acquisitions. Attacks became more organized, more nationally expansionist in aim.

By far the most successful of these later actions was carried out by Robert Blake, a portly bachelor, who, though he hardly cut an imposing military figure, was a highly capable strategist and commander. This Roundhead hero of the English Civil War, a seafarer from Bridgewater who had already achieved fame after his notable victory over the Royalists at Lyme, sailed south in 1657 under direct orders from Cromwell. After blockading Cádiz, he continued on to Santa Cruz de Tenerife.

Manoeuvring his squadron with huge skill, and using similar tactics to those he had employed in attacking Barbary pirate bases in Tunisia two years earlier, he entered the harbour, put all the land-based guns out of action with his accurate bombardments and then proceeded to sink every single one of the sixteen Spanish galleons anchored there. (These ships had just returned from the Americas and were in the process of unloading their cargo of treasure.)

Blake gave strict orders that no spoils be seized, much to the near-rebellious disappointment of some of his captains who reportedly needed his instructions to be repeated three times before they obeyed them. Blake's highly moralistic view was that the mission was punitive, not acquisitive. His men were not pirates but members of the English Navy, and should act accordingly. Not a single English ship was lost out of his own fleet of 23 though 60 of his men died. Blake himself, alas, in declining health after years of battle, did not survive the voyage back from Santa Cruz to England where the hero's welcome that awaited him was transformed into a heartfelt national memorial service.

As the endless conflicts between Spain and England spilled into the eighteenth century, British attacks on the archipelago continued. During the 1701-14 War of the Spanish Succession, when Bourbons and Habsburgs fought ferociously over who would succeed Charles II, three astoundingly inept English mini-invasions took place.

The first of these was launched by Admiral John Jennings on Santa Cruz de Tenerife in 1706, two years after Gibraltar had been taken by an Anglo-Dutch fleet commanded by George Rooke. Jennings was following the British policy of backing the Habsburgs and his main objective was to persuade the *tinerfeños* to support this cause. The defending Bourbon commander José de Ayala y Rosas refused his appeal to do so and the attack, made by Jennings' modest fleet of just thirteen ships, was soundly repulsed. The English admiral retired without further ado.

Two years later the privateer Woodes Rogers fared little better when he too attacked Santa Cruz de Tenerife and merely succeeded in capturing one Spanish ship loaded with wine and brandy. Disillusioned and bored, he then decided to broaden his horizons and spend three years sailing round the world. En route he picked up a ragged Scotsman called Alexander Selkirk who had been marooned four years on Juan Fernandez (an uninhabited isle of Chile) and later formed the real life model for Defoe's fictional castaway character Robinson Crusoe. Rogers ended his days with two terms as Governor of the Bahamas, where he rid the island of pirates, incurred debts, was imprisoned and then re-instated, ending his relative short life (he died at 53) in relative peace and comfort.

The third Canary attack, the most inglorious of the three, was made in 1744 by Admiral Charles Windham, on Tenerife's tiny neighbour La Gomera. Viera y Clavijo recounts with relish how only three Gomerans died during the assault although up to 5,000 shots were fired by Windham's fleet, and how the English soldiers were chased off by local militia when they tried to land on the beach and were forced instead to return to their ships. A faded but triumphalist fresco depicting the British debacle is one of the showpieces inside San Sebastián de la Gomera's Iglesia de la Asunción.

The Anglo-Spanish War of 1796-1808 was the last of seven conflicts between England and Spain and formed part of the French Revolutionary and Napoleonic conflicts. Amid this turmoil, in February 1797 Admiral Sir John Jervis defeated a larger Spanish fleet at Cape St. Vincent and proceeded to blockade Cádiz five months later, thereby checkmating the bulk of the Spanish fleet.

## NELSON AND TENERIFE

One of the legendary figures of British naval history, Horatio Nelson, now appeared on the scene. Jervis, while still keeping the Spanish fleet bottled up in Cádiz, ordered Nelson to head south and take Tenerife, which was defended by a relatively small force led by 68-year-old veteran General Antonio Gutiérrez de Otero y Santayana. Thanks to Jervis's blockade there was little prospect of the islanders receiving help from the Spanish Navy. Expectations in England were accordingly high; the island seemed an easy prey. But to everyone's surprise the famed admiral for once failed in his duty. He not only lost the battle but also one of his arms—thanks to a well aimed Spanish cannon ball.

Nelson's objective had not been simply to take Santa Cruz. Once that mission was accomplished his aim was to occupy all the islands, step by step, and make them British territory. The archipelago's strategic location made it an ideal Atlantic platform for basing and refuelling His Majesty's fleet.

The city's resources were hardly impressive. The Canarians had less than half as many military personnel as the English admiral. Yet after two failed landings, one at night and another at dawn, during which hundreds of British sailors perished under the withering cannon fire—in particular from one mammoth gun forged in Seville and known as "El Tigre" (today on show in Santa Cruz's military museum)—Nelson's side was coming off distinctly worse. As an added blow one of his cutters *Fox* was sunk with the loss of 97 crew and a huge supply of munitions and armaments as it was trying to launch an attack on San Cristóbal castle.

On the morning of 25 July fierce hand to hand fighting took place between the few English soldiers who finally managed to enter the city and the determined local inhabitants. The English survivors took refuge in the Santo Domingo convent and later surrendered, the agreement being signed by Gutierrez and Samuel Hood, commander of the flagship *Zealous* and a leading officer of Nelson's fleet. The Spanish loses had been minimal. One of the stipulations of the surrender was that the British Navy would never again attack the islands.

Richard Westall, *Nelson wounded at Tenerife, 24 July 1797* (1806) (National Maritime Museum, Greenwich, London, Greenwich Hospital Collection/Wikimedia Commons)

Theories as to why Nelson failed were legion. One suggested that he was lax in fully reconnoitring the coastal defences and lookout posts and that his fleet was spotted early on, thus losing him the element of surprise. Another was that his intelligence reports did not accurately show the number of armaments located around the harbour. Yet another concluded that his own excessive confidence in personally leading one of the landings was unnecessarily reckless and almost got him killed. (It was on this occasion that a shot from El Tigre removed one of his arms.) The main criticism, however, was that Nelson had simply underestimated his outnumbered enemy's united will and determination to withstand any invaders. Author Jesús Villanueva Jimenez in his historical novel *El Fuego de Bronce* describes the total solidarity of the *tinerfeños*: "Labourers, fishermen, artisans, servants, in other words the entire populace, defended the city of Santa Cruz de Tenerife."

The humiliation for Nelson and the British Navy was immense, only fully reversed eight years later when Nelson dealt his final great (posthumous) blow to the Spaniards at Trafalgar, following up his successful 1798 engagement with Napoleon at Abukir on the Nile. In contrast, the confidence and pride this defensive victory against the supposedly almighty English gave the Santa Cruz inhabitants was incalculable and every 25 July one of the city's most joyous fiestas celebrates the event.

## Changing Face of the Islands

Eventually, after two centuries of piratical and naval sieges the islands returned to a state of relative peace. But even between the constant conflicts a "normal" life of sorts had been taking place, with positive progress and changes being made. If we regard the various invaders as "takers" in one form or another there were also "givers" and "creators", a host of local people aided by a constant flow of immigrants who helped changed the very face of the Canaries.

Opulent new buildings and art works made their appearance as the main cities expanded. Among the earliest religious creations was the Santa Ana cathedral in Las Palmas de Gran Canaria, begun in 1500 but not completed until four centuries later—resulting in a mix of architectural styles from the Gothic to the neoclassical. Other notable symbols of Catholic faith were the San Juan *retablo* in Telde, Gran Canaria, the façade of the Asunción Church in San Sebastián de la Gomera, and the Iglesia de la

Concepción in Santa Cruz de Tenerife (see Chapter 11).

Simultaneously, Italian military architects were drafted in to plan and oversee the construction of impressive coastal fortifications such as San Juan Bautista and San Cristóbal in Tenerife, the Castillo de la Luz in Gran Canaria and the earlier-mentioned Castillo de Santa Catalina in La Palma.

The first factual books on the islands also appeared. The sixteenth-century Portuguese priest and writer Gaspar Frutuoso, who studied in Salamanca and was for a while confessor to Charles V, produced *Saudades da Terra*, a highly detailed historical and geographical description of the archipelago which also included visits to Madeira and the Azores; and during this same period Richard Hakluyt ("Preacher and some time Student of Christ-Church in Oxford") included a chapter by one Thomas Nichols entitled "A Pleasant Description of the Fortunate Ilandes called the Ilandes of Canaria" in his own well researched *Principal Navigations, Voyages, Traffiques and Discoveries of the English Nation* (1589), though Hakluyt himself never actually set foot on the archipelago.

## LAURENS DE GRAAF, COMIC STRIP PIRATE

During the early sixteenth century a privileged minority of nobles and aristocrats came to settle in the islands, quickly assuming prominent social roles in this, Spain's most recent colonial acquisition. So, too, did members of the zealous clergy. Below them came four distinct levels of society: bourgeois, farmer, artisan and, bottom of the rung, slave. The majority of the latter came from Africa, having been captured on expeditions there, and were destined to spend the rest of their lives in an oppressive system of bondage. Each plantation in the Canaries, producing mainly sugar, held on average 30-35 slaves in the early sixteenth century though some of the larger ones had as many as one hundred. At its peak there were, according to Antonio M. Macías Hernández, probably 5,000 slaves in the islands, that is one-tenth of the total population. From the later part of that century onwards, as the sugar industry declined, this number gradually dropped off.

Some slaves had been taken hostage further afield. One such unfortunate, a Dutchman called Laurens de Graaf, was captured as a child in his very own country during a Spanish raid and transported with his family to Tenerife where he was forced to perform menial duties on a banana plantation for several years.

The story of how he managed to elude a dismal future could have come straight out of a comic strip saga. One day he escaped from the plantation, walked to the nearest town and quickly acquired a Spanish wife called Petronilla, whom he abandoned just as quickly in order to steal a boat and sail to the West Indies. There he became a notorious pirate. He never returned to the Canaries but was a scourge of Spanish vessels en route there laden with treasure and made a big name for himself in the Caribbean and Central America where he carried out raids commissioned by the French. His most devastating attacks were on the Mexican ports of Campeche and Vera Cruz. In the latter expedition he joined forces with fellow Dutchman Nicholas van Hoorn and imprisoned 5,000 of the inhabitants in the Asunción cathedral, while abducting the wealthier citizens as hostages for ransom.

Handsome, dashing and literate (some fanciful historians claim he was a great fan of Shakespeare), he was an Errol Flynn-style rogue and charmer. Latterly de Graaf married a fiery ex-female pirate nicknamed Marie-Dieu-le-Veut and became a governor in the French Caribbean colony of Saint Domingue. No doubt he was the much-envied hero of all the slaves who never got beyond the boundaries of their plantations.

## TOURISM IS BORN

Two developments stand out among the many changes that took place in Tenerife, the archipelago's largest island, in the eighteenth century. The first, in 1723, saw Santa Cruz de Tenerife replace Las Palmas as the Canary Islands' military headquarters and take over from La Laguna as the island's capital. Tenerife was now officially the leader of the group. The second, in 1788, heralded the beginnings of Puerto de la Cruz's famed Botanical Gardens. This was an encouraging and unprecedented new step. For the first time since the inception of the colony, material trade and commerce were not the main priorities. The gardens' main *raison d'être* was simply to cultivate tropical plants and flowers in a congenial climate. (Here the winters were, and are, considerably milder than anywhere in mainland Spain.) Eighteenth-century eco-tourism was born.

The project was approved and launched by King Carlos III, and overseen by the nature-loving Marquis de Alonso de Navas y Griñon. The gardens were duly planned and laid out by a La Laguna architect Nicolás Eduardo, while a French naturalist, André-Pierre Ledru, helped sow the

The Mirador Humboldt
(Koppchen/Wikimedia Commons)

seeds of the first plantations and catalogue the initial species that grew there. He also introduced the use of the Linnaean system of two-part Latinized names devised by the Swedish botanist Carl Linnaeus in 1753.

The Botanical Gardens immediately drew international interest from noted figures like the German geographer and naturalist Alexander von Humboldt who first visited the island in 1799 and declared the Orotava Valley, where the gardens were located, the most beautiful place in the world. Humboldt was especially interested in the huge local dragon (*drago*) trees and his local travel writing and observations inspired Charles Darwin to visit Tenerife later. (The *mirador,* or viewpoint, bearing Humboldt's name, now looks down on a view somewhat less beautiful, crisscrossed by car-filled highways and dotted with untidy clusters of modern buildings.)

The surgeon, traveller and folklore enthusiast Sir William Wilde subsequently wrote about Tenerife in 1840 in his *Narrative of a Voyage to Madeira, Tenerife and Along the Shores of the Mediterranean.* Viewing the island primarily from a health viewpoint he concluded that it was especially beneficial to sufferers of bronchial problems, singling out Tenerife's Orotava Valley as the driest and warmest spot of all. The French writer and politician Gabriel de Belcastel echoed his findings almost to the word two decades later (see Chapter 9). Researchers Víctor García Nieto and Justo Hernández in their survey *Los orígenes del turismo médico en Canarias,* however, point out that other nineteenth-century medical writers, while generally agreeing that the climate in the region was excellent (give or take the odd mosquito), lamented the lack of sanatoria and health-oriented establishments in Tenerife compared with the more sophisticated spa resorts that abounded in Europe at that time.

## THE POWER AND THE GLORY

If health considerations were relatively new, the Canarians' spiritual needs had been well taken care once the Castilian invaders settled in. The influence of the Catholic Church in the Canaries was soon all-embracing and the abundant places of worship throughout the islands were well attended by Spaniards, European immigrants and converted Guanches alike.

The Inquisition inevitably made its presence felt as well, though less oppressively than in Spain at the beginning of the sixteenth century when a branch of the Andalusian Inquisition was established in Las Palmas. Initially it persecuted the small Jewish sector of the rapidly growing population; later it moved on to harry the few Protestant newcomers who had settled in the archipelago. But its power was short-lived due in no small degree to the tolerant and open nature of the Canarians, who were generally far less rigid and narrow-minded than many of their mainland counterparts. By the early 1600s the Inquisition was a spent force in the islands, though not before it had carried out some horrific sentences (such as burnings at the stake during auto-da-fés, where the victims were sardonically referred to as the *relajados*, (or relaxed ones) on the flimsiest of evidence). Researcher Bill Gladstone, in a 2002 article recounts how "in 1506 one Marcos Gonceles (*sic*) was denounced for washing shirts on Saturday night and hanging them out to dry on Sunday morning. His children confessed under torture that their parents spoke Hebrew and did not cross themselves in prayer."

The Inquisition's demise was mainly due to a local lack of the fanaticism that prevailed throughout mainland Spain. Fewer and fewer Canarians accepted its strictures as the islands' religious and civic authorities sought to compromise and find more common ground, and treaties signed with Holland and England during the early seventeenth century greatly reduced the Inquisition's assets as it prevented it from acquiring financial benefits from ships confiscated from those countries. It was officially abolished in 1813 and when the new absolutist king Fernando VII took the throne shortly afterwards and tried to re-install the organization together with its former repressive measures it was greeted with a blend of hostility and ridicule. By 1820 it was finally pronounced dead and buried.

Throughout the seemingly endless invasions, which reached their apex during the seventeenth and eighteenth centuries, the Canaries were still divided administratively. The former "free" or "unattached" islands—Gran Canaria, Tenerife and La Palma—were now completely subjected to Spain's *realengo* system of rule, though their governors were named and popularly elected by the island councils.

Meanwhile, tiny westerly El Hierro and La Gomera and arid easterly Lanzarote and Fuerteventura were still dominated by the antiquated feudally-run *señorío* system and the councils were chosen by the ruling lords, who now tended to be less charismatic and colourful than the pioneering Béthencourts and Perazas of yore.

The easterly islands were also rapidly becoming the poor relations of the group. As Lanzarote's economic status and political importance declined in comparison with those of the flourishing central islands, it began to experience an unaccustomed lack of outside interest, even from pirates. The year 1749 witnessed the last recorded Algerian attack either there or on neighbouring Fuerteventura. But that was the least of its worries. That same century also saw Lanzarote, along with many of the other islands, at the heart of a disaster of apocalyptic proportions.

## Chapter Six
# UNDER THE VOLCANOES

### ON SHAKY GROUND: LANZAROTE'S SIX-YEAR UPHEAVAL

If an unscrupulous tour operator wanted to make his customers believe they had reached the moon on the world's first lunar trip, he might well pull it off by transporting them to Lanzarote's Dante-esque Malpais de la Corona region: a petrified conglomeration of solidified magma, ash sprinkled soil and gritty sand whose colours range surrealistically from jet-black to orange-brown. No trees, barely a shrub in sight. Just the odd crater, cone or congealed lava bed. And a terrain that looks as if some giant rotovator has regurgitated it from the bowels of the earth.

In some areas the phenomenon known in Hawaii as a *pahoehoe,* in which the molten lava has frozen into a smooth, swirly, circular shape, can be seen. In others the shapes are rougher and less neatly symmetrical, resembling a burnt coiled rope or even the wrinkled skin of an aging elephant. In places such as Los Hervideros, where the lava reached the sea, phantasmagorical archways of black twisted rock have been created under which, on wild days, the sea foams and crashes.

Lanzarote is living testimony to the unpredictably violent powers of nature and the Canary Island most visibly transformed by seismic and volcanic activity. Three hundred craters dot its extraordinary landscape and a third of what can be seen today was actually formed between 1730 and 1736, when the isle was rocked by 26 huge eruptions which devastated 200 square kilometres. Miraculously, not a single inhabitant was injured, but the material damage inflicted on homes and productive land was so great that many were forced to migrate to America. It was either that or remain and starve.

Among the highest points in this uncompromising moonscape is the 511-metre (1,676 foot) Timanfaya volcano, or Fire Mountain. Tourists visit the summit seated on wooden chairs precariously attached to the backs of camels which languidly lumber up the steep tangerine-grey dunes. They are met at their destination by a distinctly modern-looking, man-made construction (though it has been around for decades): a circular

Timanfaya, or Fire Mountain (Luis Miguel Bugallo Sánchez/Wikimedia Commons)

glassed-in restaurant called El Diablo with symbols of little devils holding pitchforks emblazoned on its glass doors. These, and the restaurant, are the creation of César Manrique, Lanzarote's legendary architect and artist. Just a few feet beneath the topsoil adjoining the restaurant the volcano is very much alive. The local guide's party piece is to pour water down a funnel leading six metres into the earth and stand back, surrounded by clicking cameras, as a geyser of steam erupts two seconds later. Alternatively he will insert a straw into a shallow crevice in the earth's surface and watch everyone's expression as it bursts into flames. Steaks are barbecued over a well which contains no water but from which roasting currents of air rise and cook the food.

That six-year period of eruptions had its own local eighteenth-century chronicler: Andrés Lorenzo Curbelo, the *cura*, or priest, of Yaiza. Thanks to him, we have a lucid, on the spot account of what happened. His description of the first eruption is as follows: "The first day of September, 1730, between nine and ten at night, the earth split open near Timanfaya two leagues away from Yaiza. On the first night an enormous mountain rose up from the bowels of the earth and from its peak you could see flames which continued burning for nineteen days." He goes on to describe the apocalyptic events which continued to plague the island over the following years, annihilating scores of villages and hundreds of houses and spreading panic and dread among the island's inhabitants. "The eighteenth of October three new openings formed at the top of Santa Catalina and expelled masses of thick smoke which spread all across the island, accompanied by a great quantity of debris, sand and ashes which were scattered all over the area. The explosions which accompanied these phenomena, and the darkness caused by the great mass of ashes and the smoke which covered the island, forced the inhabitants of Yaiza on many occasions to take flight." Among the safest hiding places for them and other island villagers were the Cuevas Verdes, or Green Caves, which had been formed by earlier eruptions.

Many weird and wonderful physical features were created by the upheavals: such as the giant Jameos de Agua cavern (a large volcanic "bubble" alongside the Cuevas Verdes) whose saline waters are home to colourless blind spider crabs; or the Lago Verde, or Green Lake, in the coastal bay of El Golfo (a mixture of algae and the mineral olivine gives the water its dark emerald hue). In some places the products of past eruptions have been put to practical use. At La Geria tiny volcanic stones known as *lapilli* form crescent-shaped barriers that protect the vines growing on the area's dark grey slopes. The *picón* (volcanic ash) used to cover the soil around the vines is also regularly used in gardens to keep them irrigated by drawing moisture from the air.

## ANCIENT ISLES

Lanzarote is very old. Its sprawling neighbour Fuerteventura is even older, with an estimated age of around twenty million years. Both are perennially dry and sunny, resembling large fragments of the Sahara thrust into the sea, and both are covered with Pleistocene and Holocene cinder cones and lava flows left by early eruptions.

Fuerteventura not only managed to escape Lanzarote's disastrous eighteenth-century cataclysms but has suffered hardly a single eruption in the last thousand years. It did, nevertheless, experience various seismic upsets and volcanic explosions before then and much of its surface bears witness to this activity. Large, undulating and arid, it consists of a series of basalt plateaus covered by a calcareous crust and topped by tiny volcanic cones. Its highest point, the southerly Pico de Jandía, reaches 807 metres.

The two ancient islands are located just above a slow-moving, thick oceanic base, categorized by Tenerife researcher Cándido Manuel García Cruz as the "African Plate". Originally these were volcanic "hot spots", the most likely places to experience eruptions in the whole archipelago. Now they have reached what volcanologists describe as the "erosional stage", which means that the risk of eruptions has greatly diminished. Westerly El Hierro, the "youngest" of the group at barely two million years of age, has recently taken over as the most volatile and vulnerable location (see below). A series of recent underwater eruptions on that tiny island bear out the eminent volcanologist Juan Carlos Carracedo's 1998 claim that the current "hot spot" has now moved to the other end of the archipelago.

A multitude of other noted scientists and theorists, such as the twentieth-century researcher Dominique Frizon de Lamotte, still argue over exactly how the group was originally formed: was it by mantle plumes, uplifting blocks, elevation craters, or thermal anomalies? Or by a possible contractional deformation of the Atlas system in the late Miocene, Pleistocene and early Quaternary stages? Most visitors have little interest in such jargon or theories. They are simply captivated by the result of these creative processes, and especially in the strange, spare, eerily haunting beauty of the easterly duo.

## GRAN CANARIA: BASALT PEAKS AND BARREN *BARRANCOS*

Gran Canaria, the next island west, has suffered no eruptions at all in the past two thousand years. Its post-shield phase volcanic landscape, tempered by humid Atlantic breezes, offers more scenic variety than Lanzarote and Fuerteventura. Here, during its active period, radial flows of lava penetrated deeply into the rocks producing steep gorges like Tejeda and elliptical erosion craters like Tentiniguada and Tirajana. Other craters on Gran Canaria, such as Bandama and Los Marteles, which were formed either by explosions or simply sank, are circular, like the island itself. Bandama, the largest, was created two thousand years ago by the island's last serious eruption.

Most seismic activity took place, in fact, during the Holocene period when 24 moderate explosions shook the north-east of the island, releasing lava flows and producing small Strombolian cones, the most familiar of which is located on the tiny peninsula of La Isleta just above the capital Las Palmas. The very first eruption occurred ten thousand years ago at El

Draguillo on the eastern side of the island. The centre, meanwhile, experienced a variety of emissions from different sources and is today a ruggedly undulating mountain zone of thick basalt, covered by a further conglomeration of mainly acidic lavas. Its most emblematic feature is the massive upright Roque Nublo, which stands atop a 1,813-metre peak overlooking plunging pines and dusty *barrancos* (gulleys).

Alejandro Rodriguez-González, a renowned geologist from the University of Las Palmas, published an article in 2010 in the *Journal of Quaternary Science* detailing all the eruptions that have ever taken place on the island. He also produced a map showing Gran Canaria's main volcanic danger spots. He predicts that there will probably be an eruption during the next two or three hundred years in the heavily populated north-east, where Las Palmas and its expanding suburbs now boast nearly 400,000 inhabitants—though it is unlikely that the eruption will be strong enough to cause loss of life.

Ironically, the damage to the eco-system caused by deforestation and over-use of the island's limited water resources to accommodate the increased population, agricultural irrigation and tourist resources has actually made the dangerous combination of red hot magma and cold water, which produces the more powerful eruptions, less likely. Unwittingly, the Gran Canarians themselves, by "drying out" their island, have created a protective shield against such future violent upheavals.

## Teide: Gods versus the Devil

Further west lies the largest of the island group, Tenerife. It is shaped roughly like an isosceles triangle, and from its high central point on clear days there are bird's eye views of the entire island (as well as one or two others). The remarkable contrast between the humid north side, which falls away in dense pine forests to a coast bordered by lush banana plantations and richly black-sanded volcanic coves, and the dry south, a dusty, barren and ochre-hued semi-desert fringed by long yellow sand beaches, is clearly delineated, as if two scenically opposite islands had been neatly joined together.

Tenerife's massive conical post-shield phase Teide mountain is categorized as a "decade volcano"—one of sixteen in the whole world—by the International Association of Volcanology and Chemistry of the Earth's Interior (IAVCEI) due to its destructive power over the years. The Canaries'

Teide mountain
(Daniel Tenerife/Wikimedia Commons)

Astrophysics Institute has been operating an observatory on the mountain since 1964 though in recent years its star has been eclipsed by the rival island La Palma's famous San Roque observatory which makes use of highly advanced optical telescopes.

Now dormant, Teide gave vent to its last full eruption in 1909 and emitted small tremors as recently as 2004. Its size and appearance are intimidating. World-wide, it is dwarfed only by the awesome Hawaiian twins Mauna Kea and Mauna Lau, and at 3,718 metres is the highest point above sea level both in the Atlantic and in all Spain. Other major island eruptions came from the Boca Cangrejo vent in 1492 (whose mountain-top flames Columbus witnessed on his way west), Montañas Negras in 1706 resulting in the destruction of Garachico (see below), Narices del Teide in 1798 and Chinyero in 1909. Greater than all these, though, was the 150,000-year-old eruption, possibly rated 5 on the VEI, or Volcanic Explosivity Index, that formed the huge Las Cañadas *caldera* (crater) at the high centre of the island. Both Teide and the second highest peak, Pico Viejo, are located inside its rim.

Understandably, a giant such as Teide inspired legends in the past. A sort of Hispanic Mount Olympus, it was regarded by the Guanches as the home of their god of sun and light Magec, who was imprisoned there by Guayota the Devil (see Chapter 1) thus depriving the world of light until the supreme deity Achamán came to the rescue, killing Guayota and setting Magec free. That fear of darkness could have originated from early eruptions when black volcanic clouds would virtually blot out all sunlight for days at a time. The Guanches also lit bonfires to ensure Guayota was kept at bay. Another of their beliefs was that Teide supported the sky, sometimes seeming to fail in this task as dense mists and clouds sank over its summit.

## THE END OF GARACHICO

The worst Tenerife eruption came in 1706 when for nine days lava poured down from a vent in the Arenas Negras volcano and completely destroyed the north coast town of Garachico, brutally ending its role as the island's most flourishing port. (It had profited in particular from the export of its universally popular wine.) The town was founded in 1496 by a Genoese banker Cristóbal de Ponte and at its zenith of prosperity was known as the "Carrera de las Indias" (Road to the Indies). Indicative of its wealth in those days was the fact that some of the streets—so it was claimed—were paved with marble.

In a bizarre recreation of the lava flow that engulfed the port during those fateful days three centuries ago, burning barrels are rolled down the cliffside in the Fuegos del Risco (literally, "Fires of the Cliff") celebration which takes place once every five years. (Proof that in Spain any event, good or bad, is fair game when it comes to conjuring up a *fiesta*.) The riotous fireworks display which follows this event is clearly a further recreation of the violent volcanic explosions that took place then. The eruptions are also remembered in other ways. Garachico's flag has three horizontal stripes honouring its past: black, representing the lava flow, white—included in two of the quarters of the coat of arms, and blue representing the harbour and its waters.

Today, like frozen souvenirs of that awesome eruption, rock pools of various shapes and sizes fill the crevices along the wild shoreline where the lava had cooled, linked by walkways that meander between the petrified outcrops of black pumice. Not everything in the town itself was destroyed, though. The sixteenth-century San Miguel castle emerged miraculously unscathed from the onslaught and today is now a national monument, and other survivors include the fifteenth-century Puerta de la Tierra (Land Gate) and the original old wine press.

The priest and poet Fray Andrés Abreu, who lived both through and after the port's destruction, nostalgically described its pre-volcanic heyday in his personal diary: "The joyful and lovely town of Garachico is located at the foot of a cliff which rises on its southern side… It's a veritable delight to the eye, blessed with a perennial spring like climate, an admirable compendium of gardens and mountains where lush vines and fruitful plants blend with the perennial freshness of wild trees. To the north is an area ruled by the sea—and from here fierce winds furiously deviate from their course to whistle down the streets."

In his *Noticias de la historia general de la Islas de Canarias* (in which Abreu is quoted) José de Viera y Clavijo went on in his own words, to pour more praise on the town. It was a place, he says, where you could go hunting or fishing with equal facility as the forests came right down to sea shore, where aristocrats and generals resided, where merchants carried out international business transactions with docked ships from Europe and the Americas as easily as going shopping, and where packed-to-the-gills warehouses and palatial houses were complemented by a fine parish church, three convents and a hospital. Everyone referred to it simply as "Garachico, puerto rico" (Garachico, rich port).

Perhaps a faint sense of doom was already in the air, as in the preceding two years minor explosions from the central Siete Fuentes volcano had damaged the easterly town of Fasnia and Arenas Negras itself—Garachico's nemesis—had erupted, albeit mildly. But for the town's inhabitants the events of that initially sunny May morning in 1706 still came as a total shock, leaving them almost too stunned to react.

"The inhabitants barely had the time or nerve to flee," continues the redoubtable Viera y Clavijo:

> Women, old men, children, clerics, sick persons, some on horseback, others on foot, some hand in hand, others in scattered groups, all headed for Icod, loaded with their most treasured possessions. The town hall's generosity was remarkable: it provided a grant covering the nuns' transport to La Laguna; but much more to the generosity of General don

Modern-day Garachico
(Diego Delso/Wikimedia Commons)

Agustín de Robles who spent 3,000 pesos of his own money to help. The "emerald parapets" [of the terraced hills] looked as if they were covered with toasted cloth. Vines, waters, birds, the Port, the trade and neighbourhood all simply disappeared.

Another chronicler of the disaster was the highly praised twentieth-century Cuban poet and novelist Dulce María Poynaz, a lover of Tenerife and "adopted daughter of the island". After she died in 1997 in Havana a statue was erected in her memory in Puerto de la Cruz. She recounts in her lyrical 1958 opus *Un verano en Tenerife*—by far the finest "travel book" on the island ever written—how that heavenly spring morning turned into a living hell as the most lovely and prosperous port on the island disappeared under a mantle of choking volcanic ash and a viscous, slow-moving sea of molten lava.

Like Fray Andrés before her, Dulce María portrayed the port's bustling trade in treasured exports like Malvasia wine and silkworms, the flourishing waterfront business houses, urbane negotiators and skilled artisans. "All professions concerned with the managing and developing the wealth of the island were represented there… to the East were the sheds of the shoreline carpenters who hammered all day as they caulked the frames of the ships; to the West were the workshops of the coopers and saddlers; further off were the mulberry woodlands and further still, in the vine-covered foothills of the Teide, were the great winepresses which had by necessity been built outside the city limits because of the overpoweringly heady juice fumes that emanated from the fermenting grapes at harvest time."

Previous eruptions and seismic disturbances on the islands had only destroyed small communities at their worst; this was the first time a rich expanding community, the entire lifeblood of an island, had been eradicated. The Tenerife economy took a long time to recover and commercial and political attention switched from what remained of Garachico to the bustling and strongly fortified city of Santa Cruz de Tenerife, which was named capital and chief port in 1726.

## LA GOMERA: *LAURISILVA* HAVEN
Tenerife's satellite La Gomera, a circular and smaller topographical version of Gran Canaria, is the most eroded of all the islands with barely a cone

or crater visible today to indicate that any land shattering events ever occurred. Extraordinarily, in view of its proximity to such a volatile neighbour, it is the only one of the Canary Islands to have experienced no eruptions or earthquakes whatsoever since the Quatenary Age, well over two million years ago.

Here, instead of dusty ash-filled craters dominating its centre, we have a magnificent high altitude *laurisilva* (subtropical laurel forest) of towering broad-leafed evergreen trees. They blanket its 1,400-metre high Garajonay National Park, named after the Guanche lovers Gara and Jonay, and now a protected UNESCO heritage site.

Set amid an ever changing background of mists and clouds and filled with a cornucopia of natural life, the forest is home to several varieties of wild doves and rare plants like the *madroño canario*. Many a visitor has got lost in this mystical wonderland, which owes its verdant lushness not to rain but to the moisture taken from the trade winds that constantly blow from the north. Porous volcanic rocks deep below the earth absorb the moisture like a sponge while at the same time streams filled with pure drinking water, formed on the surface by this same captured moisture, flow down a myriad of gullies into the valleys below.

In the north of the island trees give way to drier zones of old basalt rocks marked by zeolite minerals and red tufts. Petrified obelisks formed by lava chimneys, such as the Roque Cano above Vallehermoso and a surreal quartet of smaller pillars at La Zarcita, are among the main formations showing evidence of ancient volcanic activity. But the most riveting sight of all is on the coast: the phenomenal north shore cliffs known as Los Órganos, whose basalt structure of long exposed lava pillars resembles an array of massive prehistoric organ pipes. As the land plunges sheer into the sea at this point the pillars can only be clearly viewed by boat—an exhilarating experience for excursionists in those perennially choppy offshore Atlantic waters.

## LA PALMA AND THE TSUNAMI THEORY

Only forty miles away from La Gomera to the north-west, La Palma is home to the largest crater in the archipelago and one of the biggest in the world. For many its subtropical lushness and wealth of rare plant and animal life makes it the most beautiful of all the islands. It is accordingly a magnet for naturalists and nature lovers rather than a getaway haven for sun and beach *aficionados*. Most of the time the sky is overcast and the island's handful of beaches are comprised of uninviting black volcanic sand. Like La Gomera it has little rain and compensates for this by extracting moisture from the humid winds that blow constantly across its towering terrain. *Minas galeras* (man-made channels and gulleys) then filter the water down and across the island, irrigating flatter agricultural areas like Llanos de Argual, where in the past sugarcane plantations flourished.

Today, along with El Hierro, La Palma is located above the archipelago's current "hot spot"—the area where the submarine plates covering the earth's ever-incandescent magma are closest to the surface. Roughly heart-shaped, the island boasts the second highest summit in the whole Canary group: the (just under) 2,400-metre Roque de los Muchachos, which—as previously mentioned—is home to one of the world's most important observatories.

The peak is part of a chain of peaks bordering the vast Caldera de Taburiente, which was initially formed by a huge volcanic explosion. Its steep slopes comprise the entire steep northern side of the island while to the south loom two other massive ranges, the Cumbre Nueva and Cumbre Vieja, the latter dominated at its southern tip by the San Antonio volcano. The Teneguia cinder cone volcano, also on the Cumbre Vieja, was the scene of the last eruption in 1971 though no damage was caused on a Garachico scale. This was the seventh eruption since 1492 when the Montaña Quemada finally reached the end of a marathon continuous 22-year-spell of lava discharges.

One theory, which in recent has received much publicity in the international media, claims that there was a massive landslide from—again—the great Cumbre Vieja lava ridge during the sixth eruption, caused by a 1949 earthquake. Today many experts are concerned that there is a renewed risk of this highly unstable section of the island being pushed up by a mass of magma-heated subterranean water reserves which could again dislodge a great section of the mountain and send it plunging into the sea. This would in turn cause a tsunami wave to surge westwards across the Atlantic, sweeping over the Caribbean islands to reach the United States' eastern seaboard where it would wreak havoc among a multitude of highly populated areas stretching from Boston down to Miami.

La Palma's authorities, unsurprisingly, dismiss this idea as scare-mongering. (They even single out, among a diverse range of groups they see as key "alarmists", irresponsible Florida insurance companies of trying to sell policies to cover such an event.) On a more restrained level they are backed in this opinion by objective bodies such as the Hawaii-founded Tsunami Society. Heavyweight experts such as Californian Stephen Ward and top British researcher Simon Day think the tsunami is a real possibility. As part of their evidence they point out that the triple rift system has now been reduced to single rift system, making the whole area more vulnerable to vent fissures, splits and escapes of magma.

The islanders and their supporters have produced various arguments rejecting this possibility. These include assertions that there was no discernible fault line separating "blocks" on the island; that all the rocks close to the subterranean water are of porous rock whereas solid impenetrable granite would be needed for the water to be trapped sufficiently to heat up and cause an explosion; and that the maximum length of a split in rock detected is four kilometres and not the 25 kilometres that has been claimed as evidence for the danger. They also add that there is no definite confirmation that a mega-tsunami ever crossed the Atlantic in spite of the many eruptions and landslides that have taken place over millennia of instability.

A Dutch specialist concluded in 2006 that no subsidence of the magnitude predicted was likely to take place for at least ten thousand years. Among the many videos—some sensationalist, others more down to earth—that have been made on the subject, one ironically concludes: "You've only 10,000 years left to visit La Palma". The general consensus is that some time or other in the future this massive subsidence will definitely occur. On what scale and exactly when remain to be determined.

## EL HIERRO: LATEST "HOT SPOT"

What is largely believed—and feared—will sooner or later happen in La Palma occurred one hundred thousand years ago in diamond-shaped El Hierro, around forty miles away and the most westerly outpost in the Canary Island chain. During that volatile Quaternary period a particular violent volcanic eruption loosened a huge chunk of the northern flank of the island and sent it plunging into the sea, leaving in its place the valley of El Golfo, a frozen basaltic lava flood dotted with small Holocene cinder cones. The gigantic gravitational collapse is also calculated by theorists to have unleashed waves that several hours later crossed the Atlantic to reach the then uninhabited eastern shores of America (but as this went un-recorded and unseen by human eyes, there is no solid evidence to contra-dict the La Palma disclaimer that a transatlantic tsunami ever occurred.)

After tens of thousands of years of relative peace a sizeable eruption oc-curred in 1793 at Lomo Negro at the western end of the island. But this palled in comparison with the latest series of underwater explosions which took place between 2011 and 2013, when at least one new midget islet was formed. Such was the violence of these eruptions at one stage that the evacuation of the island's entire population of 10,000 was contemplated.

With today's media coverage the whole world has been able to see more clearly than ever before the real effects of this latest seismic activity. The first eruptions, producing "harmonic tremors" as the submarine magma began to move, started just before dawn in October 2011. Dark ochre stains, "phreatic" bubbles, chunks of lava-based pumice, hollow "bombs" of basaltic rock and drifting flotillas of dead fish appeared on the sea's usually cobalt blue surface just off the port of La Restinga. The diminutive coastal outpost temporarily evacuated its 600 inhabitants to safer corners of the island, and repeated the operation a month later when further heavy tremors shook sea and land and ominous Jacuzzi-like bursts of steam rocked the area. The whole bay of El Golfo reeked of sulphur. The Devil himself looked set to make an appearance. Perhaps feeling left out, the main inland volcano, Tanganasoga, now started emitting huge gaseous clouds of carbon dioxide.

While the land threat quickly subsided, the undersea eruptions con-tinued, at their worst coming as close as sixty metres to the surface. A trio of sophisticated scientific vessels, loaded with state-of-the-art equipment that included seismic intensity measuring instruments and sediment col-lectors, surveyed and monitored the disturbances and their effects.

A lull in the activity occurred in the spring of 2012, but the eruptions started up again that summer when tiny earthquake "swarms", evidenced by more steam clouds and geyser effects, demonstrated that a further mass of magma was inexorably moving below the sea bed. It first headed west-wards and then, as September began, south. At the time of writing (summer 2013) the island is still in a highly unstable situation—much to the consternation of both the population and tourist authorities.

Yet regardless of all these apocalyptic scenarios, the islands have con-tinued to develop and flourish, initially through trade and then, as com-

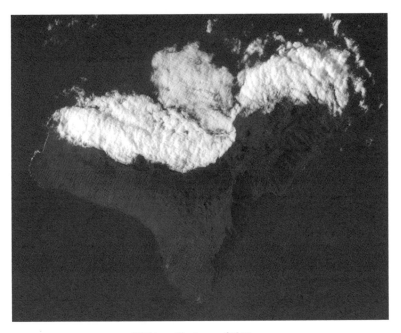

NASA satellite image of El Hierro
(Pepelopex/WikimediaCommons)

merce declined, by embracing the world's unstoppable new industry: tourism. The energy that was once expended on keeping outside invaders at bay is now put into warmly welcoming them.

*Part Three*

---

# SPLENDOUR AND MISERY

Peasant family, Gáldar, 1893 by Carl Norman
(Archivo Fotográfico de la FEDAC)

## Chapter Seven

# THE NATURALIST INVASION

Mere rumblings and eruptions from the bowels of the earth did not deter a fresh wave of invaders from heading to the islands. In fact the seismic upsets positively encouraged some of them. For many of these erudite and civilized visitors were interested not in conquering people but in investigating and recording the origins of the islands' geological wonders. Other ecologically oriented newcomers were in turn fascinated by the Canaries' rich conglomeration of flora and fauna and compiled copiously detailed reports and observations.

Many explored the island on foot. The year 1524 saw the very first recorded ascent to the summit of the Pico del Teide by a Frenchman, Père Feutrée. The peak was also scaled half a century later by an Anglican Jesuit priest called Thomas Stevens, who followed this up for good measure by making a historic journey round the Cape of Good Hope to India.

### NICHOLS AND SCORY: PIONEER INVESTIGATORS

One of earliest first pioneering Englishmen to arrive and actually settle in Tenerife, initially for business reasons, was a Bristolian called Thomas Nichols, whose exploits Romanian-born historian Alejandro Ciorianescu recounts in his 1963 book *Thomas Nichols: mercader de azúcar, hispanista y hereje* (Thomas Nichols: Sugar Merchant, Hispanist and Heretic). Religious differences between Protestant England and Catholic Spain, however, caused Nichols' arrest and imprisonment for many years in Seville as a heretic.

On his eventual return to England his now fluent grasp of the Castilian language enabled Nichols to translate many Spanish works on the Canaries and inspired his own investigations into the islands' culture, history and nature. This resulted in five books, which he began in 1577 and which also covered the exploration of territories as far afield as China and Peru. Francisco Javier Castillo points out that Nichols' own most relevant island work, *A Pleasant Description of the Fortunate Ilandes, called the Ilandes of Canaria, with their strange fruits and commodities* (1583), was the very first monograph in any language to be published on the islands.

Castillo also mentions another visitor and writer who introduced the Canaries to the sixteenth century English public: Sir Edmund Scory. Like Nichols, Scory praised the heady local wine of the time, known as Canary Sack and mentioned in the works of Shakespeare and his contemporaries. But, more importantly, he painted a vivid picture of the geography and inhabitants of the island of Tenerife that he saw during his stay in La Laguna. He describes the town and its neighbouring wildlife simply and naturally:

> The buildings are all of an open rough stone, nothing faire, they are very plaine in their buildings, two or three storeys, no more, and commonly but one storey high in the remoter parts of the City. It is not walled, they have no chimneys, no not so much as in their kitchins [*sic*]. They make only a flat hearth against a wall, and there they toast their meate rather than roast it. The decency of their streets is commendable, for when you are in the centre of the city, your eyes reach almost to the extreamest parts thereof. They have no want of water. The City hath its name from a great standing Lake at the West end of it, upon which there are divers sorts of fresh waterfowles. The haggard Falcons do every evening fly upon this lake and the Negros with slings beate them, which is the noblest kind of sport...

## J. EDENS AND THE HEBERDEN BROTHERS

The first scientific institutions to show interest in the Canaries were London's Royal Society in 1660 and the Parisian Académie des Sciences six years later. The Royal Society published the very first report of an ascent of Mount Teide by "merchants and men worthy of credit", in which they referred to a group of six worthies led by Philip Ward and John Webber who scaled the peak in 1650.

In their wake 65 years on came a certain J. Edens, who wrote a clear unadorned report of his climb and subsequent observations of the great peak, "An Account of a Journey from the Port of Orotava in the Island of Tenerife to the Top of the Pike of that Island", which appeared in the Royal Society's journal *Philosophical Transactions*. Castillo regards Edens' work as "characteristic of the Enlightenment, written in a plain style without any concession to a superfluous erudition, and which reveals to us that the author is a man of his time, who is determined to read Nature's book from science, and to provide rational explanations to what he sees." The august Fundación Canaria Orotava de Historia de la Ciencia considered Edens' report the "first account of the Canary Islands' contribution to the history of European Science" and the ever reliable Viera y Clavijo also briefly mentions this climb in his *Noticias de la historia general de las Islas de Canarias*.

During his historic ascent Edens identified and named several key landmarks, including La Carabela, Cruz de la Solera and the Fuente de Dornajito, which is located halfway along one of today's most popular *gran recorrido* (long distance) walks: the ninety-kilometre Camino Natural de Anaga-Chasma. He also encountered and explored many caves containing human remains and reflected on the myths created by the mountain in the time of the Guanches. Though little is known or recorded about Edens himself (even his Christian name remains a mystery) the tireless Castillo surmised that he was principally involved with the wine trade—which had reached its zenith then—but had a real interest in accumulating scientific knowledge of the island.

Edens wrote his subsequent account of the climb in a single night just before leaving the island and later apologized to readers for his hastiness and lack of revisions. He need not have worried. The resultant text is unpretentiously conversational in style and makes engaging and informative reading. Here is how he describes the meaning of the place called Cruz de Solera: "A *solera* is a long pole with a hole at each end and which Spaniards use to draw wood with, by fast'ning one end to the wood and the other to the oxen. This cross was made with a piece of *solera* and for that reason it is so call'd, but why it was set up in this place I can't tell, unless it was because someone was kill'd thereabouts."

During the eighteenth century more foreign visitors came and climbed Teide. An account of one such ascent was written in 1715 by the physician William Heberden, who scaled the mountain with his brother Thomas, a resident of neighbouring Gran Canaria. They discovered salt—which they named *natron* or *salitron*, according to its appearance and origins in Las Cañadas crater. The Royal Society's *Philosophical Transactions* published two of William Heberden's articles recounting the climbs and his findings.

While William continued his working life in the comfort of his homeland, his brother Thomas worked in more trying and uncertain circumstances as a doctor and surgeon at the Compañía de Jesus in Las Palmas. Although he carried out his duties there in an exemplary fashion he, like Nichols before him, fell foul of the Inquisition in the 1730s. His "crime", according to Manuel Hernández González, was to declare that sexual relations were not a sin. Worn down by harassment and imprisonment, Thomas converted to Catholicism and eventually gained his release. He moved to Tenerife where he spent seven years, but still feeling victimized as long as he was in Spanish territory he finally moved to Madeira where he lived for the rest of his life, concentrating on astronomical research.

## FEUILLÉE AND THE EL HIERRO MERIDIAN

Mathematicians and geographers were another group of learned professionals increasingly drawn to the Canary Islands. In 1724 the famed French astronomer Louis Éconches Feuillée—a highly religious man who was a devote friar of the Catholic Order of Minims (and thus risked no problems with the Inquisition)—also made an ascent of Teide, which he calculated by geodesic means to be 2,213 *toises* (at 3.713 *toises* per metre) high. He and his climbing companion Esteban Porlier found that the wine and *aguardiente* (brandy) they carried with them lost quality as they got higher (a fact disputed by others such as Viera y Clavijo). Among his botanical discoveries was the Teide violet, according to Hernández Gonzaléz, the highest flowering plant in Spain.

The main purpose of Feuillée's visit, however, was not climb mountains but to measure the meridian on El Hierro and compare its longitude with that of the Paris observatory, as Louis XIII had decreed that the smallest Canary Island was in fact the prime meridian. (Two and a half centuries would pass before this privilege was transferred to Greenwich.) At the age of 64, commissioned for this task by the Académie des Sciences, Feuillée here crowned a distinguished career and in doing so was a pioneer of subsequent scientific Canary expeditions. He also mapped the island's coastlines and tiny towns like Valverde, and after travelling over to Tenerife made the by-now obligatory Teide ascent.

He then spent three months back in El Hierro working on other aspects of his interest in the islands, drawing botanical specimens and living creatures that ranged from the *orchilla* and dragon tree to the gecko. To aid him in his main astronomical and mathematical investigations he also took a five-metre-long telescope, a micrometer for observing eclipses,

Dragon Tree, La Laguna, 1898 (*Popular Science Monthly*/Wikimedia Commons)

and various clocks, compasses and thermometers. With the aid of these in-struments he was able to calculate the Paris readings as being 20º 02'E from the El Hierro meridian. The original manuscript of his account of the expedition is kept in Paris.

In 1749 a Frenchman of Scottish descent called Michel Adanson stopped for just eight days in Tenerife and made observations on the island's topography, flora and fauna. He subsequently continued on south to spend four years as an employee of the Compagnie des Indes in Senegal, but his true passion was botany and he created a natural system of classi-fying and naming plants and creatures based on their physical features and grouped them in natural family groups. Over the years more than thirty plants have been dedicated to him and animals named after him include the *pelusios adansonii* (a turtle he later encountered in northern Senegal). Such was his fame in France that a biology-oriented journal published by the Natural History Museum in Paris is called *Adansonia* and a street is named after him in his birthplace, Aix-en-Provence. At the time of his brief Canary visit he believed Teide to be the highest mountain in the world and set about determining its height in order to confirm this.

Scottish seafarer, merchant and doctor, George Glas (already mentioned as the able translator of Abreu Galindo's *History of the Discovery and Conquest of the Canary Islands*), made several commercially oriented trips to the isles, mainly focusing on fishing, which was one of his passions. Glas wrote about harbours, coasts, winds and currents and gave good technical advice on caulking ships. He also studied island anthropology and recommended Teide's suitability as a spot for an observatory. He even spent ten months in prison for criticizing Spain's colonial policy. (The Spaniards arrested him on a charge of espionage.) He published his own book on the archipelago in 1764 in London (just before he started the translations of Abreu Galindo's earlier historical work).

## THE "ROMANTIC PERIOD" OF SCIENTIFIC EXPLORATION

The half century from 1770 to 1830 became later known as the "Romantic Period" of expeditions to the Canaries and is well documented by the Spanish academic José Montesinos Sirera of the Fundación Canaria Orotava de Historia de la Ciencia and Jürgen Renn, of the Max-Planck-Institut für Wissenschaftgesichte. These two diligent researchers have divided such trips into those paid for by the state in liaison with scientific institutions and others which were private affairs carried out by informed, enquiring and wealthy enthusiasts.

One of the initial state-funded expeditions was undertaken by the geodesist, mathematician and military engineer Jean-Charles de Borda, who made trips in 1771 and 1776 to measure the precise height of Teide and the longitude of all the islands. He was accompanied on his first visit by Alexandre Guy Pingré, a multifaceted character who was as adept in his scientific roles of astronomer and naval geographer as he was as an Augustinian priest and theology teacher back in his home region of Oise. Today he has an impact crater on the south-west limb of the moon named after him and even an asteroid, 12719 Pingré, discovered in 1991.

The disparate duo made a joint ascent of the Tenerife giant, and Borda is recognized as the first person to have accurately calculated Teide's height as 1,905 *toises* using trigonometric methods to measure triangles which had apexes in Puerto de la Cruz, Orotava and the Teide summit. But his overall objective, following a reconnaissance made by an earlier visitor, mathematician and naval officer Charles Pierre Claret de Fleurieu, who had paved the way with astronomical and cartographical surveys in 1768 and 1769, was to determine the exact locations of various points throughout the archipelago. To achieve this monumental task Borda employed forty assistants including members of the Spanish Navy. His eventual findings were published by l'Imprimerie Royale in 1778. (A famous personage also made a brief appearance at this time. Captain James Cook, on the third of his world voyages, docked for just a few days at Santa Cruz de Tenerife, coinciding with Borda, with whom he exchanged ideas and information.)

In 1785 an expedition of 400 men under Jean-François de Galoup, Count of La Pérouse, stayed long enough to scale Teide and perform observations and various experiments, before continuing on to the South Pacific where, three years later, they all disappeared off the island of Vanikoro never to be heard of again. Naturalists La Martinière and Lamanon, as well as the astronomer Monge, all recorded Galoup's brief sojourn on Tenerife. Expeditions in search of Galoup also docked in at the main port of Santa Cruz de Tenerife. Captain Antoine Bruni d'Entrecasteaux, leader of one such sortie, stayed ten days in 1791 making with accompanying scientists and astronomers the mandatory ascent of the island's great peak.

## THE BAUDIN-LEDRU EXPEDITION

The most important state-financed scientific expedition to the Canary Islands took place almost accidentally in 1796 when Captain Nicolas Baudin and André Pierre Ledru arrived on the schooner *Belle-Angélique*. Baudin (described enigmatically as "a controversial figure in the French Navy" in a Fundación Canaria Orotava de Historia de la Ciencia report, presumably as in the past he had included slave trading among his many business dealings) was a cartographer and a globally renowned collector of natural history objects. The scholarly Ledru, a professor in law and physics and one of four accompanying botanists on the trip, wrote about these objects Also on the expedition were noted gardener Anselme Riédlé and astronomer Pierre-François Bernier.

Originally Baudin had only intended to make a brief stop in the islands to take on provisions before continuing on to the West Indies to collect natural history samples he had left behind the previous year in

Trinidad, but between the Azores and Madeira the expedition experienced a terrifying storm that lasted several days. Baudin and most of the crew doubted they would escape alive on more than one occasion. The ship was battered, helmless and virtually mastless when they finally anchored, exhausted and—so says Ledru—weeping with relief, in Santa Cruz de Tenerife. Ledru sent highly atmospheric letters home recounting his experiences on the voyage, describing the unique combination of terror and elation he had felt at seeing the elements at their most violent.

Baudin's vessel was forced to stay four months in Tenerife due to the severe damage sustained. This accidental extension of the spare time they found themselves enjoying on the island allowed them to establish a good rapport with the native *tinerfeños*—Ledru in particular was a friendly and amenable man—and for both of them to study the island's nature in detail. Ledru and Baudin met the Marquis de Villanueva and stayed in his La Laguna palace for a while. Ledru subsequently wrote an in-depth book on the flora and fauna of the archipelago and produced the first catalogue on the Marquis' Botanical Gardens using a systematic listing method based on the 1753 Linnaean classification. Many of the valuable specimens originally obtained from the duo's explorations are now in French museums.

## Humboldt and the Orotava Valley

The first and most famous of the private expeditions was made by the flamboyantly rich (and, in Schiller's rather waspish opinion, "childishly vain") Prussian Baron Alexander von Humboldt, whose energy and enthusiasm were as legendary as the depth and scope of his interest in all things natural and botanical. He only spent six days on Tenerife in 1799, accompanied by his naturalist companion Aimé Bonpland, but the influence he had on the island was, from a scientific viewpoint, both invaluable and long-lasting.

Though this was only his initial brief stop in what would become a five-year world-wide journey, Humboldt included many scientific and historical references to the island in his monumental 36-volume work *Voyage aux regions équinoxiales du nouveau continent*. He fell in love with the northern half of Tenerife, in particular the green Orotava Valley. Canary Islanders claim he would rather have stayed there than continue west and today you can see a statue of the German naturalist beside the *mirador* that overlooks the valley.

A genuine blue-blooded aristocrat, Humboldt was a kindred soul of other later privileged but nature-obsessed Central Europeans like the Austrian Archduke Ludwig Salvator (1847-1915) whose love for the Balearic Islands was such that he bought land and property on the beautiful northwest coast of Mallorca, which he avidly protected from woodcutters and other "destroyers of nature", and praised in a highly detailed, monumental, multi-volume work called *Die Balearen*. Though Humboldt's vision was more global and his stay in Tenerife much briefer than Salvator's in Mallorca he brought the charms and natural wonders of this and the other Canary Islands to international attention and encouraged many others to follow in his footsteps.

Humboldt's overall viewpoint as a naturalist differed radically from those of most of his eighteenth-century contemporaries in that he saw a fluidly harmonious link between nature and the historical internal movements of the earth. He combined botany and geodesy with a profoundly human element and saw an almost mystical interaction between animals, plants, rocks and men.

## CORDIER, BUCH AND SMITH EXPEDITIONS

Among those who did follow in Humboldt's Canarian footsteps was the French mineralogist Louis Cordier who paid a month-long visit in 1803 to Tenerife, dually attracted by its colourfully mythical past and exhilarating landscape. He climbed Teide twice, accurately re-ascertained its height and made many revealing observations on minerals he found there. One of his major practical discoveries was the effect that the Chahorra volcano had made on the geological formation of the great Las Cañadas crater. No mere dispassionate specialist, however, he was moved beyond mere scientific speculations in this nocturnal description:

> The night was magnificent, cloudless and almost calm. The sky was a deep black, the twinkling stars emitted a light so vivid that we could see through the vaporous darkness that hid everything we found at our feet… Raised to this altitude, sitting peacefully on those heaps of ruined smouldering rocks, isolated from the ocean, alone and vigilant in the silent midst of nature, devotedly admiring its dreamlike majesty, evoked memories and patiently awaited the moment when the curiosity that

had drawn me this far to one of the oldest volcanoes on earth would be satisfied.

Shortly after Cordier came two more highly-regarded experts, the German geologist Leopold von Buch and the Norwegian doctor and botanist Christen Smith in 1815. Von Buch was a disciple of Abraham Gottlob Werner (his former teacher) who had preached Neptunism, the theory that rocks were formed by the crystallization of minerals in the world's oceans. After initially following this hypothesis von Buch rejected it in favour of Plutonism, which expounded the idea that rocks were elevated to form land. His magnum opus *Physicalische Beschreibung der Kanarischen Inseln* (1825), with its highly detailed morphological descriptions, was the very first full geological work to effectively cover the whole archipelago. He introduced the term *caldera* (Spanish for cauldron) into the geological lexicon and the term "elevation craters" for Las Cañadas in Tenerife and Taburiente in La Palma, after concluding that the islands' two largest *calderas* had been pushed, or "elevated", to the surface by molten magma.

View of the Caldera de Taburiente, La Palma (Michael Apel/Wikimedia Commons)

Christen Smith was a highly diligent collector, and in all he assembled over six hundred different varieties of Canary plants and trees and even named certain local species like the long-needled *Pinus canariensis*. He also sent seeds of local plants to the Botanical Gardens at Cristiana in his homeland. Unfortunately his planned written works on the subject never materialized as he died on a Royal Society-organized trip to the Congo barely a year after leaving the islands.

Two decades before Smith's premature demise the Montpellier-born naturalist Auguste Broussonet, who was also French consul in Tenerife from 1800 to 1803, had classified a lesser number of the islands' plants. He was also responsible for the construction of an *orangerie* in Montpellier's Jardin des Plantes and held a professorship in botany at that city's renowned university. During the course of his investigative tours of the islands he presented his findings to key European botanists like Joseph Banks, who had earlier organized the transport of breadfruit on the notorious HMS *Bounty*, and René Desfontaines, who eventually became a director of Paris's Muséum National d'Histoire Naturelle. The itinerant naturalist Jean-Baptiste Bory de Saint-Vincent also used information provided by Banks in his *Essais sur les Îles Fortunées et l'antique Atlantide*(1802) and later accompanied the ill-fated Baudin on his Australia expedition before moving on to explore Indian Ocean islands.

## WEBB AND BERTHELOT'S MAMMOTH ANTHOLOGY

Of all the islands' erudite chroniclers during this enlightened period it was the Frenchman Sabin Berthelot (1794-1880) who went to the greatest lengths with his compilations and who stayed longer than any other foreign researcher in the region. He began making his naturalist investigations during his initial stay in Tenerife, where he had consecutive bases in Santa Cruz, La Laguna and La Orotava, and during this period was overseer of the Orotava Botanical Gardens for the Marquis of Villanueva del Prado with whom he had become good friends.

In due course his efforts resulted in the most comprehensive scientific encyclopaedia on the archipelago produced to date. It proved too large a task for one man alone to achieve, however, and his great magnum opus *Histoire naturelle des Îles Canaries* was in fact written with the invaluable help of a wealthy British botanist, Peter Barker Webb, who met Berthelot in Tenerife while on his way to Brazil after having already done similar research work in Europe and Morocco. Webb promptly hit it off with the Frenchman and after continuing with his intended Brazil visit he returned to join Berthelot in his investigations.

To gather first-hand material Berthelot and Webb then spent two years travelling extensively throughout the islands, though they never managed to reach La Gomera or El Hierro due to transportation problems. Altogether their close collaboration spread over a couple of decades and in order to expand the work and gain a variety of perspectives they obtained contributions from a wide range of botanists and zoologists, including Alphonse de Gandolle and Sir Joseph Dalton Hooker. They also commissioned a host of talented artists and engravers to supply the relevant illustrations. The ornithological section was mostly compiled and written by Alfred Moquin-Tandon, a professor of zoology from Marseille who later became director of the Jardin des Plantes and the Académie des Sciences. (Berthelot, incidentally, has a tiny bird named after him: Berthelot's Pipit (*Anthus berthelotii*), found both in the Canaries and Madeira.)

As main author, Berthelot dealt with the sections on ethnography, history, the original Guanche inhabitants and the physical and botanical geography of the islands, while Webb contributed mainly to sections on geology and zoology. The Englishman further collected specimens between 1828 and 1830 and first published an article in 1833 in Paris entitled "Notice générale sur la géologie des Îles Canaries". By the time they had finished the two men had produced a global treatise containing 106 different fully-researched instalments.

In 1847, after Webb had returned to England, Berthelot was appointed French consul in his beloved Tenerife and renewed his private research alone, embarking on new studies of fishing practices along the island's and neighbouring Africa's shorelines, and cultivation—particularly of the red-dye-producing cochineal insect. In his new official capacity he also took an enthusiastically active part in the social and cultural scene of Tenerife, where he remained until his death in 1880. Six years before his retirement he was given the freedom of the city of Santa Cruz de Tenerife.

Three volumes of Webb's work dealt exclusively with the Canaries while other areas of the world he covered included Macronesia. Other collaborators included the French entomologist Justin Pierre Marie Macquart. The herbarium in the University of Florence, Museo di Storia Naturale di Firenze, contains many of the plants and flowers they originally brought back from the islands which had been bequeathed there after Webb's death.

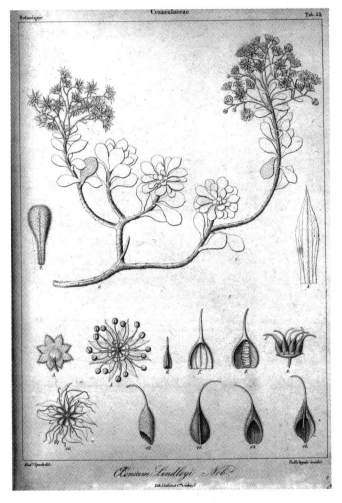

*Aeonium lindleyi* from the *Histoire naturelle des Îles Canaries*
(Wikimedia Commons)

## STUDYING THE HEAVENS

More and more scientists came, exploring ever wider fields. Some looked upwards towards the stars above rather than at the islands themselves. The clarity of the skies here, especially at high altitudes, was remarkable. Stars were visible with a stability and sharpness that made them ideal for detailed studies. A pioneer in this field was the Scotsman Charles Piazzi Smyth (who owed the Piazzi part of his name to his astronomer godfather Giuseppe Piazzi and the fact that he himself was born in Naples).

Ten years after being Appointed Astronomer Royal at Edinburgh in 1846 Smyth was commissioned to carry out work in the islands by the British Admiralty and accordingly sailed south in famed railway engineer Robert Stephenson's yacht *Titania* on a combined business and honeymoon trip. He stayed two months and closely investigated the heavens from both inside the Las Cañadas crater—in particular from its 2,717-metre Guajara and 3,250-metre Altavista peaks—and from sea-level Puerto de Orotava, later renamed Puerto de la Cruz. He worked with the aid of a 188-centimetre equatorial telescope and a smaller eighteen-centimetre refracting telescope loaned by Hugh Pattinson, a dynamic entrepreneur who was also an industrial chemist, and his focal interests ranged

Piazzi Smyth's telescope, from *Teneriffe, An Astronomer's Experiment: or, Specialities of a Residence Above the Cloud* (1858)

from ultraviolet solar radiation to the surface of the moon. He also checked out the phenomenon of thermal inversion caused by trade winds and the anticyclone conditions that existed further north round the Azores. In 1858 he published his findings in a book called *Teneriffe: An Astronomer's Experiment or Specialities of a Residence above the Clouds*. (In another quite different field, and one for which he is more famous today, Smyth made important studies of the Pyramids of Giza and wrote comprehensive reports on his findings there.)

Smyth was followed by a more international cross-section of meteorologists and astronomers, including the Swedish H. Ohrwall in 1884, the Englishman Ralph Abercrombie three years later, Americans Oskar Simony and David Webster Edgcombe in 1888 and 1890 respectively, the Swede Knut Angstrom in 1895 and Germans Hugo Hergesell and Robert Wenger at the beginning of the twentieth century. The stream of scientific explorers continued unabated and other notables followed them in turn to observe phenomena like Halley's Comet, which made a dramatic appearance in 1911.

### ANTHROPOLOGICAL DISCOVERIES

Another of the multifaceted Berthelot's keen interests was anthropology (his key work here being *L'Ethnographie et les annales de la conquête des Îles Canaries* in 1842) and he eventually led the way for a host of further investigators in that field. Leading successors were Paul Broca who seventeen years after Berthelot's work founded the Parisian Société d'Anthropologie and in 1871 identified similarities between the Guanches and Cro-Magnon man at a rock shelter in the Dordogne.

Though Broca barely set foot in the Canaries in the course of his investigations, most of which were carried out in French laboratories and libraries, a paleoanthropologist colleague and follower by the name of René Verneau went to the archipelago in 1876 and spent two years uncovering remains, measuring and examining mummies and sending his findings back to the Muséum National de l'Histoire Naturelle in Paris. Verneau made several subsequent visits to the islands, established a particularly close relationship with the Museo Canario, which opened in 1880 in Las Palmas, and wrote a book *Cinq années de séjour aux Îles Canaries* in 1884. (In appreciation of his work Gran Canaria's only French college, run by the Maison Laïque Française organization in Paris, adopted his name in 2005.)

By making the Canaries' special attractions more widely known than ever to the world Verneau boosted the possibilities and benefits of further trade and in many ways set the ball rolling for the huge global tourism market that mushroomed in the following decades.

## Chapter Eight
# TRADE AND EMIGRATION

### ACROSS THE ATLANTIC

Columbus' pioneering voyages west opened up a whole new transatlantic world of commerce for the Canaries. The islands became vital stopping off points for *conquistadores*, traders and missionaries en route across the Atlantic.

The main islands soon began to profit from this new global market, but they were not yet free agents. All Spanish commerce was still in the rigidly controlling hands of Seville, whose ultra-bureaucratic government agency, the Casa de Contratación (or House of Trade), was quick to establish strict rules to ensure the crown's monopoly on trade with the Americas. In 1526 it published a brief entitled "Secret Instructions for Navigation between Spain and the Isles of Santo Domingo" which laid out an official nautical itinerary called the Carrera de Indias—the Route to the Indies—in which ships were instructed to follow the clockwise pattern of trade winds via the Canaries across the Atlantic to the Lesser Antilles and Southern Caribbean. Javier Méndez summarizes the archipelago's role in this itinerary:

> ...once the ships have emerged from San Lucar, where the River Guadalquivir empties into the Ocean Sea, they set sail for the Islands of Canarias, called the Fortunate Islands... especially Gran Canaria or La Gomera or La Palma, because they lie on the most direct route and they are fertile and abound in the provisions and what is needed by those making this long journey. There the ships victual with water and wood, fresh bread, chickens, calves, kids, cows, salt meat and cheeses, fish, salted chickens and other provisions.

As soon as the first Spanish colonies in the Americas were settled, the Casa de Contratación opened administrative centres in the Canary Islands with the aim of countering smuggling and contraband activities between them and the New Continent. In 1566 it set up a Juzgado de India, or ju-

121

dicial zone, whose duties included inspecting vessels coming to and from the Americas to make sure they were following Spanish legal stipulations.

Santa Cruz de Tenerife was the main port for most commercial transactions, though later Puerto de la Luz, at Las Palmas de Gran Canaria, also received authorization to export goods. The Canarians, for their part, were enticed by this new promised land on the other side of the Atlantic which offered work for everybody. They mainly migrated from the two biggest islands, Tenerife and Gran Canaria, and spoke with distinctive local accents that were more strongly influenced by Andalusia than those of the smaller, more linguistically idiosyncratic islands. Consequently the first Spanish spoken in the New World was often a sort of hybrid Canary-Andaluz, which is strongly reflected in the Cuban, Dominican and Puerto Rican accents heard today.

Transatlantic trade was hindered again by restrictive Spanish practices which allowed only a few Latin American ports to do business with the Canaries. As a result the initial volumes of trade were low. But from the early eighteenth century onwards Seville eased its controls, which became even more relaxed when independence was achieved by the bulk of Spanish colonies in the 1820s. Spain gradually allowed a more open exchange of commerce, mainly to placate the increasing dissatisfaction expressed by both transatlantic colonists and Canarian traders but also because it had become aware of the economic advantages of taking such a step. Canary-based ships were allowed to sail regularly across the ocean to a wide variety of ports ranging from Havana and Santiago de Cuba to Cartagena de las Indias (Colombia) and Veracruz and Campeche in Mexico. Free to organize their own agendas and equip and maintain their own vessels, the Canarian merchants evolved into a new independent seafaring breed, intent on going their own way and professionally matching their more experienced Spanish mainland rivals from Galicia, Asturias and Andalusia.

## SUGAR AND SPICE...

The first major Canary export was sugarcane, which grew in abundance on the central islands after plantations had been laid out by experts from mainland Spain in the 1480s. On his second trip across the Atlantic Columbus took sugarcane seedlings with him to Hispaniola and in doing so paved the way for undermining future Canary production, for it soon became clear that it would be cheaper to grow the crop there on large slave-run plantations. Of all the Caribbean locations, Santo Domingo was the pioneer in successfully producing sugar and by 1516 it was already exporting the raw product in substantial quantities to Europe.

In spite of this early competition the sugar business flourished in the Canary Islands throughout the sixteenth century, attracting foreign entrepreneurs who ran their businesses from trade agencies, houses and stores in three main towns: Las Palmas de Gran Canaria, Santa Cruz de Tenerife and Santa Cruz de La Palma. English merchants such as Thomas Nichols (see p.105) formed a particularly strong presence and made profitable two-way transactions, importing much-needed manufactures like London cloth and exporting sugar and wine. The Flemish also played a major role in the sugar trade, and a large sector of it was run by two Flemish families, Van Dales and Groenbergh (later hispanicized into Van Dalle and Monteverde). Incidentally, many Flemish were targeted by the Inquisition during the sixteenth century, both because of their Protestant beliefs and because they were resented for allegedly taking business away from local workers.

Sugar had long been very highly valued. Considered a "fine spice", according to William Bernstein in his *A Splendid Exchange: How Trade Shaped the World*, (2009), it was first grown in Southwest Asia. From there production moved slowly westwards via Cyprus and Sicily before reaching Madeira and the Canaries, and then, as we have seen, continuing further west across the Atlantic to the West Indies and the Americas. The crop was very profitable due to the high prices it obtained, but it needed large, costly tracts of land to grow on. In order to cut overheads much of the labour was provided by slaves, though this practice was less common in the Canaries than in the Latin American and Caribbean colonies where it had become a business in itself.

The Canary sugar boom was short-lived. The famed "white gold" was exported principally to the Spanish mainland, Flanders and Italy, but the bubble burst after the sixteenth century when Caribbean and American prices seriously undercut those of the archipelago. During its brief heyday there were over sixty sugar mills in the islands producing a joint total of up to 320,000 *arrobas* (units weighing 25 pounds) practically all of which was exported. The strongest competitors were the Caribbean islands and mainland Brazil, whose Portuguese colonizers had become Spain's main rival in the sugar stakes. By the mid-seventeenth century the cost of West

Indies sugar was only half that of sugar produced in the Canaries.

Its popularity was such that it soon became available to a wider spectrum of the public. Larry Gragg writes: "From the mid fifteenth century increasing supplies transformed sugar from a luxury for a few to a commodity widely consumed by Europeans of all classes. Beyond the jobs provided by refineries in places like Antwerp, the growing popularity of sugar created opportunities for those who made the wide array of utensils used in serving sugar as well as for the confectioners who sought to satisfy the cravings of the European sweet tooth."

Today residual sugar products are almost exclusively found in the islands' modestly resurging wine industry, where they are used to aid the fermentation of grapes such as Lanzarote's Malvasia Volcánica from which the smokily fragrant La Geria dry white wine is produced. Along with other new-style "sophisticated" island wines this vies in popularity with the sweet heavy traditional Malmsey dessert wines which need even more residual sugar in the fermentation process, though neither of these wines is today exported in sufficient quantities to compete with the superior mainland Spanish vintages.

## In Vino Veritas

The wine trade, in fact, enjoyed a great deal more success in the past, when as Canary sugar exports waned the islands' rich Malvasia wine, whose original varietal had been brought over from the ancient wine-producing island of Cyprus, was produced in prolific quantities to further satisfy "sweet tooth cravings". It then took over as the number one earner of Spanish dollars, also known as *pesos de ocho* or pieces of eight, and the standard currency throughout the Canaries and all other Spanish territories during the sixteenth and seventeenth centuries. It was mainly exported to the Americas, Europe and Portugal's Cape Verde Islands, but was especially popular in England where one radical seventeenth-century doctor called Thomas Sydenham (who also advocated laudanum and cinchona bark for health purposes) prescribed it as a medicine which could—when taken in moderation—help cure gout and diabetes. For many English imbibers it was more popular than similar rival heavy-style French and Italian vintages.

A "Wine War" broke out between England and the Canaries in the 1660s when rocketing prices compelled King Charles II to form an organization baptized "The Governour and Company of Merchants Trading to the Canary Islands to Regulate Prices". Its role was to persuade Canary producers to deal only with the Company in the hope of reducing prices. In response the Canarian authorities banned English ships, and England, in a counter-response, prohibited imports of Canary wine unless they came via an English run co-operative known simply as the Canary Company.

This monopoly proved too much for the islanders who, understandably, wished to export wine independently. Their dissatisfaction and frustration took a violent turn in 1666 when 340 mask-wearing Tenerife locals attacked the Company's cellars in Garachico and in a memorable event known as the *derrame del vino* (literally, "spilling of the wine") smashed every single barrel they found, producing, in Viera y Clavijo's words, "one of the strangest floods you'll ever read about in the history of the world". The streets, lanes and gulleys of the town literally ran red as oceans of the lucrative Malvasia wine flowed into the harbour, darkening its clear blue waters into an opaque purple and leaving a rich odour of wine hanging over the town for weeks after. (This was a few decades before the famous eruption virtually wiped the town off the map, but spared the rest of the island.)

The conflict over wine was thankfully brief, and eventually the monopoly was relaxed and the islands' wine sales in England rose to higher levels than ever. Tenerife was considered to be the home of the best wines in the archipelago, while La Palma was highly regarded for its rich Malmsey versions which, according to the Hogshead wine blog, "in a few years gained a bouquet like a ripe pineapple". Exports to England of Canary wine reached an 1827 peak of around 418,000 gallons, but have declined ever since. A severe but temporary setback in the islands' wine production occurred in 1852 when vines were hit by a destructive "powdery mildew", though they were spared the dreaded phylloxera disease which ravaged most of Europe's vineyards. The vines successfully recovered after a long period of treatment and exports were resumed by the end of that century, though they never returned to the heights previously enjoyed. Apart from Europe, and England in particular, a major recipient of exported Canary wines was America, especially the North American English colonies.

Irish Catholics who also opened businesses had understandably little or no trouble from the Inquisition. As many as 50,000 of them had fled from Ireland to Spain and other parts of Europe after William of Orange's Protestant victory over the Catholic Jacobites at the Battle of the Boyne in 1690. In mainland Spain the Irish refugees settled mostly in Cádiz and Málaga. In the Canaries their preferred destination was Puerto de la Orotava (today's Puerto de la Cruz) in Tenerife where family names like Cologan, Walsh and Fitzgerald live on today. The pioneer families started many of the island's businesses, especially those involved with the wine trade, thus giving them an opportunity to take on the established English vintners. These two religiously and politically opposed rivals from the north battled for dominance of the lucrative Malvasia wine market.

One of the Cologans' descendants, Carlos Cólogan Soriano, wrote a book about his family's wine legacy, *Los Cólogan de Irlanda y Tenerife*. Another historian, José Antonio Álvarez Rico, recounts in his *Descripción histórica del Puerto de la Cruz de la Orotava* how many Irish merchants grew rich very quickly. (He also observes acidly that in some instances the sudden transition from underdogs to top dogs "went to their heads"—like the heady wine itself—and made them insufferably conceited.)

Malvasia did not completely dominate the market. There were other popular, less fortified wines as well. As early as in the nineteenth century Tacoronte reds from Tenerife were regarded as the islands' best vintages and by the following century they had received the archipelago's first *Dominación de Origen*. There have been nine more such awards since, four in Tenerife and the rest divided between the other islands, even including tiny El Hierro. *Listán negro* is the favoured grape from which most island table wines are produced today.

## GONE FISHING

George Glas (*The History of the Discovery and Conquest of the Canary Islands*) divided the Canaries' sixteenth-century commerce into four categories: trading with Europe and the English colonies in America; exporting products to the West Indies; inter-island exchanges of goods; and—his favourite topic—fishing off the Barbary Coast in North Africa, an activity which proved modestly profitable for the islanders themselves. Canarian fishermen found their main catches not way out in the mid-Atlantic as one might imagine, but just off the neighbouring Barbary Coast. They may not have been as sophisticated in their techniques as their European counterparts but were positive experts in comparison with their Guanche forefathers, who were notably unaccomplished in the piscatorial arts.

In Glas' time the total fishing fleet of the islands amounted to some thirty rigged brigantines, all locally built, with between fifteen and thirty fishermen in each vessel. All crew members carried their own equipment and provisions and together they all ensured there was a good supply of salt to cure the fish. Each man shared the profits with the owners and fellow crew, according to his status. There was little competition from North African ships as they did not venture as far south into the Atlantic as the Canary vessels, which regularly sailed down to Cabo Blanco on the lower north-west Moroccan coast.

The top catches were *sama* (sea bream) and *cherney* (grouper): both better tasting than most other varieties, according to Glas, who regarded this particular area as "the best fishery in the universe", far superior to the much-vaunted Newfoundland waters favoured by European fishermen. Here the fine weather and dry winds minimized the possibility of the fish putrefying, unlike the effect cold, humid conditions had on catches further north. Thanks to their large fore topsails the brigantines were able to reach relatively high speeds (for their time) and were often able to make the 400-kilometre journey to Gran Canaria from Cabo Blanco in just twelve days.

The profits from this hardworking business, which demanded extremely long hours and almost limitless stamina from its workers, were hardly huge, though. Glas wrote of the early eighteenth-century rates: "The common price is three half pence per pound, of thirty two ounces, which is the weight used here for flesh or fish, sometimes they are sold for a penny, never higher than two pence. The *regidores* (regulators) or *cabildos* (local councils) in the islands always regulate the price."

Glas complained of the excessive taxes and duties imposed by local magistrates who, in his eyes, seemed intent on undermining, rather than encouraging, the activity. They even forbade the Canary fishermen to have any form of social contact with the Moroccan inhabitants, a course of action the fisherman would tacitly agree to but in secret ignore, as their very existence was dependent on keeping on good terms with their North African neighbours (especially when bad weather drove them ashore for desperately needed food and water).

The fisherman then had little or no knowledge of the interior of that—or any other—corner of Africa. They were fishermen pure and simple and all they knew was the coast and its offshore waters. Anything beyond that simply did not interest them. They were not explorers, nor did they have an explorer's mentality.

## LA PALMA'S GOLDEN ERA

As their wealth increased, the Canary Islands attracted more interest from Europe. Many fine buildings were built both on the two main islands of Gran Canaria and Tenerife and on their smaller, but surprisingly successful, neighbour La Palma, whose compact capital Santa Cruz soon boasted grand houses and monuments that would not have looked out of place in much larger cities. The sense of affluence was palpable, with a strong international flavour. Prominent La Palma businesses were often run by Europeans such as the German Welzers who from 1513 controlled the waters of the Tazacorte Valley, where the island's two richest and most sumptuous *haciendas* (country estates) once stood and an original aqueduct still towers today; and the Englishman Thomas Malliard, who in partnership with the Genoan Francesco Spinola ran a company at Río de los Sauces.

Richard Hakluyt, a noted sixteenth-century Hereford-born chronicler, who wrote widely about the colonization of North America, cites one typical example of a European, Nicholas Thorne, who had settled in La Palma and made good. Thorne originally came from Bristol and from his new La Palma base he imported—as did many others in his line of business—much-prized cloth and other quality materials from London. In return he sold sugar, *orchil* and goatskins of varying qualities to Europe and the Americas.

The total amount of exports, mainly to Portugal, Italy and the Netherlands, allowed from the islands was 1,000 tons and La Palma's share was a moderately generous third of this. Seville subsequently tightened the reins and reduced this overall allowance to 600 tons, but somehow in spite of these restrictions trade continued to flourish. Shipbuilding was also a major industry in Santa Cruz de la Palma's heyday, and its success encouraged skilled immigrants from Galicia, the Basque Country, Portugal, Italy and northern Europe to move there and seek work.

As the three main islands prospered there was a corresponding fall in importance of Lanzarote and Fuerteventura, although Lanzarote produced a fair amount of wheat and wine. La Gomera and El Hierro were too small to compete internationally and only traded with the other

Canary Islands, importing the basic provisions they needed for their own local consumption.

In 1852 Queen Isabel II declared both Las Palmas de Gran Canaria and Santa Cruz de Tenerife free ports, an act which eventually turned them into two of the busiest seafaring cities in the world. Their dual success, perhaps inevitably, made them great rivals in the contest for the role of Canary capital. Not even the 1927 division of the archipelago into two provinces (with Gran Canaria governing Lanzarote and Fuerteventura, and Tenerife governing La Gomera, La Palma and El Hierro) helped lessen the ambition of each city to be considered more important than the other, however.

## CANARIANS ABROAD

After its initial sixteenth-century boom the economy underwent an alarming succession of ups and downs. Spain's attitude to the Canaries was ambivalent. Islanders had less prestige than mainlanders and were often regarded merely as cheap labourers, ready military conscripts and potential settlers for the new colonies. Initially (at least this was the theory) work-seeking Canarians could only travel to the Americas as soldiers. The Spanish government was also less interested in helping the poorer islands like El Hierro or others that suffered from periodic droughts (especially Lanzarote and Fuerteventura, which at one stage endured a devastating plague of locusts) than in extracting wealth from the Americas, so the financial aid and relief those areas sought was seldom forthcoming.

Whenever the situation became markedly unsettled, many Canarians found themselves compelled for various reasons—sometimes financial, sometimes because they were offered firm jobs by the Spanish government in the "colonies"—to emigrate. Some of them were familiar with the Americas as they had already visited or even been briefly employed there. By 1870 a serious economic crisis following the collapse in first sugar then wine exports precipitated a major exodus, and Canarians headed west in droves to Cuba, the Dominican Republic, Puerto Rico, Uruguay, Venezuela (which welcomed up to 40,000 *isleños,* or Canary Island immigrants, over a period of fifty years from 1840 to 1890) and the United States (where they were encouraged to settle in Texas and Louisiana to counter the increasing numbers of respective French and British military movements in those areas).

Two Caribbean islands, Puerto Rico and Cuba, were the most popular destinations for Canarian workers in the nineteenth century. Álvarez Nazario, a Puerto Rican essayist, journalist and philologist, has traced the successive waves of Canary Island immigration to his native island, where entire villages were populated by relocated islanders. Of 28 *pueblos* founded on the island between 1714 and 1797 no fewer than 19 of these were colonized primarily by Canarians, the first being Río Piedras, where the newcomers, mainly of Tenerife origin, introduced their traditional religious cult of La Candelaria.

In Cuba, meanwhile, the *isleño* became an even wider-known personage, characterized by a combination of industriousness and peasant superstition, and the speech and behaviour of Canary Islanders figure prominently in Cuban literature of the nineteenth and early twentieth centuries. In 1690 thirty Canary families founded the Cuban coastal town of Matanzas, which they originally named San Severino de Matanzas. They were second only to Galicians in numbers of Spanish nationals who migrated to Cuba. The move had been initiated twelve years earlier when the Spanish king ordered a *tributo de sangre* (or "decree of family rights") with the purpose of sending Canary islanders to inhabit Spanish territories in the Caribbean. The agreement stipulated that five Canary families would go for every hundred tons of goods exported there. In the following centuries increasing numbers of emigrants found their way to Cuba, reaching a peak between 1835 and 1850 when a total of 16,500 Canary *isleños* settled on the island.

Some later returned from Cuba to their homeland and as a result of this exchange the Canary archipelago and Cuba share many common traits, from regional accents to music. In La Palma the Spanish spoken resembles the Cuban version more than anywhere else in the archipelago—in fact linguistically the situation is now reversed as originally it was Canarian accents that affected how Cuban Spanish sounds today; and throughout the Canaries musical genres such as the *mambo, salsa* and *punto cubano* are commonly heard at festivals and shows. Canary emigrants returning from Cuba also, incidentally, introduced the tobacco plant to La Palma, where it eventually became one of the island's main products (see below).

Canarian cuisine, too, has much in common with its Cuban counterpart. The garlicky fully-flavoured potato and meat stew known unappetisingly as *ropa vieja* (literally, "old clothes") was first introduced to Cuba by Canarians, and other shared culinary delights include the flour-based *gofio* and pungent *mojo* sauce which form a staple base to meals eaten throughout all the islands. Idiosyncratic words commonly shared include *guagua* (meaning bus, though actually derived from the klaxon sounds emitted by the vehicle) and *socio/a* (partner) as an intimate—rather than business—term.

The low esteem in which some "salt of the earth" Canarians were sometimes held on the other side of the Atlantic is epitomized in an anecdote recalled by George Glas. It concerns the father of a simple rustic Tenerife family who migrated to a certain island in the West Indies (he does not specify which one), where many of the gallant local ladies (in Glas' words) "swim in luxury and pomp". When after many years the father had not returned to his native island—and none of the money he had promised to send his patient home-bred wife had arrived—his spirited young son went across to the Caribbean in search of him and, Glas tells us, found him "settled in a certain place, in great affluence, and married to a lady of rank and fortune".

> He [the son] made himself known to his father, who seeing him such a rustic, called to his remembrance his former low situation, which so wrought on his mind that he disowned him, and denied that himself had ever lived in Tenerife. The young man was so struck with this unexpected treatment, that he publicly challenged him and made known the whole story, to his father's confusion, and the astonishment of all the inhabitants.

This shaming of an "awkward clown" (Glas' words again) who had presumed to rise above his station was probably a rare instance of just desserts being meted out to one of these simple, self-gratifying, go-getters. Many must have vanished into their new world of well-being and never been traced, leaving the family back home disconsolate and probably ruined.

That said, the vast majority of single emigrants were more honourable men, who saw their families well provided for, and even returned home with funds they had amassed. Like the *Indianos* of Galicia, Asturias and Catalonia on the Spanish mainland, having made their fortune in Latin

Canarian migrants arrive in Uruguay, 1729 (Carlos Menck Freire)

America, they sometimes returned with enough money to build sumptuous (and sometimes outrageously vulgar or eccentric) houses.

Not all Canary emigrants ended up in the West Indies. Some went to the great agricultural countries of Argentina or Uruguay. Others went—or, rather, were dispatched—into the deep heart of the American mainland. The very first Canary settler in those regions was a captain and explorer Bernabé de las Casas who in 1604 planted roots in the Salinas Valley in the Kingdom of Nuevo León, as Mexico was then known.

The following century saw the American mainland invaded by a much larger number of immigrants. In 1779 lower Louisiana experienced an influx totalling 352 families and 100 single men, all the male members of whom had been sent as recruits for the local militia in order to defend the area against British colonizers. The Canary Islanders Heritage Society of Louisiana, formed as recently as 1996 to honour the state's Canary past, observes in one of its newsletters: "The recruits had to be 17 to 36 years old, healthy, without vices, and more than five feet tall. In fact, recruiters were paid extra for every half inch their recruits stood over five feet. Though it wasn't in the written agreement, these men understood that they would be staying in Louisiana permanently." Such was the new Canarian militia's success that they eventually conquered and occupied substantial areas of British territory on the lower Mississippi River. Evidently, the fighting spirit of the Guanches lived on.

Under Governor Bernardo de Galvez's supervision the new settlers were sent to occupy four separate small Louisiana towns: Villa de Galvez (now Galveztown), situated at the meeting point of the Amite river and Bayou Manchac; Barataria, at Barataria Bay; San Bernardo (now St. Bernardo) at Terre aux Boeufs; and Valenzuela, along the banks of Bayou Lafourche. Only four years after those first arrivals the total number of Canary colonizers had reached 2,363 and today over 120 Hispanic surnames, mainly of Canary origin, feature in the list of Louisiana residents. All the early arrivals appear to have adapted reasonably well to their new environment though not without suffering some hardship for in that southern region's flat, humid, undeveloped countryside mosquitoes were rife and malaria common. (Immigrants were later given guarantees by regulators that they would be sent to "healthier" areas where possible.)

The other mainland American state which saw a large eighteenth-century influx of Canary newcomers was Texas, which between 1690 and 1821 formed part of New Spain. In 1730 fifteen Canarian families and four single men totalling 56 individuals arrived in San Fernando de Beixar (a military town already founded eleven years earlier) after an arduous six-month journey across Mexico from Vera Cruz where they had first landed. (An original, more ambitious plan by the Marquis de San Miguel de Aguayo and Philip V of Spain to authorize a party of four hundred families to make the trip had been aborted and replaced by this more modest venture.)

San Fernando de Beixar was the first organized civil government centre to be formed in Texas and by 1736 it was renamed San Antonio, which today has grown into the tenth largest city in the United States. Then, it was a modest *presidio*, or garrison, built to protect missions in the area and serve as a way station between the Rio Grande and West Texas missions. The aims of this community were to establish further *presidios* to help Christianize and "civilize" the local Indian population and to fend c hostile tribes and keep out the menacing French forces that were bent

*"Spanish" (probably Louisiana Isleño) trapper and his children taking muskrat pelts into the FSA (Farm Security Administration) auction sale which is held in a dancehall on Delacroix Island, Louisiana. The fur buyers come from New Orleans*: photo by Marion Post Wolcott, January 1941 (Farm Security Administration/Office of War Information Collection, Library of Congress)

on seizing the region from Spain and colonizing it. Five Spanish missions were founded in the area by Canary Island settlers. One of these—destined to become an American legend—was San Antonio de Valero, later known as the Alamo.

At first the Canarians were coolly received by the racially homogenous community that already existed there, but mounting attacks by Apaches and Comanches drew them all more closely together in the common need to protect the community. "Shared roles, kinship ties and the frontier experience tied much of Beixar's population into a dynamic community," says Jesús de la Teja, a professor at the South West Texas State University, and a leading spokesman for the Canary Islands Descendants Association of San Antonio.

## NEW EXPORTS
Even when emigration was in full flow there were valiant attempts to improve the islands' welfare and self-esteem. From 1778 onwards Carlos III gradually liberalized trade and added cotton, silk and tobacco to the

list of permitted exports. By the nineteenth century honey, beeswax and other varied products were also being sold into the Iberian Peninsula and other European destinations. A further new money-spinner was cochineal, named after the parasite which was found in *tuneras* (i.e. *chumberas* or prickly pears) and which produced carmine: a crimson substance used for dyeing. Many peasants and farmers started cultivating this insect, especially on the island of La Palma. It proved to be a major source of income (though nowadays Canarian output is only one-tenth of Peru's).

Tobacco, famously launched by Sir Francis Drake, was slow to take off as a business proposition in the Canaries. Cigar production dates from the eighteenth century and though its heyday has passed it still provides a good source of income for the islands. Most of the standard cigars seen on sale today in Spanish *estancos* (tobacconists) are manufactured in the archipelago and much of the tobacco used to make them comes from Havana, where many emigrating Canarians set up the first Cuban cigar factories. Now, with less tobacco available from Cuba, the cigar makers are having to look elsewhere for fresh supplies.

CITA (Centro Industrial de Tabaqueros Asociados) is the islands' largest cigar producer, but even today a score of small family-run businesses like Puros Richard in Breña Alta can still be found on La Palma alone. During its boom period that particular island had no fewer than forty tobacco factories, but only one of these now remains. The main two islands make up for this deficit by producing around eight or nine million Canary cigars annually.

The nineteenth century saw the advent of yet another new crop, bananas, which soon took over as a pillar of the economy, representing at the industry's peak a third of all island exports. Originally introduced from Southeast Asia via Africa in the sixteenth century, bananas were not grown commercially till the 1880s when the first plantations were laid out. Today these plantations cover 4,200 hectares throughout the islands (mostly in Tenerife) and jointly produce around 150,000 metric tonnes of the fruit every year, ninety per cent of which is exported to mainland Spain while the remainder goes to other corners of Europe. Though profits have dropped in recent decades the Canaries are still by far the most prolific growers of bananas in Europe, their output controlled by ASPROCAN (Association of Canary Islands Producers). Being an autonomous region of Spain gives the Canaries unlimited access into the European market in

Banana plantations surround Agulo, La Gomera (Andree Stephan/Wikimedia Commons)

spite of their southerly location. They are accordingly covered by all EU-related legislation, rights and obligations.

The islands' many banana types are best grown between sea level and 500 metres, principally in the northern sections of Gran Canaria and Tenerife, and they are supported in today's export market by tomatoes and exotic flowers and plants, all of which thrive naturally in the benign Canarian climate. Bananas remain the archipelago's main agricultural product, followed closely by tomatoes, which are similarly distributed.

So what next in the ever-changing world of Canary commerce? Sugar, wine, tobacco, cochineal, bananas and tomatoes all made their mark as big money-spinners over the years. Still to come, though, was the industry which would outstrip them all. Mass tourism, in all its splendour, was about to burst upon the scene.

## Chapter Nine
# HEALTH AND HEDONISM: THE TOURIST BOOM

Given their location and marvellous year-round climate the Canary Islands were bound to become tourist attractions. Playa del Inglés' excesses today are echoed in sister island Tenerife's Playa de las Americas and in various well-known Spanish mainland resorts like Torremolinos and Benidorm. The only difference here is that in the Canaries resorts are recent, purpose-built creations built on virgin shoreline, while those on the mainland are usually extensions, albeit enormous ones, of existing villages.

## EARLY DAYS: HEALTH TOURISM

Before looking closer at these hedonistic jet-age creations, it is worth re-calling how Canary tourism really started. During the second half of the nineteenth century, as we have seen, groups of informed and affluent people—scientists, journalists, artists, politicians and the like—began coming to the islands almost solely for health reasons, having been en-couraged by the abundance of reports by qualified doctors and medical researchers extolling the virtues of the archipelago's climate and curative qualities of its waters and thermal springs. They produced detailed records of their stays and published articles and books that also described the landscapes, towns and local life customs, recommending the Ca-naries as an ideal destination to escape the chill European winters. They praised the climate and mountain air of various areas which were be-lieved to be beneficial for ailments such as bronchitis, tuberculosis and asthma.

They had been encouraged to visit by a number of island chroniclers who abounded from the previous century onwards. Especially prolific were the English. Among the first was the traveller-doctor William Anderson, who died of tuberculosis on board Captain Cook's ship during the latter's third voyage in 1778. Ironically in hindsight, he had earlier praised Tener-ife's climate as ideal for curing the illness and recommended doctors send their patients there rather than to southern Europe or Madeira, which at that time were the fashionable destinations for TB sufferers.

Another early observer was John White who, while transporting 700 convicts to Botany Bay in Australia, stopped off in Tenerife and noted: "The climate here is pleasant and healthy. I know of none better for convalescing patients. People who come here, furthermore, can even choose their preferred climate due to the mountainous nature of the isle."

English visitors to Tenerife in this period made a point of visiting the beautiful and tranquil Sitio Litre gardens, which were laid out by a British merchant Archibald Little beside the mansion he built here in 1774. It is the earliest of all Tenerife's floral oases, and many famous tourists from Humboldt to Agatha Christie (see below) have visited it over the years to admire, in particular, its lovely orchid selection.

As the nineteenth century dawned writers continued to emphasize the health attractions of the archipelago. The Scottish doctor John Cleasby Taylor in his book *Grand Canary: its Climate and Springs* (1889) compared two rivals in this era: Puerto de la Cruz and Las Palmas, concluding that the Gran Canaria capital enjoyed the sunnier and drier climate but that Tenerife's famed northerly seaside town had a much more attractive natural setting, especially in the nearby Orotava Valley. After an 1859 visit the Frenchman Gabriel de Belcastel wrote *Les Îles Canaries et la Vallée d'Orotava au point de vue hygiénique et médical* (The Canary Islands and Orotava Valley Seen from a Hygienic and Medical Point of View), described by historian Nicolas González Lemus (see below) as the "genuine *leitmotiv* of tourism in the Canaries". González Lemus attributed the book's instant success to the fact that Belcastel spent six months in the Orotava Valley and came to know its inhabitants and their customs well, unlike other medical investigators who barely stayed more than a few days and could only produce a superficial account of their findings. Belcastel became so much a part of the community that he was even accepted—a rare honour—as a member of the local *casino* (not a gambling locale, incidentally, but a social meeting and drinking spot for leading citizens).

The continuing flood of English writers, all fascinated by the islands' salubrious attractions, are particularly well-documented in José Luis García Pérez's *Viajeros ingleses en las Islas Canarias durante el siglo XIX*. He identifies one of the most accomplished of these as Ernest Abraham Hart, a distinguished doctor and director of the *British Medical Journal*, whose *Winter*

*Trip to the Fortunate Islands* and *Notes of Travel in the Islands of Tenerife and Gran Canary* (1887) aroused considerable interest in Europe.

Hart stayed mainly in Las Palmas and became acquainted with the English residents of both islands. He was keenly interest in the dress and customs of local people and describes the women he saw wearing "head-scarfs whose corners fell on their shoulders to protect them from the heat" and the children "who wore a light piece of calico which, open in front, reached their knees like a skirt, which both served their needs and observed the rules of decency." Both mothers and children alike, he adds, begged for money and if a visitor made the mistake of giving them some they followed him or her everywhere, even into shops and sticking to the benefactor like glue.

George W. Strettell's *Personal Experiences of the Islands as a Health Resort* (1890) was even more eagerly devoured by English readers in search of new places to rest and treat their diverse ailments. Strettell arrived in Tenerife in 1888, stayed on and lived the rest of his life in a house he bought in the Orotava Valley. He wrote so quickly and enthusiastically that accuracy on specific facts and locations sometimes took second place, but at other times he made lucid and valid comments such as his observation that the island had a more stable climate than that of the French Riviera and a less humid one than Madeira.

After Hart and Strettell came Edward Paget Thurston, whose *The Canaries for Consumptives* (1889) was written after a ten-day visit to Gran Canaria and Tenerife; and Douglas Mordey, who a year later produced *Grand Canary as a Health Resort for Consumptives and Others*. Unlike the here-today-gone-tomorrow Paget Thurston, and more like Strettell who attached himself to Tenerife, Mordey settled down and lived in Las Palmas together with his family from Dublin. He greatly preferred Gran Canaria to the then fashionable northern part of Tenerife which he criticized for its poorer health facilities and frequent damp and cloudy weather. In addition to making all the usual medical and health observations he was probably the first writer to include standard travel information such as hotel rates and relevant sea travel fares in his book.

Three distinguished doctors now appeared on the scene, the first group of experts to make a point of examining the benefits of the islands' climate in detail. Two of them, James Clarke and William White Cooper—who practised ophthalmology from his surgery in Berkeley

Square—jointly wrote *The Invalid's Guide to Madeira with a description of Tenerife, Lisboa, Cintra, Mafra etc*. Unlike Mordey, they sang Tenerife's praises, pointing out that its climate was less humid than Madeira's (30 days of rain a year compared with Madeira's 73 days).

The Banff-residing Clarke (1788-1870) also wrote the most detailed works, *The Influence of Climate in the Prevention and Cure of Chronic Diseases* (1829) and *The Sanative Influence of Climate* (1841), even though he was the only one of the three never to actually visit the islands. The third doctor, William Roberts Wills Wilde (father of Oscar, no less), was an Irish ear and eye surgeon who wrote a similarly-oriented tome entitled *Narrative of a Voyage to Madeira, Tenerife and Along the Shores of the Mediterranean*, based on his own travels in those areas.

Next came a globetrotting dilettante observer, Samuel Greene Wheeler Benjamin, London-based though born in America. His non-specialist book, *The Atlantic Islands as a Resort of Health and Pleasure*, was among the earliest to introduce a leisure-oriented concept of tourism rather than a purely health-angled one. He wrote articles for the *Illustrated London News*, had been a diplomat for two years in Persia and spent large parts of his life flitting across the ocean between his homeland and Europe. His love of islands was such that he took an ambitious trip from the Isle of Wight via the Canaries to the Bahamas. Stopping off in Tenerife, he stayed at the Hotel Turnbull, one of Puerto de la Cruz's very first hostelries (see below) and made his many inland and coastal sorties from there.

Yet another nineteenth-century specialist, this time a distinguished medical expert, was William Marcet, president of the Royal Meteorological Society, who carried out research at London's Brompton Hospital on digestive processes and the effects of alcohol on the body. He visited Madeira and then Tenerife in 1878 and like Wheeler and others before him stayed several weeks at the Hotel Turnbull.

During his Tenerife sojourn Marcet made a detailed study of the trade winds which favourably affected the islands' climate, forming clouds which kept the summer temperatures moderate. He selected Puerto de la Cruz as the ideal climatic location, rather than La Orotava which often became unpleasantly cool at night. He was also the first medical specialist to study the climates of Teide and Las Cañadas in depth, focusing on the extreme temperature contrast between night and day at those altitudes and its effect on visitors' health.

He was closely followed by Alfred Samler Brown who published *Madeira and the Canary Islands - A Practical and Complete Guide for the Use of Invalids and Tourists* in 1889. Brown saw Tenerife as the most important island in the archipelago and favoured and supported its capital Santa Cruz in its rivalry with Gran Canarias' Las Palmas, describing the former as a "picturesque and pleasant city, full of lovely balconies with cool patios and interesting corners".

In contrast to Samler Brown, the soldier-author Alfred Burton Ellis, a seasoned Captain in the First India Regiment, had demonstrated in his *West African Islands* (1885) a marked preference for Las Palmas, which "seen from a boat, has a semi-oriental appearance. Its houses are all white and rectangular-shaped with flat roofs, piled one on top of the other on the slopes of a bare mountain, whose summit is crowned by a long, low wall of fortifications. Its numerous cupolas and church spires and chapels could well be minarets and mosques." Santa Cruz de Tenerife, on other hand, struck him as sombre and enclosed due to the small windows of its houses and the dark volcanic stone used to build them.

## TRAVEL GUIDES

The very first objective, non medically-oriented travel guide describing landscape, atmosphere and local customs was published in 1891 by the Liverpudlian J. H. T. (John Henry Townsend) Ellerbeck, who provided charming illustrations and hand-drawn maps for *Madeira and the Canary Islands: Being Notes Written to Illustrate Certain Photographs and Lantern Slides Taken and Published by J.H.T. Ellerbeck*. With en eye for the exotic, he also took many photographs of the isles which he exhibited in a catalogue and sold to early tourists staying in the Taoro and Aguere hotels.

A number of spirited female authors also appeared at this time, flouting the tacitly prevailing Victorian view that they should "stay at home and mind the babies". Among them was the much-travelled British consul's wife Elizabeth Murray, whose books included material gleaned from studies made by her during her adventurous lone expeditions around the heart of Tenerife where she ended up living a total of ten years. In her most famous work, *Sixteen Years of an Artist's Life in Morocco, Spain and the Canary Islands*, she makes an interesting contrast between the inner comfort of the houses of Puerto de la Cruz, with their bequeathed English-style comforts and accoutrements, and the lifeless world outside, all changed since the exodus of the town's erstwhile thriving businesses and commercial operations to Santa Cruz and La Laguna:

> The once busy town now has a very desolate and lonely appearance. The grass grows freely in the principal streets and the sight of a human being is so rare that a cannonball might sweep from one side of the town to the other without doing any injury. There is nothing stirring all day except the north east wind which blows right bravely through the town for nearly nine months of the year, there is nothing to make itself felt or seen.

Even more adventurous was Olivia M. Stone, whose *Tenerife and its Six Satellites* (1889) was the fruit of her tireless visits to every island in the archipelago, each of which she explored and reported on assiduously. She could be evocative in the simplest way. Her timeless view of the Lanzarote capital lives on in the memory: "Arrecife, with its curiously coloured mountain backdrop, forms a pleasant picture and is a place where one could stay and dream of past days, letting time move backwards and the years pass in peaceful succession."

Other notable nineteenth-century women writers who visited the islands included Frances Latimer, Margaret d'Este and Florence du Cane, while John Whiteford, Charles Edwardes and Harold Lee were prominent visiting male authors.

As well recommending the Canaries as a winter resort, all these writers focused on depicting their landscapes, the locals and the lifestyles of towns and villages at a difficult—but for writers fascinating—time of transition when the islands were emerging from the shock of colonial abandonment and poverty and trying to merge with not just with the culture and society of mainland Spain but also with other corners of Europe. In *The English in the Canary Isles: Being a Journal in Tenerife and Gran Canaria, with Latest Information* (1888)) Frances Latimer describes the lushly contrasting appeal of a "pretty country house", whose familiar homely appearance vies with its exotic surroundings, as follows:

> Clambering creepers and mantling roses cover one side... a big pond for goldfish, myrtle and English greenery, make us fancy ourselves within an old-world garden at home, until a turn of the eye reveals a fine "dragon",

a small thicket of bamboo and a few steps take us to two palms of great height and girth that stand as sentinels to a piece of land given up to maize. Those glorious palms! One never tires of the tower-like strength, cleanliness of stem, and elegant top-knot of these Oriental trees. At hand or afar they are alike shapely, and the shapeliest of all is the Royal palm, broad at the base, then rising round and slim, elegant as a column of grey marble, crowned with a plume of feathery green.

Nicolás González Lemus, the author of several books on foreign visitors and expatriates, is the main expert on both early English travel writers and the tourist situation today. As well as cataloguing past authors and their observations he describes the factors that draw holidaymakers to the archipelago now: "The islands enjoy a tourism in which people come to buy things, attend congresses, take boat trips, and enjoy the sun and sea on our splendid sandy beaches." He adds that the islands' benign winter climate remains one of the Canaries' biggest selling points.

In the early days, when access by was less easy, travellers went there by necessity for two main reasons: business or health. González Lemus points out that the great "romantic illness of the nineteenth century" was tuberculosis, which reached epidemic levels in Europe, largely caused by unhygienic conditions in major cities due to poor sanitation and industrial emissions. Jules Vallès, a radical French author exiled in London in 1880 referred to the British capital then as "the city of fog and smoke". Bronchitis, consumption and pneumonia were other major diseases of the time.

## THE FIRST HOTELS

The initial steps taken in health resorts—by now in increasing demand thanks to the awareness spread throughout Europe by these writers—were taken by Tenerife's Compañía de Hoteles y Sanatorium del Valle de La Orotava, which was formed in 1886. This organization opened the first sanatorium the following year in Puerto de la Cruz in a colonial mansion re-named the Orotava Grand Hotel. This was followed by the Buenavista and the Monopol, two other nearby converted mansions designed to cope with the overflow from the Orotava Grand Hotel (which was grand in name but not in size and only able to accommodate a few guests).

Shortly afterwards three separate boarding houses, all owned by English settlers, appeared: Fonda Jackson, which was run by a former carpenter; the now legendary Hotel Turnbull, whose Scottish owners John and Elisabeth would soon host a series of eminent guests; and Nixon's Boarding House, founded by a nurse who specialized in giving personal care to invalids. In 1888 an ambitious Irishman with business agents based in London, opened a fourth hostelry, the Hotel Tremearne.

Following this small-scale arrival of "international" hotels in Puerto de la Cruz, the health and leisure industry quickly spread to Las Palmas de Gran Canaria where it began with the opening of the Hotel Santa Catalina, which, remarkably and thanks to intervening periods of tasteful renovation, is still going strong. Other Gran Canaria hotels of this era were the ravine-side *balneario* Los Berrozales in Agaete, which, according to reporter Javier Bolaños in the local paper *La Provincia*, is earmarked for renovation and reconstruction plans at the time of writing (2014) and the Hotel Quiney, an English-run establishment founded by Charles Baker Quiney in 1884 and later renamed the Continental. (Today it still stands as an attractive period house.) Another vintage hotel of the past, the Santa Brigida, was originally located near the extinct volcano crater of Bandama. It was subsequently transferred to the outskirts of Las Palmas where it now operates as an hoteliers' training school.

Thanks to these initial hostelries a variety of services related to tourism began to develop and different nationalities started arriving. At first the newcomers were almost exclusively British. Then the Germans appeared at the beginning of the twentieth century, concentrating mainly on visits to Tenerife. Nevertheless it was two British businessmen Charles Howard Hamilton and Edward Beanes, who in conjunction with a rich Irishman called Arthur Henry Pring formed the island's Taoro Company in May 1888. They launched one of the island's very first large-scale, non-health-oriented hotels in Puerto de la Cruz: the eponymous but alas now closed Gran Hotel Taoro, which hosted a variety of international guests—many of them famous—during its glory years from 1888 to 1950.

Health-oriented establishments were now also opening in other islands such as La Palma, where the Hotel La Fuente Santa, named after a thermal spring, was built as an early sanatorium-style retreat. It has long since closed the site and spring remain.

More sophisticated, state-of-the-art sanatoria were established to satisfy the public's increasing need for such establishments. The best-equipped resort of this kind to materialize in the early twentieth century

Gran Hotel Taoro (private collection)

was Puerto de la Cruz's Thermal Palace, brainchild of the Wildpret brothers Gustav and Wilhelm, whose father Herman was a distinguished German botanist and landscape artist. The hotel opened in June 1912 during the fiesta of San Juan. It was the first project of such magnitude that the brothers had been involved in, having previously been confined to running several of their father's shops in the same area.

Their ambitious gamble initially paid off. According to reporter Dave Penny in a *Tenerife News* piece, the Thermal Palace was conceived in the grand old tradition, with a huge ballroom, a well-stocked library, a billiards salon, a spacious restaurant and even a cinema that could accommodate up to 400 filmgoers. Health and sports amenities included a skating rink and Turkish baths fed with water from the Martiánez spring. Horse riding exhibitions were arranged on Sundays and fiestas and there were traditional island folklore shows that included dancing and wrestling. Energy was supplied by the hotel's own generator. For two short years wealthy British and German visitors, who—as was then the fashion—only came in winter, filled the hotel to capacity. Then the First World War erupted and the mini-boom was over in a flash. After four years of trauma and mass destruction, business slowly returned. The hotel tried to recover, but never saw a period of grandeur again, and continuously operated at a loss until it closed for good in 1925.

Today the Lago Martiánez volcanic swimming pool complex stands on the site once occupied by this illustrious hotel, bordering the restless ocean waters that lap the coastline around Puerto de la Cruz. The lido was launched in 1940, closed some years later and finally re-opened in 1977 after being revamped and redesigned by the great Lanzarote artist-architect César Manrique (see below).

## DISTINGUISHED VISITORS

Past luminaries who visited the islands tended to patronize Puerto de la Cruz's famed Gran Hotel Taoro in particular. They were a varied bunch, ranging from the naturalist André-Pierre Ledru (see Chapter 7) to explorer-writer-translator Sir Richard Burton of the (then-scandalous) *Kama Sutra* and *Arabian Nights* fame.

Sir Winston Churchill was a later eminent visitor who discovered the charms of the Canaries after taking a break from his earlier painting sorties on the island of Madeira further north. He first came in 1940 in full wartime mode with a military plan codenamed "Operation Pilgrim" aimed at thwarting possible Spanish-German joint defences setting up Stuka bases on the islands from which they would easily be able to attack Allied Atlantic convoys.(The plan was considered unnecessary and aborted three years later due to Franco's fading support for Hitler.) Churchill subsequently continued to visit the islands on a more casual basis, hobnobbing with jet-set socialites like Aristotle Onassis on several occasions between 1959 and 1961.

Agatha Christie also came to stay at the Taoro with her twelve-year-old daughter in 1927, though reportedly she disliked the black volcanic coves and uncomfortable swell of the rough seas, which often made swimming difficult. After a few days there she sailed across to Las Palmas where she fell in love the calmer, golden-sand twin city beaches of Las Canteras and Alcaravaneras (the latter port-facing beach had not then been polluted by the constant sea traffic). She had come to recuperate from a nervous breakdown after marital problems. In 1979 a fanciful movie about her secretive disappearance—nobody supposedly knew then where she had gone—starred Vanessa Redgrave as Christie who is tracked down in Bath by an American reporter (Dustin Hoffman) with whom she purportedly has an affair.

Another striking hotel of this period was the castle-like Quisisana in

Santa Cruz de Tenerife. Originally built by a rich Jewish businessman, Enrique Wolfson, it was transformed into the religious Colegio de las Escuelas Pías de Santa Cruz in 1940 and at the time of writing is in the process of being renovated.

The number of hotels continued to grow as more tourists arrived, albeit still in relatively small numbers. Ship travel was leisurely and romantic for some but what was really needed was an efficient means of air transport to usher eager visitors in more quickly. A major step forward was taken in 1930 when Gando international airport opened in the south of Gran Canaria. The anticipated increase in tourism proved short-lived, however, as Spain's devastating Civil War broke out only six years later and the Second World War followed closely. It took two decades for the barely-begun tourist business to really recover. Then at Christmas 1957 the very first European charter flight (Transair AB from Sweden) landed in Gando with 54 passengers. A new era had begun.

The year 1960 marked the start of a real surge in tourism as European holidaymakers arrived at the Costa Canaria's first leisure-based hotel in San Agustín in the south of Gran Canaria. Health-based holidays were still as popular as ever and three years later Eduardo Filiputti opened a spa

An early aviation pioneer, 1939

hotel in neighbouring Maspalomas featuring treatment based on solar therapy.

Amid today's super-abundance of large, multi-bedded, fully equipped, pleasure-palace-sized hotels boasting every amenity under the sun, modern health resorts continue to proliferate in Gran Canaria (as well as on other islands) but in a more sophisticated form than in the early days. Today they provide thalassotherapy pools, anti-aging (algae based peeling) and anti-cellulite treatments, shiatsu and Turkish massages, stone therapy, seaweed wraps, mud and iron-rich sea therapies, Chakra and relaxation massages. A major example, the 7,000-square-metre Talasoterapia Canarias San Agustín, which forms part of the Hotel Gloria Palace, is one of the largest spa resorts in all Europe.

## BACK TO NATURE

Health and hedonism apart, nature-oriented tourism was becoming increasingly popular by the end of the nineteenth century. It was limited principally to the three most westerly islands, El Hierro La Palma and La Gomera, though the two central islands and easterly Lanzarote and Fuerteventura also provided their own brand of natural attractions.

All seven islands have today been declared Biosphere Reserves by UNESCO. All offer, to some degree, quiet, outdoor, retreat-style holidays where visitors can stay in small traditional hotels or *casas rurales*—converted or purpose-built houses and cottages—that blend in with the landscape and atmosphere, and enjoy the unspoilt nature of this climatically blessed area.

It is the westerly trio that boast the most uncompromisingly "green" surroundings with barely a hint of mass tourism. The smallest and most peaceful island, El Hierro, probably provides the most satisfyingly different break of all. In complete contrast to the giant establishments now widespread in the two largest islands it actually boasts, according to the *Guinness Book of Records*, the smallest hotel on the planet: the Punta Grande near the mini-*pueblo* (600 inhabitants) of La Frontera on the wild south coast in an area that has been declared an official marine reserve.

Accommodating just four guests, the volcanic-rock hostelry stands on a miniature outcrop overlooking a bay. Guests can actually fish from the balcony of one of the two rooms. Owner Miguel Torres claims that the strange, isolated location (surrounded by the sounds and smells of the sea)

Valverde, El Hierro
(Mataparda/Wikimedia Commons)

unsettles some guests who need time to adjust to this total surrender to nature. But when they do succumb they are hooked: "some guests have returned up to sixteen times," he says.

The "small is beautiful" theme dominates the island and its landscape of black-rocks inlets, plunging cliffs, coastal *matorral* (shrub), juniper and pine woods entices visitors who walk along paths that for centuries have been used mainly by goatherds and their flocks. Its inland capital Valverde, often swathed in mists caused by trade winds, has barely a thousand inhabitants. Its highest point, 1,501metres, gives the island—like its neighbours—a conical aspect.

Nearby La Palma's top spot, the towering Roque de los Muchachos peak, is a further 900 metres up, making the island one of the most mountainous places(for its size) in the world. It seems to rise sheer from the ocean with its famed observatory perched above a near-permanent covering of clouds near the summit. Here the main eco-tourist attraction is the huge central Taburiente crater, filled with magnificent woodlands whose vegetation and wildlife, including a varied range of exotic birds, are best seen on foot. Trekkers follow an intricate network of narrow earthy lanes that were used by mules to transport goods across the island well into the mid-twentieth century, when the construction of the first good roads saw the end of that timeless mode of transportation. Today only tourists and hikers use these pathways, which are shunned by the business-like locals.

For nature lovers exploring La Gomera, its World Heritage Site, the Garajonay National Park, is the principal attraction. It is an inland sea of humid subtropical *laurasilva* (laurel) woodlands and giant rocks created by eroded volcanoes, most famous of which is the once sacred Fortaleza (fortress). As in La Palma, the island's mountainous interior is crisscrossed by well-worn paths used by enthusiastic trekkers—mainly German and English—who often become lost in the treacherous mists that descend in a flash. This usually requires the intervention of local rescue teams who come up from the coast and help them find their way back down. A devastating forest fire in 2012 mercifully failed to destroy too much of this prized parkland and eco-tourists still climb its heights (up to 1,487 metres) as before. Near the summit of Mount Garajonay stand a Guanche sanctuary and two small simple wooden statues honouring the mythically fated lovers Gara and Jonay, who gave this area its name.

Few people visit these three islands for swimming or beach holidays. The sea is often rough and beaches are mainly coves of dark sand enclosed by steep cliffs and difficult to reach. In contrast, easterly Fuerteventura comprises almost one extended beach. The island won its UNESCO award mainly for the quality of its endless expanse of sand and the cleanliness of the waters that wash it. Correlejo was singled out as the setting for a natural park that epitomized the uniquely elemental Fuerteventuran character.

The whale-shaped island looks like a dune-covered section of the Sahara that has strayed into the Atlantic. A haven for naturists and windsurfers, its development is tastefully low-level in the traditional style, and though there are bars and clubs they come in smaller sizes. Here the main attractions are the sun and the sea—and the sense of space. Though the second largest of all the islands Fuerteventura's population is small and it is still easy to find a secluded corner.

## TASTE AND TRADITION: CÉSAR MANRIQUE'S LEGACY

Fuerteventura's neighbour Lanzarote, though smaller, is more startlingly multifaceted. On the natural side there is the extraordinary Timanfaya National Park with its eerie moonscape and endless craters. And on the less natural, more mass-market side is a welter of hotel and apartment conurbations lining many of its lovely beaches. Yet here the modern face of tourism is rarely brash and ugly, even in the big resorts such as Puerto del Carmen and Costa Teguise. As in Fuerteventura, tourist development has been confined almost entirely to the low-level traditional island style, enhancing and blending in with the landscape rather than ruining it.

One man in particular, the energetic and resourceful César Manrique, almost singlehandedly managed to give modern Canary tourism this individual and tasteful character. Born in 1919 into a family of comfortable middle-class *lanzaroteños* in Arrecife, he loved the island ever since his father first built a seaside house in 1934 at Caleta de Famara, where he recalled spending the happiest moments of his life: "five-month long summers on Famara beach with its fine clean sand enclosed by 400-metre ridges which reflected on the beach like a mirror. That image is engraved in my soul like an object of extraordinary beauty that can never ever be erased."

He fought in the Civil War (on Franco's side), studied technical architecture at La Laguna University and art and painting at Madrid's Real Academia de Bellas Artes de San Fernando. He considered himself first and foremost a painter and had his first exhibition in Lanzarote in 1942. In the mid-1960s he spent two years in an artists' colony in New York's Lower East Side staying at the house of a Cuban painter Waldo Díaz-Balart. He then rented his own studio and succeeded in opening his own exhibition at the prestigious Catherine Viviano Gallery. Thus apprenticed, he returned to his own beloved island, desperate to see people living in their own natural habitat again and not existing "like rats" in the artificial concrete world of the great American metropolis. "I wanted to convert my island into one of the most beautiful places on the planet, given the infinite possibilities that Lanzarote offered," he explained.

Manrique was regarded as a driven, almost puritanical figure, athletic, energetic, early to bed and early to rise, never touching alcohol or tobacco. It was tragically ironic that, hating the increasing congestion of roads even on an island as small as Lanzarote, he should have died in a car accident in 1992 at the relatively young age of seventy-three.

Yet the legacy Manrique left is indelible. Thanks to him Lanzarote has become a model for tourism development to follow in its respect both for the environment and the individuality of the island's many attractive locations. He struggled tenaciously and successfully against the construction of those featureless condominiums and *urbanizaciones* that have marred so many other popular island and mainland holiday destinations, and instead promoted a unique style of architectural work that formed an integral part of the landscape.

Manrique produced a series of dazzling architectural scenarios among which his work on the spectacular Jameos del Agua caves in the north of the island particularly stands out. His enchanted sunken Jardín de Cactus—created in a former quarry—and the cliff-top Mirador del Río—with its panoramic vistas of La Graciosa islet and beyond—are no less spectacular. Other masterpieces include his Yaiza restaurant, recreated in the only three houses in the village that were not buried by lava during the great eighteenth-century eruptions, his trademark spindly Juguetes del Viento (Wind Toys) sculptures—always rustling in the Canary breezes—and his dignified Monumento al Campesino in Teguise with its central cubist white "fertility" symbol and adjoining subterranean house museum where Manrique himself lived till his relatively early death. He was a more robust, less ascetic counterpart of the Catalan Antoni Gaudí.

Manrique did not just transform Lanzarote, which for many admirers represented his greatest single work of art. If in his native island he influenced a host of followers and helped to create an architectural originality

The Mirador del Río, Lanzarote (afrank99/Wikimedia Commons)

that extends from the Mirador del Río in the north down to Playa Blanca in the south, his vision also encompassed other islands. Memorable tourist spots such as La Gomera's Mirador del Palmarejo viewpoint, El Hierro's La Peña restaurant and Tenerife's north coast Lago Martiánez lido in Puerto de la Cruz, where turquoise open air pools are embedded in the jet black volcanic rocks, show his guiding touch as does the similar Parque Marítimo César Manrique in the capital Santa Cruz. Further afield he designed the La Vaguada commercial centre in northern Madrid and the Canarian Pavilion for the Expo 92 trade fair in Seville.

## BIG BROTHERS: GRAN CANARIA AND TENERIFE

It is on the two largest Canary Islands that the tourist contrast is seen in its most striking form. Gran Canaria, like Tenerife, home of the biggest mass tourism developments, also has unspoilt zones such as the central Roque Nublo peak and surrounding natural wonders. Tenerife, in turn, boasts Las Cañadas and the imposing Teide mountain, which jointly comprise yet another UNESCO-approved national park.

The polar opposite to these gems of nature is to be found in the giant man-made resorts of Playa del Inglés in Gran Canaria and Playa de las Americas in Tenerife, mentioned at the beginning of this chapter. Both islands' resorts, representing the tackier, money-making face of *turismo*, were launched simultaneously in the late 1960s. Both are located on their respective islands' sunnier south side and have expanded considerably since their modest beginnings. They are examples of just how far speculators and developers are prepared to go in their attempts to accommodate as many visitors as possible, though unlike certain Spanish mainland resorts they have a comparatively small number of high-rise buildings. What is to be found instead are seemingly endless *urbanizaciones* containing hotels, apartments, bars, cafés, restaurants and nightspots. The latter tend to be grouped together in what look like miniature cut-price versions of Las Vegas. Playa de las America's garish neon-lit Veronica's Strip offers cheap drinks, drunken teenagers en masse and a seemingly endless array of bars, discos and clubs.

Both resorts also have superb beaches covered in golden sand imported from the Sahara, which attractively masks the natural local darkgrey sand (in turn lighter than the soot black coves of the rugged north coasts). They are the real money-makers of the tourist industry and will

153

Playa de las Americas (palmbeachclubtenerife.com)

doubtless continue to expand and prop up the islands' economies. But, as we have seen, the modern resorts are only a part of the rich tapestry that makes up the archipelago's multifaceted appeal for visitors. In tourism, as in other aspects of their life and culture, the islands are not easily labelled and categorized. Neither are its people as they face the complex social and political challenges of the twenty-first century.

*Chapter Ten*

# WAR, POLITICS AND PROGRESS

## TWO PROVINCES, TWO CAPITALS

As the islands' two major cities, Santa Cruz de Tenerife and Las Palmas de Gran Canaria, continued to grow, so did their traditional rivalry. In 1927 the archipelago was divided into its two present provinces with Santa Cruz administering La Palma, La Gomera and El Hierro and Las Palmas governing Lanzarote and Fuerteventura. Their elevation to the status of joint Canary capitals did not so much sooth as exacerbate the tension. Like Madrid and Barcelona on the Spanish mainland, each city was convinced of its superiority over the other and each wanted to be top dog.

Both have highly distinctive characters. Las Palmas is a narrowly jutting surrounded by the Atlantic on three sides in the manner of Cádiz and La Coruña and blessed with a reef-protected and sandy city beach. Santa Cruz de Tenerife is less sea-dominated and more gently exotic, backed by hills dotted with brightly coloured houses, its wide avenues filled with flowers and palms that emphasize its proximity to Africa.

Las Palmas is the more cosmopolitan. It has the business edge. A burgeoning professional British presence had already ensured by the mid-1920s the introduction of water mains and an electrical system and telephone network that were more efficient and sophisticated than those in Santa Cruz de Tenerife. Both ports were refuelling stopover points for transatlantic shipping, though Las Palmas was able to accommodate more vessels.

The twin capitals currently (2014) have to endure the urban inconveniences suffered by all similar-sized cities. The sprawling Gran Canaria capital, complete with industrial estates and unlovely suburbs, is the larger of the two, with a population of around 380,000, compared with Santa Cruz de Tenerife's 205,000. In spite of the sharp difference in these numbers both cities now have serious traffic congestion and parking problems, not to mention pollution which even the ocean breezes cannot always disperse.

Santa Cruz, surprisingly, has bettered Las Palmas with the introduction of an electric tram service—similar to those in Spanish mainland cities from Barcelona to Bilbao—in an attempt to avoid possible gridlock. (The previous trams in Santa Cruz, of the vintage variety with rails down the streets and overhead power cables, had ceased operations in 1951.) But there is still no underground metro system in either capital.

In Las Palmas, where the congestion is even worse, electric trams are still awaited. The delay in installing such a much-needed service is surprising since in 1974 the city seemed all set to surge ahead with an innovative overhead city rail system known as the *Vertebrado TV2*. Invented by a brilliant Basque engineer called Alejandro Goicochea, who also created the Talgo high speed train, it was ambitiously intended to connect the city with Gando airport and Maspalomas in the south and reach speeds of up to 180 kilometres per hour (well ahead of its time). Unfortunately it failed to live up to expectations for a variety of technical and practical reasons and the project was abandoned, as was Goicochea's subsequent TV3 model, which was also unsuccessfully tried out in Santa Cruz de Tenerife and Caracas in Venezuela.

Currently the Gran Canaria capital waits in hope and enviously watches Santa Cruz take over in the intercity communication contest. Yet progress is being made. According to the Las Palmas newspaper *La Provincia*, a 23-year-old engineering student called Cristo Eseú González Navarro recently designed an urban tram service, similar to others already operating in many cities in mainland Spain, which has been approved by the local authorities but not yet given a go ahead.

## Franco and the Civil War

Both cities received a severe jolt in 1936, barely a decade after they had been named twin capitals. Mainland Spain, for some time falling apart socially and politically, then found itself on the brink of chaos. Plots to "save" the country had long been in the making. One of the chief intriguers was General Francisco Bahamonte Franco, who had been appointed Commandant General of all the islands. The ruling democratically elected government, knowing his anti- democratic views and capricious pro-coup tendencies, had sent him there to distance him from the decision-making circles of Madrid. As it turned out, the islands proved an ideal base for Franco to finalize his part in the plan to stage a military coup.

When he and his fellow conspirators decided it was time to strike he flew incognito from Tenerife to Tetuán in Spanish Morocco in a de Havilland Dragon Rapide which had been contracted by Luis Antonio Bolín, the right wing *ABC* newspaper's correspondent in London. The plane, which took off from Croydon on 11 July, was piloted by Captain Cecil Bebb from the airport's Olley Air Services. Also on board also were his colourful navigator-friend Hugh Bertie Campbell Pollard ("a retired army officer, ex secret service agent and sexual adventurer", according to historian Paul Preston in his book *Four Women of Spain*) and two female companions—one a relative—to make it look like a pleasure trip. The idea of using a British plane in the first place had been to avert any suspicion the flight might have a military aim. (Today, incidentally, that very same aircraft can be seen in Madrid's Museo del Aire). Franco had a surprising number of British allies at that time and the flight was planned over lunch by Bolín and Douglas Jerrold, the right-wing Catholic editor of *The English Review*, at Simpsons restaurant in London.

From Tetuán Franco continued to the Spanish mainland to join his fellow Nationalist military rebels. Originally it was thought they would achieve their takeover objective just in a couple of days. It the end, it took three years, cost hundred of thousands of lives, severely traumatized a whole nation and led to 36 years of harsh dictatorship.

During his absence (and unexpectedly meteoric ascent in power in Spain as one by one a quartet of Franco's senior rivals disappeared) the archipelago came fully under the control of the *franquistas*, or Nationalists. Though the islanders were spared the slaughter that devastated the mainland there were small pockets of resistance to the new regime in La Palma and Vallehermoso in La Gomera that were quickly suppressed, and all the islands were forced to toe the line dictated by the new-right wing ideology. The twin capitals' boom was accordingly curtailed until the mid-1940s when both the Civil War and the Second World War were over.

During the latter conflict the islands came close to being fully involved on one or two occasions, but in the end escaped largely unscathed. Roosevelt initially saw them as a "springboard" for attacks on Germany, and Churchill, who had plans for them to be used as a "spying centre", considered an all out assault on the archipelago in the event of an attack by Franco on Gibraltar. Neither of these projects came to fruition. During the early stages of the war there were strong suspicions that the Germans

Monument to Franco, Santa Cruz de Tenerife
(Koppchen/Wikimedia Commons)

were using some more remote corners of the islands to hide their U boats, though not a scrap of evidence was ever produced to support this theory. (Tall tales of Nazi submarines being hidden in coastal tunnels in Fuerteventura particularly lacked substance, even if they would have made a splendid premise for one of Ken Follett's early novels).

There was some alarm when Franco authorized the construction of a military base at Las Palmas in 1940 but he effectively scotched Allied threats to intervene when he officially switched his role in the war from non-belligerent to neutral, and refused to let the German Navy refuel its ships there. (Though many Allied ships were sunk in this corner of the Atlantic in the first half of the war, this was most likely due to the fact that the Portuguese dictator António de Oliveira Salazar had authorized the Germans to install U-Boat bases in the nearby Azores. Salazar subsequently switched his allegiance to the Allies and allowed their fleets to refuel there instead.)

## AIMS FOR CANARY INDEPENDENCE

It was perhaps inevitable that some expression of island individuality would eventually find its own voice, especially after the years of rigid authoritarian rule. Two and a half decades into the Nationalist dictatorship, during which any attempts to assert a form of Canary identity in local government were forcibly repressed by Madrid, a splinter group called Movimiento por la Autodeterminación e Independencia del Archiépelago Canario was created by a local lawyer called Antonio Cubillo. It originally aimed at promoting its policy in a non-violent manner and achieved recognition from the Organization of African Unity in 1968. Yet the movement fell prey to factionalism, and a group named the Fuerzas Armadas Guanches (Guanche Armed Forces) perpetrated a bomb attack on a shopping mall in Las Palmas in 1976. The following year the FAG blew up a shop in Las Palmas airport, seriously injuring several members of the public.

A threat of a further attack at Gando airport forced the authorities to close down air traffic temporarily while they carried out security searches. Many aircraft destined for Gran Canaria were accordingly redirected to Tenerife's smaller and less well-equipped airport at Los Rodeos (which, coincidentally, had opened in 1941 with a short inter-island Dragon Rapide flight from Gando). This led, indirectly, to the worst tragedy in civil aviation history. Two Jumbo jets, one Dutch (KLM), the other American (PANAM), collided on a runway at Los Rodeos in dense fog, causing the death of 583 passengers and crew. Subsequent findings established the cause of the accident as human error on the part of the KLM pilot—a highly experienced and respected professional who had nevertheless succumbed to impatience after a three and a half hour delay—though there was also a possible misunderstanding between his plane and the control tower over his authorization to take off. Another contributing factor was the airport's lack of ground radar at the time.

How the FAG regarded their role in this is hard to say. Perhaps in the spirit of their aims they saw it as a means of deterring tourists and returning the islands to their former unsullied glory, though it was hardly likely they welcomed a tragedy of this magnitude.

In 1978 Cubillo was the victim of a failed assassination attempt, allegedly perpetrated by the Spanish secret service. This took place in Algiers, his main base of operation, and left him handicapped and confined to a wheelchair. He received little public sympathy. His group had scant support from the Canarian people, who, though largely interested in achieving personal freedom and autonomy from Spain, preferred to do so by peaceful methods. They eyed with distaste the ruthless actions of ETA in support of the Basque cause in mainland Spain. In all events the FAG, already shaken by the Los Rodeos tragedy, now renounced all further violence.

Both Cubillo and his group were pardoned by the Canary Autonomous Community, which was created by the Spanish government in 1982 with the aim of easing tensions and resentment within the islands' political community. Cubillo, no longer threatened with arrest, was able to return to the islands and subsequently create the more politically accepted Congreso Nacional de Canarias (CNC), which still listed its radical priorities as ridding the islands of foreign corruption and Spanish "colonialism". It aspired to forge an independent "Third State" on a par with Morocco and Tunisia that would have a seat in the UN and enjoy "liberty, equality, and respect for human rights for all citizens of the Canary Islands".

Cubillo's original party had been broadcasting propaganda radio programmes in exile from Algiers (La Voz de Canarias Libre), urging the islanders to assert their independence, rediscover their pre-conquest origins and adopt the Amazigh (original Berber) language used by their Guanche ancestors. Today that linguistic aspect is as much academic as political and increasing numbers of Canarians remain strongly interested in their islands' heritage. In addition to the CNC other political parties encouraging regional independence still abound. These include the left-wing FREPIK-AWAÑAK (Canary Islands National Front), NC (Nuevas Canarias), APC (Alternativa Popular Canaria), ANC (Alternativa Nacional Canaria) and UP (Unidad del Pueblo). Further independent socialist groups and another youth group, Azarug, also encourage interest and pride in pre-conquest culture and aim at promoting and reviving the original Guanche tongue, with its resonant Berber influences. Magazines have been produced with poems and pieces in Amazigh, and a number of folksongs in the language such as the musical group Almogaren's *Wanche Berber* have been performed at Berber-oriented social events in the islands.

## DEMOCRACY COMES TO THE ISLANDS

When the Spanish state returned to democracy after the death of Franco in 1975, the Canaries were at last able to begin their move towards self rule, and in 1982 Madrid approved the Estatuto de Autonomía (Autonomy Statute). The intervening seven years had still presented a variety of troublesome incidents, however, with the police apparently acting at times with the same impunity as under the fascist *caudillo*. In addition to the attempt on Cubillo's life two young student dissidents, Bartolomé García Lorenzo and Antonio Padilla, were murdered (allegedly by the authorities) and violent action taken against striking protesters resulted in at least one further death, including that of a sixteen-year-old female bystander.

In 1983 the socialist PSOE won the general elections and the islands seemed at last to have entered a genuinely democratic era. They were led by Jerónimo Saavedra, a doctor in law and qualified expert in business administration. In 2000 he "came out" as a homosexual, a revelation which if anything enhanced his prestige as an honest and outspoken politician, and seven years later was elected Mayor of Las Palmas by a huge majority. Four years on there was a swing back to the right when the PSOE lost out to the Centro Democrático y Social, founded by Adolfo Suarez, but in 1991 the PSOE, again presided over by Saavedra, was returned to power.

In 1993 the Independent Canary Party won at the polls, repeating its success in 1995 and 1999 with the support of the Partido Popular led by José María Aznar. Among these signs of increasing influence from the right, the House of Representatives in Madrid approved the new Autonomy Statute in 1996.

The uneasy links with Aznar's party continued, and in 2007 the combined Canary Coalition and Partido Popular were voted in with 61-year-old Tenerife-born former teacher Paulino Rivero Baute as president of the Canary Autonomous Community. A self-made man from a rural working-class background who did not attend school until he was thirteen, RiveroBaute had fought tenaciously to attain his place in politics.

"My childhood was very hard, like that of many families at that time in small villages like mine [El Sauzal]," he explained to journalist Esther Esteban in an *El Mundo* interview. "My parents got up early and I would be left looking after my six younger brothers and sisters—four boys and two girls—and doing the housework. I also helped my mother in her work." He spent much of his early youth collecting vegetables from nearby fields and taking them for sale to Tacoronte, three kilometres away. When he finally did get to school, unlike most children of his age, it was like a dream come true. He loved studying, excelled in all his subjects and went on to university. At 26 he was mayor of his village. His ascent was unstoppable.

In 2011, heading yet another PP/CC coalition, Rivero Baute was re-elected president, but faced now a far less stable economic situation than before with alarming increases in unemployment and inequality. In spite of recent calls for a "new face", Rivero Baute is still set to re-run as president in the 2015 elections.

## ECOLOGY AND NATURE

While profound political changes were taking place positive steps were also being taken in terms of development and environmental policy. The number of protected natural areas in the Canaries is the largest—in relation to the total area involved—not just in Spain but in the whole of Europe. The bustling capitals in the north and over-developed tourist zones in the south of the two main islands are notable exceptions to the predominance of wild and richly varied natural landscapes. No less than forty per cent of the total area, covering fifteen designated "parks" (national and natural), is under strict ecological control.

The four most extensive of these—Teide, Timanfaya, Taburiente and Garajonay—are national parks, representing a large share of the total of fifteen located in all Spanish territories. (Teide and Garajonay are also World Heritage Sites: see below). Each has its own individual attractions. The biggest, the 14,000-hectare Teide mountain and its surroundings (the most visited natural area in all Spain), encompass the seventeen by twelve kilometre Las Cañadas crater whose otherworldly landscape of cones, lava fields and strangely coloured sands also houses tiny recondite gems like the vividly hued mountain violet and bright yellow Canary bird (which is, as we know, not the origin of the islands' name).

Lanzarote's Timanfaya is even more extravagantly lunar while La Palma's Taburiente and La Gomera's Garajonay parks are home to dense green forests of, respectively, tall pine and *laurasilva*, both of which shelter a wide range of birdlife ranging from crows, finches, wagtails and kestrels to doves, pigeons, great spotted woodpeckers and partridges.

Off shore there is yet more abundance of life, including five types of marine turtle—Loggerhead, Green, Hawksbill, Leatherback and Kemp's Ridley—and a range of marine species that covers sharks, moray eels, jellyfish, octopus, groupers and rays. Over twenty species of whales also live year round in the waters off south-western Tenerife and La Gomera. Among this array of lumbering cetaceans are the large blue and killer varieties though the most common is the Pilot whale, which together with the Bottlenose dolphin, can be seen most days of the years on the many popular excursions that sail out along the islands' shores. Monk seals (of the kind Gadifer de la Salle hunted in the fifteenth century on the Isla de Lobos) also used to proliferate but are now alas rarely seen. Most common of all are the almost countless species of sea urchins, while around Fuerteventura swimmers delight in their frequent sightings of the colourful and ubiquitous parrotfish.

The smaller natural parks are, in turn, Las Cumbres and Las Nieves in La Palma; Majona in La Gomera; the Archipiélago Chinijo and Los Volcanes in Lanzarote: the Islote de los Lobos, Jandia and Correlejo in Fuerteventura; Pilancones and Tamadaba in Gran Canaria; and the immense *Corona Forestal* surrounding the Teide park in Tenerife. Together they comprise a spectrum of totally diverse panoramas and flora, uniquely rich and varied for such a small area.

The only island without a national or even natural, park to date is tiny El Hierro, whose Tibateje Special Nature Reserve may well soon qualify for such a rating. The whole island has a stark solitary beauty and at least one unique form of wildlife that the local authorities are doing their best to preserve: the recent re-introduced giant Hierran lizard which was close to extinction a few decades back.

Careful steps have been taken to protect and enhance the environment in a range of different sectors: the above-mentioned national and natural parks, national monuments, protected areas, integral and special nature reserves, rural parks and sites of scientific interest. Foremost among the latter is the Astrophysical Observatory which was inaugurated at the 2,400-metre-high Roque de los Muchachos on the island of La Palma in 1985. It is the most important space observatory in the northern hemisphere and has the largest international concentration of telescopes. Its location is perfect for night time observations and solar physics. The quality of the skies around it for optical infrared astronomy is only bettered in the northern memisphere by Mauna Kea Observatory in Hawaii.

Roque de los Muchachos is part of the Instituto de Astrofísica de Canarias, which also supervises the Mount Teide observatory. On site facilities include day and night time dormitories, kitchen, dining room and

The Nordic Optical Telescope, Roque de los Muchachos
(Bob Tubbs/Wikimedia Commons)

games room, which are all used by the scientific and technical staff working there. In 2003 two highly sophisticated telescopes were added to the observatory's state-of-the-art assortment: the MAGIC (or Major Atmospheric Gamma Imaging Cherenkov) for detecting high energy cosmic rays, and the MERCATOR: an optical telescope named after the sixteenth-century Belgian astronomer and cartographer. But the most impressive of the other twelve telescopes at the institute is the Grantecan or Gran Telescopio Canario, whose 10.4-metre segmented mirror makes it the largest optical telescope in the world.

Among the many expatriates who have settled in the islands and become experts in their fields is Leeds-born Sheila Crosby, who provides a unique insight into the workings of the observatory in her factual book *A Breathtaking Window on the Universe*. In it she recounts her experiences at Roque de los Muchachos where she worked six months before moving into tourism and writing. She has now been living over two decades on La Palma and is both an accomplished authority on both that island and El Hierro and an imaginative author of science fiction tales.

Other biosphere reserve improvements are also on the move. In order to make the luminous night skies above the island even clearer to observers, La Palma is now evolving an intelligent energy-efficient lighting system which will minimize light pollution and facilitate a deeper study of the universe, while in El Hierro a hydro wind project is destined to create the first electricity-sufficient island in the world. There are also plans to reduce carbon emissions on the latter island, increase energy efficiency and look into public transport alternatives. The Canaries' other impressive biosphere reserves are headed by Gran Canaria whose huge protected area covers seven municipalities: Agaete, Atenara, San Nicolás, Mogán, Tirajana, Tejeda and La Vega de San Mateo.

Irrigation on the islands is a constant problem as there are no rivers. The westerly outposts, especially La Palma, occasionally experience flash floods that pour torrents of rainwater down the gulleys—on more than one occasions causing the deaths of unwary and unguided foreign hikers—but most of the time the moisture, known as horizontal rain, comes from the *alisio* sor trade winds that keep the trees lush and green year round.

Easterly, rain-deprived Fuerteventura, meanwhile, has no such relief and often suffers years of drought. It has, however, taken decisive moves to make the countryside more productive for its residents and entice more discerning visitors to explore its strangely beautiful hills and coastline. One of its most successful steps has been to seed and grow a crop called *Jatropha curcas*, a small tree which originates from Cabo Verde and Brazil and is used to protect the dry soil against erosion, simultaneously preventing desertification and producing a biodiesel fuel supply. The project, directed by soil expert Marisa Tejedor of La Laguna University in Tenerife, is called Biocombustible Jatrofa. Other plans for the island include a renewable water project linking water cycles with the production of biofuels, and a wind farm that connects with a water desalination plant.

In addition to making progress in such biodiversity fields, the Canaries also boast three UNESCO-approved World Heritage Centres. Two of them are the already-mentioned National Parks of Garajonay in La Gomera and Teide in Tenerife. The third is the old quarter of San Cristóbal de La Laguna in Tenerife, the island's cultural centre and a historic repository of narrow lanes and wooden balconied eighteenth-century mansions surrounded by a more modern zone of wide, tree-lined avenues. Considered to be "of outstanding universal value", it is the first example of a non-

Vineyards, La Geria, Lanzarote
(Yummifruitbat/Wikimedia Commons)

military Spanish colonial town laid out and built according to a complete plan inspired by sixteenth-century concepts of urban design. With its geometric grid system, it served as a model for future towns built by the Spanish in the Americas. Later, more eclectic, nineteenth- and twentieth-century architectural works have added style and variety, while somewhat "chic" tourist-conscious contemporary plans include transforming the town's old San Pablo market into a Covent Garden-style food emporium similar in style to Madrid's gastronomic San Miguel *mercado* near the Plaza Mayor.

Newest of the applicants for consideration as a World Heritage Centre, meanwhile, is Lanzarote's La Geria region, home to the small crescent stone wall-protected vineyards of the island, long famed for their production of Malvasia wine. Uniquely surreal in appearance, the system is also eminently practical as the walls protect each cluster of vines from breezes while the black *picón* soil strewn around them helps absorb lifegiving moisture from the air.

## GETTING AROUND: TRANSPORT IN THE ISLANDS

Apart from the modern tram system in Santa Cruz de Tenerife there is no rail service anywhere in the archipelago. Tenerife alone is earmarked for train line development in 2018 and there are still undetermined plans for Las Palmas de Gran Canaria to have a tram service similar to Santa Cruz's that may eventually extend down to Maspalomas.

Partly as a consequence of financial and political constraints, roads and highways, especially on the two main islands, are highly congested, especially in and around the two capital cities. Again, the only plans to ease this problem so far have come from Tenerife where a circular round-the-island road is projected to operate between southerly Adeje and northerly Icod de los Vinos, linking the island's two main motorways.

Air transport facilities, on the other hand, have improved immeasurably in recent decades. A year after Tenerife's 1977 twin jumbo tragedy a second airport, Tenerife South, was opened near Los Cristianos in a location close to the sea and less prone to foggy conditions. Los Rodeos in the meantime was renamed Tenerife North. Facilities and safety standards in both are now highly sophisticated and with increasing traffic every year, especially from tourism, they have joined the ranks of major Spanish airports. The number of annual visitors to all the islands is today twelve million, predominantly British, German and mainland Spanish.

The archipelago's smaller airports are also highly efficient, and regular scheduled flights between them and the Big Two (or Three, if burgeoning Lanzarote is counted) are quick and relatively economical. The planes actually use up less fuel than the high-speed ferries and jetfoils that also provide an efficient linking service, though the latter are indispensable for transporting vehicles from island to island.

## THE CANARIES TODAY

Thanks to the tourist boom which drew north Europeans south beyond the Spanish mainland in search of year-round benign weather, the islands' economy really took off in the 1960s and has proceeded by leaps and bound since. At present, however, the economy is decidedly in the doldrums, as in most of Europe, and practically all industries except tourism are struggling.

Unemployment stands at around 34 per cent, a figure only exceeded in Ceuta and Andalusia in all Spanish territories. At its worst in the cities, it is slightly higher in Las Palmas than in the Tenerife capital. The youth unemployment situation is particularly dire, estimated by some at over sixty per cent, and there is a huge exodus of young people—two-thirds of whom have a degree—heading mainly to Europe and America in search of work. (Another alarming sign of the prevailing economic climate is the fact that eight out of every ten Canarians under the age of thirty still live with their parents.)

At the bottom end of the social and economic scale, according to UNICEF's 2013 report, are the most vulnerable; child poverty affects 29 per cent of households, and 26,000 Canary families receive no income whatsoever—though charity organizations like Caritas Diocesana do their best to help them.

Yet there are always people who even in the most difficult times find a way to feather their own nests, albeit at the expense of others. *Visa Europe* estimates that the Canary Islands' informal (and untaxed) economy amounts to over 28 per cent of their total GDP. Some blame the lucrative holiday market for aggravating the problem rather than helping it, reducing economic morals to a new low. Returned native islander Álvaro Santana, a former Harvard University Sociology PhD candidate who is now studying the current economic situation in the islands, remarks in Open Democracy's "The Canary Islands: Spain's Paradise Lost": "as local and foreign experts have shown, tourism in the Canaries, while not the major cause of the crisis, continues to be a great source of political corruption, cultural indolence and environmental and heritage destruction."

In spite of such unencouraging news immigrants still continue to arrive, some looking for menial work, some to retire, some to set up their own businesses. The total foreign community—both inactive and working—now totals around 14.5 per cent of the whole population, which stood at 2.12 million at the last count in 2012.

In 2001 a flood of illegal immigrants began to arrive, consisting of mainly work-hungry refugees fleeing the impoverished African countries of Mauritania, Niger and Mali in small, inadequately provisioned boats. Osvaldo Lemus, a Spanish Red Cross emergency response co-ordinator, described to the *Daily Telegraph* reporter Michael Hirstin in a 2006 interview how the immigrants would set foot on land "dehydrated, hungry and often suffering from hypothermia" having paid (what was for them) exorbitant fees to unscrupulous traffickers who arranged these dangerous odysseys. Many of the immigrants—men, women and children alike—landed suffering from splinters and bruises incurred from rubbing against the sides of the overcrowded vessels they came in and not few died during the long journey from the Mauritanian coast.

The interview was prompted by the fact that in that same year, 2006, arrivals reached a shocking peak of 31,678, with the easterly islands of Lanzarote and Fuerteventura bearing the brunt of the "invasion". Their local Red Cross resources were overloaded and an unofficial "humanitarian crisis" was declared, causing protests, resentment and even outbursts of overt racism among the usually hospitable islanders, who were highly alarmed at the presence of these dispossessed, uninvited, and—in their eyes—potentially untrustworthy, "guests". Since then, maybe at least partly due to the subsequently dismal work situation in Spain, the number of arriving illegal immigrants has dropped drastically, totalling only 340 in 2011, according to Spanish Ministry of the Interior figures.

Most of the adult immigrants who did arrive were able to use the Canary Islands, in their capacity as an "outer member" of the European Community, as a "springboard" for work in mainland Spain. The hundreds of *menores no acompañados* (under eighteen-year-olds unaccompanied by adults) who also came were, on the other hand, kept in so-called Centros de Acogidas de Menores (Welcome Centres for Minors) until it was decided what could be done with them.

The British, as we have seen, have long had a strong presence in the islands. Formerly they were mostly to be found in business houses and shipping offices such as Blandy Brothers in Las Palmas, but in recent years they have been conspicuous in local English-language journalism, with a number of writers like Barrie Mahoney and Joe Cawley providing knowledgeable, up-to-date information on the islands. Their output embraces articles, Twitter pieces and even optimistically-cum-humorously titled books (*Living the Dream* or *More Ketchup than Salsa: Confessions of a Tenerife Barman*) that may encourage their fellow Britons to sample the islands' delights. Between them both writers have helped to launch periodicals such as the *The Canary Islander, Tenerife News* and *Island Connections*. Another Tenerife-based author, American Janet Anscombe, who was formerly a historian, has also published a number of well-researched pieces on the islands in a regular newsletter popular with readers on both sides of the Atlantic (see www.janetanscombe.com).

Though Tenerife seems to be the most popular base for these writers, other islands have their own home-based specialists. In Lanzarote Mike Cliffe-Jones (who signs himself off as "Miguel"), runs a small team of authors who prolifically produce pieces for his "Anything and Everything about Lanzarote" newsletter, covering all aspects of island life past and present. Las Palmas resident Matthew Hirtes (www.matthewhirtes.com) in turn provides a similar lowdown on his adopted island in "Going Local in Gran Canaria".

An offbeat addition to these expatriate observers is the robust Lancashire exile Alan Gandy, whose *Walking the Canary Islands: The Adventures of a Grumpy Middle-Aged Expat* describes a charity walk he made in spring 2012 across all seven islands. His chosen area of happy exile is no longer Lanzarote, where he lived for several years, but mainland Almeria, where he publishes an online magazine called *Spain Buddy*.

Not all escapees from chill European or North American winters immerse themselves in writing or running bars, though. Many come simply in search of leisure and relaxation. In addition to the endless flow of ephemeral tourists there is now a strong contingent of expatriate residents, whose intention is simply to retire and enjoy a hoped-for *dolce far niente* existence.

According to Mahoney—and this is his own subjective view—these expatriates tend to be less settled and positive than their counterparts on the Spanish mainland, who, whether or not they actually integrate into Spanish life, have at least created a world of their own in which they are both active and happy. Mainland expatriates, he claims, are less inclined to complain and to refer constantly to Britain as "home" than many Canary residents.

Of course, the British are not the only outside nationalities to experience settling-in problems in the islands, but their woes do appear to be more fully chronicled. Why so many of them should feel this way about the Canaries is a moot point. Perhaps knowing that they are much further away (1,000 kilometres) from mainland Europe has something to do with it. Or perhaps it is the feeling, if and when realization finally dawns, that they genuinely are somewhere "different". Geographically they may be in, or rather near, Africa, but that does not really explain the sense of disorientation. The truth is that the expatriates find themselves in a uniquely mystical and isolated place (Las Palmas traffic jams apart) and that can be an alarming or exhilarating sensation.

I recall only too well my own feelings on first seeing the spindly, black monolithic rock known as the Dedo de Díos, or Finger of God, which (until the "tip" unfortunately broke off in a 2005 gale) used to rise above the volcanic-pebbled cove of Puerto de las Nieves near Agaete in the north of Gran Canaria, backed by vast menacing cliffs that seemed to reach to the sky. I felt I had entered some new, ominous, yet fascinating corner of the planet. They may have been the Fields of Elysium, Garden of the Hesperides or "Fortunate Isles" to the ancients, but the Canaries undoubtedly have their darker, eerie side as well.

## POSTSCRIPT: *CARNAVAL*

The opposite to that dark side was what I experienced whenever, for a breather, relaxation or an exhilarating change of scene from my interior room (the only view there was down a shaft) and the hotel reception area where I worked all those years ago, I climbed the stairs to the roof terrace. There the ocean breezes, the dazzling silver light reflecting on the flat rooftops around me, the wheeling, wailing, mournful seagulls, the distant sighing hiss or occasional roar of the nearby ocean, the plaintive hoot of a ship heading for Las Palmas' Puerto de la Luz harbour, or the indistinct murmur of Andaluz-cum-Latin American accents as people below went about their daily business all weaved a different kind of spell for me. There was a sense of adventure in the air, of limitless horizons and possibilities. Other shores beckoned. Not those of neighbouring Africa but of Cuba and Puerto Rico and Venezuela and Brazil thousands of miles west across the Atlantic.

The Caribbean and Americas seem particularly near in February when it is *carnaval* (carnival) time and the liveliest, most exotic and colourful fiesta spectacle in all Spanish territories explodes into life in Santa Cruz de Tenerife. No other celebration on the islands or mainland Spain can compete with its sheer excitement and exuberance. It rivals its twin city Rio de Janeiro's great event and comes close to matching it. It was declared a Tourist Festival of National Interest in 1980 and now has aspirations to join the ranks of UNESCO World Heritage sites.

The festival has a long history. The first celebrations, on much a smaller scale, took place in the early seventeenth century but soon expanded when Santa Cruz graduated from a small port to a bustling international trading centre. This development saw the emergence of a new bourgeoisie who helped expand the fiesta and bring it out of the cafés and bars where it had been held till then and into the streets and plazas of the city where people of all classes and types freely mingled. The increased military presence in the city added to the *desfrenado* (wilder) aspects of the celebrations when the army cut loose on its days off and helped carnival on its way to becoming the all-out orgy of unrestrained enjoyment it is today.

Tenerife writer Alberto Galván Tudela, who made an anthropological study of the event, sees it as a form of a popular social rebellion expressed in "behavioural patterns which contradict the norms and rules of accepted behaviour and reverse the usual social relations and order of things". He points out that the celebrations take place just before Lent when fasting and seclusion are the supposed norm in a Catholic country and that flamboyant dress, ridiculing of important figures, satire, song, wanton excess and even promiscuity (hidden behind colourful masks, although on more than one occasion in history these were banned by the authorities) all cock a snook at the prospect of the austerity that lies ahead.

A modern Canary researcher, Ramón Guimerá Peña, sees hedonistic links with the early Roman saturnalia and bacchanalia celebrating the wine god Bacchus and comes up with another meaning of *carnaval*: *carronavalis*, which refers to the "boat on wheels" that carried the drunken Bacchic revellers. (Another more common explanation of the word *carnival* is that it originates from a medieval Latin expression *carne-levare* meaning "abandon meat" as a prelude to the forty days of fasting prescribed during Lent.) Guimerá Peña theorizes that the Romans helped spread this riotous form of celebration throughout Europe at the height of their imperial rule. The Spaniards and Portuguese in turn exported it to the Canaries and the Americas several centuries later—in spite of strong opposition from the Catholic Church and, most recently, from the twentieth-century dictators Primo de Rivera and Franco.

Today the fiestas host performers from the Latin American and Hispanic music and dance world ranging from Cuba's late lamented "queen of salsa" Celia Cruz (who reached *Guinness Book of Records* status when in 1987, accompanied by the Billo's Caracas Boys Band, she sang to an audience of 250,000 people in the Plaza España) to Enrique Iglesias, the iconic popstar son of the veteran Miami-based Spanish crooner Julio.

Carnival poster (todotenerife.es)

The exotic Queen of the Carnival is usually chosen before the big event and quickly attracts nationwide attention and media coverage. The highly expensive and lavish costumes are made of feathers, plastic, metal and paper, all vividly coloured. A spectacular opening ceremony is followed by nightly dancing till dawn in the streets until Ash Wednesday. Thereafter the schedule is as follows: Saturday is the all dancing day, Monday is for feasting and Tuesday is the day when a hugely lavish *coso* or parade takes place along the Avenida de Anaga.

Santa Cruz de Tenerife was declared carnival world capital in 2000 and since then its calendar of events has become even more eclectic and wide-ranging. Its multinational shows, which started fairly modestly with the theme of Rome in 1987, have changed from year to year, moving through Ancient Egypt, One Thousand and One Nights and Mexico to the futuristic Space Odyssey and, most recently, Bollywood. Artists who have designed lavished posters for the fiesta since 1962 include César Manrique.

Over the years carnival has survived numerous attempted bans and restrictions (including one on wearing masks) and complaints from hapless city centre dwellers as local *murgas* (street musicians) and *comparsas* (groups of local clubs) parade with increasing enthusiasm through the city streets. All such bids to reduce the noise have been to little avail.

Just before the final weekend, known as the *Piñata,* winds up the fiestas with a powerhouse array of set pieces by international performers and a lavish firework display, comes one of the weirdest events in the whole carnival programme: the mock-funereal *Entierro de la Sardina* (Burial of the Sardine). Characteristically, this takes place on first day of Lent and is on a larger, more extravagant scale than similar events with the same theme performed throughout the year in other parts of Spain. It is ostensibly a time for "mourning"; buildings are draped and a huge, luridly sensual, blue-scaled and red-lipped "sardine" on a float is followed by wailing "widows" along a four-kilometre route before being finally ceremoniously burned.

The mood is humorously offensive and blatantly anti-establishment and satirical allusions to the Catholic Church often border on the obscene, with Almodóvar-like transvestites amicably mingling with other participants dressed as mock bishops and priests. The climactic burning of the "sardine" symbolizes the end of the past and the birth of a new era, or transformed society. Various differing interpretations of why a "sardine" is used in this role have been offered. The less elaborate Madrid version, where a much smaller "sardine" is simply put in a tiny coffin while sombre men in top hats and black suits pay quiet homage, has clearer origins: in the seventeenth century some fish delivered to the Spanish capital were found to have unpleasantly passed their prime and needed to be urgently buried. Here the "rotten" old era receives a more drastic catharsis as the fish is dramatically cremated. The revellers can have their cake and eat it too: enjoy a riotous time and simultaneously pretend that they are making a "serious" statement in favour of changing the status quo.

*Part Four*

# ISLAND AESTHETICS

Balconies in Teror, Gran Canaria
(Guido Haeger/Wikimedia Commons)

## Chapter Eleven

# ARCHITECTURE: FROM "ATLANTIC GOTHIC" TO "VOLCANIC FUSION"

### THE GOTHIC

During the centuries-long Guanche tenure of the Canary Islands only the most basic kinds of building existed. Many inhabitants lived in caves, which were more secure and weather-proof than wooden or stone huts (see Chapter 1). Their simple lifestyle changed with the arrival of Jean de Béthencourt and Gadifer de la Salle in Lanzarote at the beginning of the fifteenth century. The Norman adventurers commissioned a talented compatriot, the *maestro albañil* (master craftsman) Jean de Macon, to build the first two fortresses, both on that island and in neighbouring Fuerteventura, bringing a second taste of Europe, after Lancelotto Malocello's earlier sojourn, to those arid eastern outposts of the archipelago.

One of these fortifications, the early Gothic San Marcial de Rubicón, was located on the south coast of Lanzarote near Playa Blanca in the province of Yaiza, and its name is said to be a corruption of the Latin *rubicundus*, or red ochre, referring to the nearby Montaña Roja (Red Mountain), whose colouring is a result of the presence of oxides in the soil. The Rubicón played a dual military-religious role. Robustly constructed with an eye to repelling the constant pirate attacks of that time, it was built as a fortress on the site of the first European settlement in the islands. It was also a church and in 1404 its status was elevated to that of cathedral when Benedict VIII issued a papal bull officially designating the Rubicón "Catedral de la Diócesis Rubicense" and naming it San Marcial in honour of a medieval Limoges saint and bishop. This honour officially made it the second bishopric to be established in all the Canaries (the first bishopric had been ordained at Telde in Gran Canaria in 1351 only to be disbanded some four decades later after its notable lack of success in fending off a series of particularly ferocious corsair raids).

The original decision to build the fortress cathedral here, made at the end of the fourteenth century during Béthencourt's rule, was partly motivated by its fine strategic headland location next to shallow waters that made it easy for ships to anchor and partly because it offered easy access to a tiny island that separated Lanzarote from Fuerteventura and served as a springboard for the consequent Norman conquest of this larger neighbour. (This was the misnamed Isla de Lobos, or Isle of Wolves, which was in fact the habitat of seals that could be hunted as food and for their skins.)

In its modest heyday the tiny outpost of San Marcial de Rubicón boasted, in addition to the church-cathedral, a watchtower, various small houses, a cemetery and even some tiny "industrial" areas. It also had seven wells extending along a dusty ochre gulley, which provided abundant water: a luxury in this bone-dry part of the archipelago. Today only four of the original wells still remain, but two of them are the oldest in the region.

The Rubicón's brief moment of glory began to fade in 1435 when Pope Eugenio IV authorized the bishopric to be moved once more back to Gran Canaria though, perhaps to soften the blow, he also decreed that the Rubicón diocese be given the title of Canariense-Rubicense in perpetuity. The actual move did not take effect until 1483 when the Lanzarote outpost's cathedral status was transferred to the Iglesia de Santa Ana in Las Palmas and Juan de Frías was proclaimed the new bishop for all the islands. The town of Teguise now assumed administrative control of the Rubicón area, while further corsair attacks added to the hauntingly evocative church- fortress's woes and it gradually faded into insignificance. Today, however, thanks to its pioneering past and evocative remains, the whole area is an archaeological park granted the title of *patrimonio nacional*.

The other main early Gothic *lanzaroteño* monument to survive from this period is the hilltop Castillo de Santa Bárbara (also known as the Torre de Guanapay), which was constructed in the fourteenth century by Sancho de Herrera in Teguise during Malocello's tenure. Solid reparation work, after many destructive attacks, was carried out two centuries later by another Italian, the brilliant engineer Leonardo Torriani, and most of what is visible there today is the result of his efforts. In its later years the castle was used as a military prison and between 1991 and 2011 was transformed into a cultural information centre recounting and cataloguing Canary Islanders' emigration to the Americas with the aid of old documents, letters, maps, ships logs and personal documents.

Castillo de Santa Bárbara, Teguise, Lanzarote
(Frank Vincentz/Wikimedia Commons)

Now languishing in its dotage, yet impressive as ever in its dominant hilltop location, the castle is home to the island's Museo de la Piratería or Piracy Museum, which relates in popular mode the centuries-long history of attacks made by African and European corsairs and mercenaries on Teguise and the island in general. Among its attractions are colourful effigies of English seafaring legends like Drake and Hawkins, video excerpts from pirate films, arrays of skulls, cannon and sabre displays and small sculptures portraying the island's long-suffering inhabitants.

In neighbouring Fuerteventura the other most notable surviving early Gothic monument is the church-fortress of Santa María de Betancuria, less well preserved than the *lanzaroteño* pair but still impressive. It was badly damaged by an amalgam of misfortunes ranging from Berber invasions and earthquakes to a devastating fire, yet still retains many of its original pillars. Seventeenth-century embellishments include a notable stone-worked façade and a bell tower constructed by master builder Pedro de Párraga. Inside the church today are three aisles separated by half arches built over small cylindrical columns of masonry while the sacristy features some ornate Arabic-style work.

The Spanish *conquistadores* who followed the Normans set up new colonial outposts and commissioned skilled architects who had already designed monuments in Spain and Italy to provide plans for similarly impressive works in the islands. These were again in the early Gothic style but had some further Moorish-influenced *mudéjar* elements added as well, since the majority of their manual workers were Portuguese or Andaluz.

The key building to appear during the early stages of this period is Las Palmas' Santa Ana cathedral. Considered one of the finest examples of "Atlantic Gothic", it was completed on the eve of Corpus Christi in 1570 after seven decades of continuous work under the initial orders of architect Don Diego Montaude (whose daily salary, according to William Scott's "Some Notes on the Cathedral of Las Palmas and Thoughts on Tropical Architecture" published in *The Ecclesiologist* in 1851, was a modest forty *maravedis*, or 16 to 18 *sous*). Work after Montaude's death was carried out by another noted Canary builder, Juan de Palacio, though the cathedral continued to grow for another three centuries, and the work of subsequent builders like Prospero Cassola (1589), Diego Nicolás Eduardo (1781), José Lujan Pérez (1809) and Salvador Fábregas (1890) resulted in a blend of additional Renaissance and neoclassical features.

The cathedral's Gothic highlights include a magnificent *retable*, high arched vaults (*bóvedas de crucería*) and a forest of huge columns whose summits divide and spread into the high roof like frozen tentacles. The aristocratic Scott (alias Baron Stowell of Stowell Park) saw a definite visual allusion to palm trees and describes their appearance as follows: "The whole effect combines the Corinthian and the Pointed. These columns are banded twice with a very rich and effective moulding, combining a cable with row of ball-flowers above it, below a deeply run chevron pointing downwards. These shafts have no capitels, they run into a horizontal fillet, from which spring plain vaulting ribs, which flow from the shafts as palm branches do from the trunk."

The seventeenth-century Museo Diosesano adjoining the cathedral in the Patio de los Naranjos has a good selection of religious artworks but attained notoriety when it became a base of operations for the Spanish Inquisition. It has various salons, of which the oval-shaped eighteenth-century Sala Capitular with its bright ceramic flooring created by Diego Nicolás Eduardo, who used traditional tiles imported from the mainland Valencian town of Manises, and a polychrome wood Santísimo

Santa Ana cathedral, Las Palmas
(Alejandroclemente/Wikimedia Commons)

Cristo sculpture created by José Luján Pérez in 1793, is the most important, though the Sala del Tesoro (Treasure Salon) with its volcanic stone ceiling and pinewood décor is equally evocative.

The geographical location of the Canaries on the sea route to the Americas explains the increasing number and variety of triptychs, *retables*, sculptures and stone-carved works from different European regions such as Flanders and Italy that gradually began to appear in the islands' many churches from the early fifteenth century onwards. They are seen to particularly fine effect in the second greatest religious monument in Gran Canaria, the Basílica de San Juan Bautista de Telde, located in the archipelago's second largest municipality, a sprawling east coast agricultural town of 100,000 souls that has in recent years become a virtual suburb of Las Palmas (though its old San Francisco quarter contains many vintage buildings and its centre boasts one of the island's largest parks). Erected by the García del Castillo family well over a century after the town had been designated the site of the islands' first bishopric by a 1351 papal bull titled *Coelestis Rex Regum* and officially named a city, San Juan Bautista still features its original Portuguese-Sevillian Gothic gate, though the neo-Gothic towers date from the early twentieth century. The extraordinary interior statue of Christ was made from corn paste by Tarasco Mexican Indians in the mid-sixteenth century, while the Gothic main altar and the Flemish triptych of the Virgin Mary, with its *retables* depicting five religious scenes, both date from the late sixteenth century.

The so-called "Atlantic Gothic" period also produced many non-religious buildings in Gran Canaria, at their finest en masse in Las Palmas' historic Vegueta quarter: a time-warp labyrinth of cobbled lanes, tree-shaded *plazas* and elegant mansions which was declared a UNESCO World Heritage site in 1990. Highlights include the Episcopal Palace, whose fifteenth-century façade, with its decorative *alfiz* (*mudéjar*)moulding magnificently reformed by the neoclassical nineteenth-century architect Manuel Ponce de León y Falcón, is still intact and whose later features include fine latticed windows and ornate balcony, and grandiose town houses like Casa Moxica-Matos, Casa de Colón, Casa del Canónigo, Casa del Dean and Casa Santa Gadea-Mansel which have similarly decorated exteriors dating from this era.

La Vegueta, 1915
(www.fotosantiguascanarias.org. FEDAC)

Two charming Baroque hermitages also survive in this quarter. One, set in the pleasant stone-paved square named after it, is the Ermita San Antonio de Abad which features a Baroque *retable,* a splendid teak wood pulpit, a rectangular lintelled doorway and a grey stone Baroque steeple. A plaque on the outside wall commemorates the notion that Columbus is said to have offered his final prayers here before sailing west. The other, in an intimate triangular *plaza* also bearing the same name and with an ornate stone fountain made (again) by the nineteenth-century sculptor Ponce de León, is the similarly styled Ermita del Espíritu Santo (The Hermitage of the Holy Spirit).

Rival Tenerife's earliest and most important Gothic monument is the sixteenth-century Iglesia de la Concepción, which has been a National Historic-Artistic Monument since 1948. Located in the heritage site city of San Cristóbal de La Laguna, it was the first parish church to be built on the island and its impressive millstone tower is the most emblematic landmark in the area. The church has three naves topped by semicircular archways and heartwood moulded *mudéjar*-style ceilings. Its outstanding features range from a fifteenth-century baptismal font of Sevillian origin (said to have been used to baptize the first converted Guanches) to a magnificent wooden Baroque pulpit created by an anonymous artisan three centuries later. Though the whole church was restored in the eighteenth century from sketches made by the architect Diego Nicolas Eduardo and rebuilt in 1974 after the naves threatened to collapse, its character remains wholly intact.

La Concepción also contains several examples of late Spanish Gothic statuary including the impressive Cristo del Rescate, but by far the most revered and important effigy of a crucified Christ in all the Canaries is the Cristo de La Laguna which resides in La Laguna's Santuario de Cristo (formerly the Franciscan convent of San Miguel de las Victorias). Of Flemish-Brabantine origin, the statue was examined and evaluated by a leading professor of art history at the city's university, Francisco Galante Gómez, by means of X-ray and ultra-violet techniques. He began his investigations after finding a tell-tale inscription in one of the statue's cloth folds and concluded that the work was finished around 1514, not by a Spaniard as originally believed, but by an accomplished Antwerp sculptor, Louis van der Vule. On its way from Flanders to the Canaries the statue made leisurely ecclesiastical stopovers in Venice, Barcelona and Cádiz province (where it was temporarily housed in the Iglesia de Vera Cruz de Sanlúcar de Barrameda) before finally reaching the island in 1520. It was listed as a cultural monument in 2003 and plays leading roles in the city on two annual occasions: one during the 14 September Fiesta del Cristo de La Laguna, when it is carried on a silver cross; the other on the eve of Good Friday when it is paraded on a simple wooden cross. (The present church, rebuilt in 1810 after a fire destroyed the original, also houses a sculpture of La Dolorosa by Rodriguez de la Oliva.)

The largest islands hold no monopoly on Gothic architecture. The Lilliputian Gomeran metropolis of San Sebastián (8,000 inhabitants) probably has more Gothic monuments per capita than anywhere else in the archipelago. These include the *portadas* (or doorways) of La Iglesia de la Asunción, built and expanded on the site of an old hermitage in a blend of *mudéjar*, Gothic and Baroque styles, and the (fifteenth-century) late Gothic Torre del Conde (or de Peraza) which was built in 1447. The latter is the best-preserved medieval construction in all the Canaries and has been an artistic and historic monument since 1990. It is also the most southerly Gothic monument in the world. Set in neat lawns surrounded by palms and shrubs, the tower measures fifteen metres high and is decorated in the traditional fifteenth-century manner with white, lime-washed walls and geometrically precise blocks of rich russet corner stones. It served as an impregnable bastion for the ruling Castilians when the Gomerans, infuriated by their rulers' arrogance and oppression, rose up against them in 1488 (see p.55).

The Torre del Conde apart, a further array of sixteenth-century military buildings continues to reflect those particularly unsettled times. The range of impressively well-preserved castles and fortifications from this period includes San Miguel and Santa Catalina in Santa Cruz de la Palma, San Cristóbal in Santa Cruz de Tenerife and de la Luz in Las Palmas.

## RENAISSANCE ARCHITECTURE

Initially merging with the Gothic, whose influence slowly faded, the Canary Renaissance movement's quasi-retrogressive emphasis on classical symmetry, geometric proportion and love of columns, arches and domes reflected the grandiose ambitions of the islands' sixteenth-century colonizers. The *conquistadores* and their city planners were quick to incorporate this stylized Italianate form, with its imitation Greco-Roman columns,

Casa del Corregidor, San Cristóbal de La Laguna
(Koppchen/Wikimedia Commons)

into their *cabildos* (council chambers), churches and other important buildings in the capitals of the larger islands.

Tenerife boasts an especially rich selection of Renaissance monuments, most of them located in San Cristóbal de La Laguna. Highlights there include the Casa del Corregidor, the cloister of the San Agustín convent and several stately houses such as the Palacio de Nava (an officially-declared National Monument since 1976). Renaissance tastes are also exemplified in private homes such as the Casa de los Capitanes.

La Orotava, too, has a wealth of Renaissance town houses, which include the Casa de los Balcones and Casa de Molina, both of which feature magnificent woodworked balconies—some of the most beautiful on the islands—as well as intimate interior galleries and moulded ceilings. Owned by the Méndez and Jiménez-Franchy families, they are open to the public as museums and craft centres. Opposite this imposing duo is a further early Renaissance house, now the official Casa del Turista or Tourist Office, which was built by a local man Francisco de Molina in 1590. Its lintelled doorways are flanked by pilasters (inbuilt wall columns) and the outside patio is regularly used for exhibitions of local crafts such as "volcanic carpets". A similar nearby vintage house, Casa Lercaro, built in 1593, has a stonework façade, an interior patio with wood carvings on the upper floor (an unusual feature in Canary houses of this period) and Renaissance brickwork and patterns. The stone staircase is supported by a dome and semicircular arch. Today the building's eleven rooms house the Tenerife History Museum and island archives.

Further fine examples of the Renaissance style can be found in many of the smaller towns such as Los Realejos, whose Iglesia de La Concepción, begun in 1697 and protected as a Bien de Interés Cultural, is a first-rate example of Canary churches built during this period. Its collateral sacristies and tiny *camarín posterior,* or rear chapel, are linked to three aisles with small bordering chapels featuring characteristic *mudéjar* roofing. Once-flourishing Garachico in turn boasts the highly impressive Santa Ana church, built a century earlier than La Concepción and virtually destroyed by the great 1706 eruption, but then quickly rebuilt and restored following the original plans and now featuring a wealth of *mudéjar* work and Gothic *retables* in its ornate side chapels. The church's most remarkable statue is its lightweight sixteenth-century Cristo de Maíz ("Corn Christ"), similar to the other previously mentioned Mexican statue in Telde's San Bautista church, but this time made by Oaxacan peasants using an art form perfected originally in their home province.

Gran Canaria's outstanding Renaissance monuments include Vegueta's sixteenth-century Santo Domingo convent (home to the island's finest *mudéjar* ceiling and designated the Museo de Arte Sacro, or Museum of Sacred Art, in 2012); and the doorway of Las Palmas' cathedral's Capilla de la Virgen de la Antigua. Among various outstanding houses in this style is the Casa Regental. Westerly Santa Cruz de La Palma, in turn, has one Renaissance pile that stands head and shoulders above the rest on this island: the Iglesia Matriz de El Salvador, first built in 1493 and the only church to emerge unscathed from the devastating 1553 Pata de Palo pirate raid. The interior, which initially contained only one nave to which others were later added, is surrounded by a host of chapels, *retables* and statues. Today the church also features an eclectic blend of multinational additions: the tower, which was built by Juan Ezquerra a dozen years after the attack; one of its seven bells which came from Seville in 1758; and a clock imported from John Moore and Sons in London in 1842. The impressive portal, flanked by two pillars and made of Cuban cedar, was imported from Havana in 1709.

## BAROQUE AND NEOCLASSICISM

The Baroque movement which followed the Gothic and Renaissance periods produced another kind of individual architecture favouring white walls and striking stonework corners, all topped with red Mozarabic (Arabized) tiling and featuring elevated patios, latticed galleries and elaborately carved woodwork.

Here Tenerife again leads the field with a wide array of Baroque churches that includes Tacoronte's Santa Catalina, La Orotava's San Agustín and the two Iglesias de la Concepción in La Laguna and Santa Cruz de Tenerife. It also preserves a cluster of interesting Baroque houses such as Casa de Ossuna in La Laguna. This was originally built by one Captain Juan Manuel Delgado in the mid-seventeenth century before being taken over by the Ossuna family and is now a centre for Canary Island studies.

The most emblematic structure to appear during this inventive period in the islands' architectural history is undoubtedly La Laguna's Episcopal Palace or Casa Salazar, which was formerly the residence of the Counts of Valle del Salazar who commissioned the building in 1664. Its sober façade, designed by Juan González de Castro Illada and completed by the expert Canary stone masons Juan Lizcano and Andrés Rodriquez Bello in 1691, is widely regarded as the finest civil architecture work in the whole archipelago. For a short time the palace housed the Porvenir Casino (a men's social meeting club) but since the nineteenth century its status has been elevated spiritually and it is now the seat of the bishopric of Diocesis Nivariense. It was declared of cultural interest in 1983, and after a serious fire in 2006 (caused by a faulty heater that took five hours and nearly fifty firemen to extinguish) it was painstakingly restored. The palace re-opened to great acclaim in 2009, and today one of its key features is the superbly refurbished Capilla del Obispado (Bishop's Chapel). Though the building is as highly regarded as ever the only part of the original that survived the conflagration is the façade.

A subsequent eighteenth-century creation, Santa Cruz de Tenerife's Iglesia de San Francisco was one of the first to feature lush frescoes, while Las Palmas' San Francisco de Borja church, built around the same time, followed the more restrained Jesuit model. Other religious landmarks to emerge at the time included Teror's Basilico del Pino, La Orotava's Basilica de la Concepción and Icod's Iglesia de San Marcos, characterized by ornate gilded wooden *retables* mainly created by two talented craftsmen: Orotava-born Gaspar de Quevedo and Las Palmas' Juan de Miranda who established a whole new school of art work and later gave way to eager disciples like Luis de la Cruz y Ríos and Fernando Estévez.

The ensuing neoclassical movement was in turn a reaction against the decorative excesses of the Baroque, creating what the *Gran Enciclopedia Visual Islas Canarias* calls "an architecture of fair proportions, with colonnades, pediments and straight lines". A number of eighteenth-century La Laguna houses were built so exquisitely in this style that the authorities have transformed them into cultural and social highlights. The Casa Lercaro, with its fine Mannerist façade and long first-floor balcony, is now La Laguna's History Museum, while the Casa Montañes serves as the offices of the Canary Island Advisory Council. The Casa de Alvarado Bracamonte, with its red stone portals, striking pilasters and superb wrought-iron balcony, has been a residence for several island governors since the nineteenth century and is now a municipal historical and artistic heritage centre.

Many of the major ecclesiastical buildings, which had been amplified and extended over the centuries, now displayed a vivid intermingling of styles. The Cathedral of San Cristóbal de La Laguna, located on a site originally occupied by a sixteenth-century hermitage called Nuestra Señora de los Remedios, is a rather unusual example of this eclectic mix. When the hermitage disappeared the church was rebuilt in *mudéjar* style, and a tower subsequently added. In 1825 the building was officially designated a cathedral. It featured three aisles and an ambulatory around the chancel— unique in the islands and more medieval European than Canary colonial in style. Seven decades later the whole building was demolished due to its dilapidated state, and what stands today is actually an early twentieth-century recreation masterminded by engineer Rodrigo de Vallabriga. As result of his work it now manages to effectively blend revived neo-Gothic and Renaissance styles while still retaining the original 1820 neoclassical façade designed by Ventura Rodriguez. Today its interior highlights also include a Carrara marble pulpit carved by the Genovese sculptor Pasquale Bocciardo which contrasts interestingly with the re-installed Gothic *reredos* originally commissioned by Pedro Afonso Mazuelos in Flanders in 1597 and whose panels are, according to Matías Díaz Padrón, curator of Flemish painting for the Prado Museum, the work of Van Dyck's maestro Hendrick Van Balen. Thanks to its phoenix-like nineteenth-century resurgence and in spite of its hybrid hotchpotch of styles, the cathedral has much of architectural and aesthetic interest and is now regarded as one of the most important religious monuments in the islands.

### *MODERNISME*, RATIONALISM AND "COLONIAL BAROQUE"

The period between the mid nineteenth and early twentieth centuries saw a further variety of architectural styles, thanks to increasingly strong European influences. Foremost among them was *modernisme* (not to be confused with functional twentieth-century modernism). Examples of this striking and sometimes bizarre architectural style are to be seen in all Spanish territories, even in outposts as far flung as the North African enclave of Melilla, which still boasts over a hundred *moderniste* buildings. The hybrid blend of Art Nouveau and Catalan eccentricity actually originated in France and Belgium but was subsequently adopted by, and re-invented in, the dynamic city of Barcelona, where its hermit like founder Antoni Gaudí and his dedicated disciples Lluis Domènech i Muntaner and Josep Puig i Cadalfach (each with the help of affluent patrons) developed a strange mix of fairy tale magic and solid workmanship in their architectural creations. Key features of the form included sinuously curved façade depictions and stylized yet unified arrays of outlandish ornamental figures that ranged from the gremlin-like to the surreal. The great *moderniste* triumvirate also possessed an uncanny knack of producing buildings so singular that each had its own clearly defined individual personality, and it was virtually impossible to confuse one with another.

The most prolific and ubiquitous architect working mainly in the *moderniste* form in the Canaries was Valladolid-born Mariano Estanga, who lived for some years in Tenerife before returning to his home in the harsh *meseta*-land of Old Castile. A lover of Greek art and the Hellenic mode of using *loggias masónicas* in temples, he tried to incorporate these two aspects into many of his buildings. Among his most attractive works are the Círculo de Amistad XII de Enero (a light blue and cream gem), the Farmacia Castelo, Clinica Pompera and Antiguo Colegio de las Madres Dominicas in Santa Cruz (in which he also incorporated classic Gothic and Renaissance motifs) and the Palacete Rodriguez Acero in La Laguna. The latter, with its fourteenth-century Granadine *mudéjar* patio, is considered to be his most accomplished work.

Non-religious landmarks over this period include the oldest of Las Palmas' four markets, La Vegueta (www.mercadovegueta.com), a huge cloister-like edifice with a large central inner courtyard lined with a myriad of stalls selling food of every imaginable kind, which dates from 1856 but was re designed by Miguel de Oraá in the twentieth century; and a city garden zone, which was strongly British-influenced.

Santa Cruz de Tenerife also features a residential garden zone, much larger than that in Las Palmas, dating from the nineteenth century. Known as the Barrio de los Hoteles (literally the "Hotel District", though it refers to privately owned mansions rather than commercial establishments), it is centred round the Plaza 25 de Julio and features many *moderniste* buildings designed by an eclectic blend of architects.

These innovators were headed by Miguel Martín-Fernández de la Torre who initially studied in Madrid under the rationalist architect Secundino Zuazo (perpetrator of Madrid's chilling bunker-like Nuevos Ministerios government offices) but succeeded in producing his own blend of post-Civil War "*moderniste*-rationalist fusion" which he effectively employed to create Gran Canaria's first government-run mountain inn, the Parador de Tejeda, and—most famously—the Pueblo Canario, or Canary Village, a popular venue for folklore exhibitions located in the old heart of Las Palmas.

The above mentioned twentieth-century rationalist, or *racionalista*, movement was noted for its unadorned and supremely functional form. The style of its buildings was pared to the bone, eschewing all excessive decorative elements and any superfluous additions. The buildings were practical, linear, unadorned and aimed solely at serving the purpose for which they were intended, be it educational, industrial or political. Though the movement began in the 1920s it was not until early in the following decade that the first rationalist buildings actually made their appearance in the islands.

A prime example is Santa Cruz's clean, white, sober Hogar Escuela, designed by Domingo Pisaca y Burgada (1894-1962). This revered Tenerife-born figure went to Cádiz as a young man to study medicine, following in the footsteps of his father, but shortly afterwards decided that

Casa Quintero, Santa Cruz de Tenerife, built in 1905
(Koppchen/Wikimedia Commons)

designing buildings was his true vocation. Both *moderniste* and eclectic in style, he created numerous impressive works such as the post-Civil War University of La Laguna and Civil Government offices in Santa Cruz de Tenerife. A rare failure was his innovative 1930s cliff-side Balneario de Santa Cruz which suffered many economic setbacks and today is in a sad state of abandon.

Also prominent was Tenerife's José Enrique Marrero Regalado (1897-1956), who specialized in a monumental style known as neo-colonial, or *barroco colonial* (colonial Baroque). He created distinctive buildings such as Santa Cruz de Tenerife's imposing Cine Victor (which opened with Michael Powell's lyrical 1954 celluloid version of *The Tales of Hoffmann*), the capital's beautiful San José church, the Cabildo Insular de Tenerife overlooking the Plaza España and the Mercado de Nuestra Señora de Africa, linked to the main city by José Blasco Robles' bridge, El Puente General Serrador, which passes over the arid Barranco de Santos and features small bronze statues of lions at each end. Last but by no means least on his list of achievements is the grandiose Basilica de Nuestra Señora de la Candelaria in the small Tenerife town of Candelaria.

Marrero Regalado's more austere-looking dream project, the Sanatorio de Abona, which tops a small hill in the east coast town of Abades, was originally conceived as a leper colony. It was an objective seemingly at odds with its stark 1940s *franquista* architectural style, whose cold, clinical forms or block-shaped edifices—not unlike those of the rationalist structures— were admired and encouraged not only by Franco, but also by his fascist counterparts Mussolini and Hitler. Alas, it was destined never to play this humanitarian role as medical progress helped cure the disease shortly after its construction. (For a while it became, instead, a military base, and in 2002 an Italian entrepreneur bought it for his own commercial use.)

## "Volcanic Fusion" and the Contemporary Scene

The twentieth-century Lanzarote genius César Manrique, whose life and key works have already been briefly discussed in Chapter 9, was in some ways the island's very own Salvador Dalí, even though these two creative spirits followed quite different paths. The flamboyant, dandified Catalan surrealist painter's topographical inspiration came from a tiny northern Costa Brava inlet called Port Lligat, whose raw-boned coastal landscape and iridescent waters are etched crystal clear by the Tramuntana wind, mercilessly cold in winter as it sweeps down from the Pyrenees. The earthier, elemental Manrique's statues and buildings were inspired not by one bleakly evocative cove but by an entire island, which, unlike the more austere and northerly Port Lligat, basks in perennially mellow sub-Saharan breezes. His work seems to burst out of the volcanic landscape itself and seamlessly blend with it.

Manrique's semi-subterranean *casa-estudio*, most of which is submerged iceberg-like in the arid volcanic area where most of the eighteenth-century eruptions occurred, was built in 1968 after his return from New York. Nature was the fundamental basis of both his existence, and his art and home are totally in tune with their geographical surroundings: five of the rooms were actually formed by lava-created bubbles, prime examples of the locally-coined term "volcanic fusion." Manrique lived and worked in the midst of this phantasmagorical creation which since his death has become the Fundación César Manrique. Its labyrinth of salons and open spaces are visited by over 300,000 people every year and the house is also a cultural rendezvous where subjects as diverse as plastic arts and the global environment are examined and discussed with equal enthusiasm at lively presentations or reflective forums.

Foremost among recent works by contemporary architects in the Canaries is the ubiquitous Santiago Calatrava's Adán Martín Auditorium (2003) in Santa Cruz de Tenerife. His work is devoid of traditional or natural island characteristics but is instead futuristic in appearance and has a global rather than regional appeal. Similar to the group of buildings Calatrava created in his Ciudad de la Ciencia beside the Mediterranean in his native mainland Valencia, this luminous silvery-hued creation features a curved protecting fifty-metre-high "wing", white concrete and *trencadis* (fragmented mosaics). It is built in series of successive platforms located in 16,000 square metres of plazas and terraces overlooking the ocean. Three regular orchestras perform concerts in its two large music halls.

The highest buildings in the Tenerife capital—and in fact in the whole archipelago—are the 120-metre Torres de Santa Cruz, or Twin Towers, designed by local architect Julian Valladares. Each tower was constructed by a separate company, one by Ferrovial and the other by Candesa between 2004 and 2006. (Wary after the 2001 New York terrorist attacks, the authorities actually delayed this project for three years before work began.)

The Gran Canarian capital also boasts a number of ultra-modern constructions, less high, less ambitious and less artistic, but more practical in their aims such as the sober Inakasa and colourful Woermann buildings which are designed purely for office or residential use. Inakasa is a stark grey cubic (some might say brutalist) conglomeration that merges public and private spaces, while the slightly more innovative Iñaki Abelos- and Juan Herreros-designed Woermann Tower and Plaza is a sixty-metre high-rise featuring yellow, blue and green Vanceva overlays and horizontal solar fins to create a glass effect that enhances light and transparency. The Woermann complex stand in a public square made of Portuguese stone with designs by the German contemporary artist Albert Oehlen.

Not all recent innovative Canary creations are on this ambitious scale. Many of the islands have also produced some human-size works: such as young architect Ilya Escario's "Volcano House" near the village of Lajares in Fuerteventura. Far from following the naturalistic Manrique style, as its name might imply, the house is modern, minimalist, long, low and rectangular using a combination of steel plate, ceramics, glass and wood to form the structure. It typifies the imaginative, forward-looking spirit of island architecture on all levels today. And it is a long way on from the Guanches and their caves.

## POPULAR ISLAND ARCHITECTURE

One particularly attractive feature of traditional Canary houses, especially those located in the old quarters of cities such as Las Palmas de Gran Canaria and San Cristóbal de la Laguna and La Orotava in Tenerife, as well as in smaller island towns like Teror and Santa Cruz de la Palma, is the prevalence of expertly crafted balconies, made from the resilient heartwood that comes from the tall pines of inland hills and valleys of the more fertile central and western islands. The balconies feature lattice work louvres and pronounced overhangs that afford the occupants good views of any activity below. They are ubiquitous in simple homes and stately houses alike and are more ornate in the central and western islands than anywhere in mainland Spain. This is less the case in the easterly semi-desert environs of Lanzarote and Fuerteventura, however, where traditional homes tend to be of a pared down, quasi-Arabic appearance: simple, cubist, white and balcony-less (except in some of the more recent tourist *urbanizaciones* where new wooden terraces have been tastefully added).

Casa de los Balcones, La Orotava, Tenerife
(Berthold Werner/Wikimedia Commons)

Common to many island dwellings are the thick exterior walls and shady inner patio, both legacies of Andalusian and Portuguese architecture introduced by immigrant constructors from those southern Iberian regions where buildings need protection against a fiercer heat than is experienced in this Atlantic-cooled archipelago. Here the temperate ocean breezes lend the houses a more subtle, gentle and distinctly Canarian aura. Pebbled or tiled patios are usually lined with clay or ceramic pots filled with brightly coloured flowers and sometimes feature a central "distilling stone" designed to both filter and cool water, and above the patio an inner supported pinewood gallery, reached by a wooden stairway, leads to the bedrooms. (Their layout roughly resembles, though in a much warmer and homelier way, the basic *corralas* to be seen in old corners of Madrid, and in spite of their stark simplicity—they served as communal homes for the Dickensian poor described in the nineteenth-century Canarian writer Pérez Galdós' bulky novels—are now preserved cultural buildings.)

The islanders love to paint their houses in different colours and the simple urban homes of the central and western islands, whether clustered in rows overlooking the enclosed, amphitheatre-like waterfront of tiny San Sebastián de La Gomera or scattered across the cliff-tops that serve as a backdrop to sprawling Las Palmas, run the full spectrum from sunset red to violet, making even the simplest home appear exotic. Certainly nowhere else in Spanish territory are there houses with such vivid colours as those in the islands.

Unlike in the urban areas, fewer Canarians now inhabit the old traditional country houses. As farming decreases, tourism expands and more locals gravitate to the cities and the coasts in search of work many former farmsteads and *campo* (countryside) homes have been converted by property developers (often with commendable taste) into *turismo rural* establishments.

*Chapter Twelve*

# CANARY ART: FROM CAVE PAINTINGS TO MODERN MISTICISMO

## CAVE AND ROCK ART AND THE FIRST SCULPTURE

In the dim distant past the only artistic creations were primitively, uniquely Canarian. They mainly came in the form of cave wall paintings and the most important findings in this genre to date were uncovered near Gáldar in Gran Canaria in 1873. That northerly region's Cueva Pintada (Painted Cave) is the only cavern in the whole archipelago to feature not only etchings and paintings of Guanches on its interior walls but also neat geometric designs, coloured squares, triangles and circles whose meanings are ambiguous and whose appearance is disconcertingly modern. It has been calculated that the muted reds and whites that feature in these designs were obtained, respectively, from ochre and burnt nitrates.

Petroglyph, La Palma (StMH/Wikimedia Commons)

On La Palma rock markings have also been found which roughly resemble the rings on the inside of a tree trunk, while other images look like small crosses or possibly even miniature weapons like crossbows. Similar markings have been found at La Zarza (Garafía) in Tenerife and others can be seen in some parts of North Africa.

The most extraordinary solid image to survive from that era, however, is the emblematic Idolo de Tatra: a squat, honey-coloured mini-sculpture with bulbous arms and thighs and a tiny head made from terracotta which was discovered near the village of Tatra near Telde and can be viewed today in Gran Canaria's Museo Canario (see p.119).

## EARLY BAROQUE ARTISTS

After those primitive creations no new form of Canary art evolved until the sixteenth century, when stylized, atmospheric paintings in the approved Early Baroque style made their appearance, dutifully reflecting the strong Catholic themes imported by Hispanic invaders and conquerors. As yet there was no attempt to interpret traditional *costumbrista* or *indigenista* notions relevant to the culture of the islands' own inhabitants.

Those Early Baroque works remain deeply impressive. The Canaries' first great artist in this field, Gaspar de Quevedo, who was born in Orotava in 1616 and as a talented youth trained in Seville under the city's Baroque *maestro* Miguel Güelles, became proficient in the form's rich but sombre style. His work also reveals the darkly realistic influence of Francisco de Zurbarán, especially in paintings such as *La Concepción con Felipe Machado* in Tacoronte's Santa Catalina Martir church and his *Inmaculada Concepción de la Familia Lercar o Justiniani* which is now displayed in Santa Cruz de Tenerife's Museo Municipal de Bellas Artes. Both make maximum use of the *chiaroscuro* effect (strongly contrasting light and shade) that characterized the Extremaduran genius's work.

Close on de Quevedo's heels came Cristóbal Hernández de Quintana (1651-1725) another Early Baroque master who was also born in Orotava but did most of his work in La Laguna. An illegitimate child brought up by a *mulata* in humble circumstances, he was a quiet and reflective artist who lived to an advanced age. He already showed talent as an artist when barely out of childhood. Strongly influenced by Murillo and again Zurbarán, he worked with oil on canvas, employed strong pure colours such as red and green and tended to differentiate men and women by the tone of their skin. Most of his paintings were austere in mood and featured a dominant figure in the foreground. He was widely regarded as the most outstanding painter of this period in the islands and his masterpieces included *San Pío V rezando por el triunfo de Lepanto* (St. Pío V Praying for Victory at Lepanto) which can be seen in La Laguna's Santo Domingo de Guzmán church. In this majestic work (created when he was 75) he employed strongly emphatic brushstrokes to create depth of character and mood.

His paintings can be seen in churches throughout the islands, especially in Tenerife and Gran Canaria, and his highly praised *ánimas*—portrayals of "purged souls"—are found in two parts, one in La Laguna's cathedral and the other in that same city's Iglesia de la Concepción. The lower sections of each part depict Purgatory, the middle sections the Virgin, Joseph and the archangel St. Michael and upper sections the Trinity, surrounded by saints. Hernández de Quintana also created the beautiful *retable* in the Basilica de Nuestra Señora de Candelaria.

Cristóbal Hernández de Quintana, *Virgen de la Candelaria*
(Museum of Art of Ponce/Wikimedia Commons)

As fashions changed, his work became less sought after. Towards the end of his own lifetime it was judged to be of little aesthetic value and (by some) even of poor artistic execution, and his 1724 painting of San Sebastián, after being commissioned by the *canónigo* Domingo Pantaleón Álvarez de Abreu, and displayed in Las Palmas' Santa Ana Cathedral, was eventually replaced by a work by the up and coming Juan de Miranda (see below). His style was much imitated in subsequent years in spite of his supposed fall from grace and today he is recognized as a seminal figure in the Early Baroque world of art.

His "successor" Juan de Miranda (1723-1805) was born in Las Palmas de Gran Canaria and died in Santa Cruz de Tenerife. He received formal training under another famed Canary painter Fernando de Rojas y Paz as well as at the Academia de Bellas Artes in Seville. His key work, *Expulsión de los mercaderes del templo* (Expelling the Merchants from the Temple), can be seen in the Museo Municipal de Bellas Artes in Santa Cruz de Tenerife. Like Hernández de Quintana he was of a quiet, melancholic nature and a great lover of solitary activities such as walking in the countryside and fishing. Still waters run deep, though, and his private life was not without its melodramatic moments. In1757 he was sentenced to serve six years in Oran prison for having an illicit relationship with one Juana Martin, by whom he had several children, and for brandishing a "naked weapon" at the moment of his arrest.

On his release he delayed returning to the islands in order to live and work briefly in Madrid, Seville and Valencia. His other fields of activity during that itinerant but fruitful period include engravings and ponderously atmospheric paintings emulating the Sevillian school. He also employed a symmetrical rococo style, mastered the use of contrasting light and shade and completed several Venetian school-influenced portraits. Later he created colder and more sober images in the neoclassical mould. Strongly religious themes with the Virgin as centrepiece featured in many of his paintings. According to the historian Sebastian Acosta, his depictions of angels, as in his *Elias alimentado por un angel* (Elias being fed by an angel) in La Laguna's cathedral, were the finest of any Canary painter.

NEOCLASSICISM
The first talented sculptors now appeared on the scene. Foremost among them was José Miguel Luján Pérez (1756-1815) who was born in Guía,

Gran Canaria, and produced many evocative religious statues. He was probably best known for his moving *La Dolorosa* which can be seen in Las Palmas' Santa Ana Cathedral (in whose construction he also devoted his talents as an architect). One of the islands' most famous schools of painting, founded by a host of talented artists, was later named after him (see below).

Next, still strictly conforming to Spanish mainland trends, came the neoclassical artists led by Fernando Estévez (1788-1854). A disciple of Luján Pérez, Estévez was an artist of the court for Fernando VII and in this capacity painted portraits of the Canary aristocracy. His major religious works included the serene Magdalena in La Laguna cathedral and the dignified El Nazareño in Santa Cruz's Santo Domingo church. In his later years he was named "Profesor de Dibujo y Modelado" in the Tenerife capital's newly opened Museo Municipal de Bellas Artes.

His only real competitor at that time was Puerto de la Cruz-born Luis de la Cruz y Rios (1776-1853) whose multifaceted talents included painting, wood carving and refined enamel art work. He was appointed painter of the King's Chamber by Fernando VII in 1815 and spent his final years in Andalusia. He also tutored Carlos de Haes, a Spanish painter of Belgian origin who later specialized in realistic landscapes.

## IMPRESSIONISM AND LANDSCAPES

The growth of a more open and cosmopolitan society in the nineteenth century opened different avenues for artists of all kinds. A new wave of landscape painters materialized, coinciding with the emergence of European markets which used the islands as a platform for trade with the Americas. These were the first Canarians to look beyond Spain for their inspiration and influences and they trained mainly elsewhere in Europe. Some later crossed the Atlantic in the wake of Columbus and other explorers before them, this time searching for aesthetic inspiration.

Foremost among the trailblazers was the colourfully named Tenerife painter Cirilo Triulhé Hernández (1813-1904) who studied neoclassical art at Bordeaux's Ecole des Beaux-Arts where he assimilated the style of the French Romantics. Light was a key factor in his work, though he abandoned clarity in favour of a mystical Turner-like haziness. As researcher-critic Miguel Angel Alloza Moreno observed in his 1981 book *La pintura en Canarias en el siglo XIX*: "His romantic painting are diffuse and vague.

His images seem lost wrapped a kind of fog or mist. This is the result of the range of colour and his technique of using short brush strokes which are full of tension."

He was followed by the painter, musician and academic Nicolás Alfaro y Brieva (1826-1905) who studied first under Lorenzo Pastor y Castro in Santa Cruz de Tenerife, then under Jenaro Pérez Villaamil at the Real Academia de San Fernando in Madrid. Latterly he turned for tutelage to Luis de Cruz y Rios' pupil Carlos de Haes, who was perhaps his greatest influence. He founded the Sociedad de Bellas Artes in Santa Cruz de Tenerife on his return and to bolster his modest income gave private painting and music classes (one of his other talents was as a violinist in the island's Philharmonic Orchestra).

Alfaro y Brieva's main forte was Tenerife landscapes which he painted in both oils and watercolours with equal enthusiasm. He also produced accomplished Dutch landscapes and later came under the influence of the Escuela de Olot, where he fell in love with the gentle green Catalan countryside. Later he switched his allegiance from romanticism to realism and became one of the first Canary artists to treat landscape painting as a whole separate genre of work. His images pay homage to both human and animal figures, often with a tone of melancholic sympathy, and his techniques included the use of pencilled sketches, oil on canvas and watercolours.

The best selection of his work, including many of his outstanding Gerona countryside depictions, can be seen in Santa Cruz de Tenerife's Museo Municipal de Bellas Artes. His portraits are also exceptional, not least a nostalgically atmospheric 1870 portrayal of his wife, who poses tranquilly, illuminated against a darkening sky. His equally outstanding portrait of his nieces Joana and Julia won a prize at Las Palmas Town Hall's provincial exhibition in 1862.

The islands' first major impressionist, Manuel González Méndez, came to prominence slightly later. Born in La Palma in 1843, he was a highly talented, versatile craftsman who ably combined the professions of painter, musician, sculptor and fine arts professor. He studied landscape and watercolours in Tenerife and then came under the wing of the sculptor Aimé Millet at the École des Arts Décoratifs in Paris where he distinguished himself in all his studies. (To date he is still the only Canary artist to have ever received the French Légion d'Honneur).

He was the Canaries' leading island-oriented nineteenth-century artist. His realistic portraits captured the psychological mood of his subjects and he was much in demand with high society figures. Both the Canary countryside and its people came alive through his eyes and he eventually matured into the leading *costumbrista* painter of his age. One of his most emblematic works was the *Campesino de Garafía* (The Garafía Peasant), which is housed in the Museo Pérez Galdós. Today his most important paintings can be seen in Santa Cruz de Tenerife's Town Hall and Fine Arts museum, as well as in Las Palmas' Gabinete Literario and the Canary Parliament buildings. The writer Ortega Abraham said of him in 1983, pointing out that his all round acute artistic senses also embraced music: "He is a sharp, wide awake child, as inspired and adept in his painting skills as he is in stylishly and spontaneously singing an opera aria or a song he's just heard from the window of some illustrious house while walking down the street." He died suddenly from pneumonia in Barcelona in 1909.

Valentín Sanz Carta (1849-98) was another of the great early Canary landscape artists, skilled in his naturalistic vision of the islands' gulleys, mountains and woodlands. Supreme among his paintings is an outwardly simple work: the lyrical *Molino de Viento* in which a large windmill glows ochre-gold in the foreground, backed by a hazily muted cloudy sky. He had just reached his peak in this sphere of painting when his life took an unexpected new turn. Encouraged by the politician Fernando León y Castilla to seek wider horizons, he joined an expedition to the Caribbean. En route he stopped off at Havana and became instantly intoxicated with the city. He decided to stay on. There he quickly reinforced the fame he had already garnered in the Canaries as both a landscape and portrait artist and became one of the Caribbean islands' most noted artists, playing a prominent role in the Cuban capital's Academia de Bellas Artes de San Alejandro. Equally unexpected was his premature and tragic death at the age of 49 in his newly adopted city from a fever contracted after a visit with his wife to the United States.

Last and finest of this imposing quartet of nineteenth-century local landscapists was Nicolás Massieu y Matos (1876-1954) who was born in La Angostura in Gran Canaria and trained in Paris as a young man in the company of Monet, Manet, Degas and Renoir. Among his key works are the urban *Risco de San Nicolas,* the rural *Roque Nublo* and the great seascape *El Rincón,* all of which evoke the scenic charms of central and northern Gran Canaria. He also produced highly accomplished portraits, including one particularly warm interpretation of his mother and another of fellow artist Agustín Millares. His distinguished still-lifes include the masterful *Bodegón con olla de bronce y naranjos* in which he employs *cioroscuro* effects.

The curator, painter, poet and art critic Antonio Zaya, creator of a network of Canary artists who travelled the world with their work, concluded that the application of Massieu's impeccable Impressionist training to the open Atlantic setting of his island home transformed him virtually unchallenged into "the Canary artist *par excellence*". His niece Lola Massieu later followed in his footsteps to become one of the few female artists to make her mark in the islands (see below).

## "GUANCHE NOSTALGIA"

In the twentieth century the Canary Islands' art scene became more adventurous and varied. High in its ranks of innovative artists was Néstor Martín-Fernández de la Torre (1887-1938), who produced two symbolist works expressing an obsession with the islands' heritage and reflecting a kind of "Guanche Nostalgia". These were the exotically colourful and luminous *Poema del Atlántico*—some of which featured giant, orange-hued fish who dwarfed the puny humans—and the unfinished *Poema de la tierra*—famed for its erotic images—which together formed his prized *Poema de los elementos*. Each part of the duo is an eight-piece work representing the four seasons and four separate times of day. Two further projects, the *Poema del aire y poema del fuego* (Poems of Air and Fire), alas, never saw the light of day.

His talents were legion and he also designed Gran Canaria's emblematic Pueblo Canario or Canary Village, a charming architectural complex built by his brother Miguel in 1939 in Las Palmas' Ciudad Jardín quarter. Its central plaza, surrounded by typical Canarian buildings and bordered by a hermitage and a traditional restaurant, was originally the stage set for theatrical productions of works by Albéñiz and Strauss and is today a popular venue for folkloric dance performances.

Martín-Fernández de la Torre was also one of the first island painters to attempt ambitious murals, fine examples of which can be seen in the Teatro Pérez Galdós in Las Palmas (which he helped restore after its destruction in an accidental fire) and the Casino de Santa Cruz de Tenerife.

Néstor Martín-Fernández de la Torre, 1910 (Wikimedia Commons)

The charming Museo Néstor, located inside the Pueblo Canario, is dedicated to him and his works.

Another muralist of this era was José Aguiar (1895-1975), who reacted against the minimalism of contemporary Cubism by using an intense range of colours in key works like his large *Friso isleño* which is filled with romantic images of Canary *campesinos*. Born in Cuba, he emigrated with his family to the archipelago when young and in his later years moved to Madrid where he died. During an interim period of European travel he studied in Italy under the right-wing Novecento group and later adopted Baroque and Expressionist styles in his work. There is a huge mural by him in the Cabildo de Santa Cruz de Tenerife and another in the Basilica de Candelaria, which was finished by his son.

## TWENTIETH-CENTURY SCHOOLS: EXPRESSIONISM, SYMBOLISM AND CUBISM

A second wave of landscape artists dominated the islands' art scene during the late nineteenth and early twentieth centuries. Among them was Francisco Bonnín Guerín (1874-1963), who studied in Madrid and Segovia and was involved with two institutions: the Círculo de Bellas Artes and the Agrupación de Acuarelistas Canarios (Association of Canary Water-colourists), both in Santa Cruz de Tenerife. At his peak he was recognized as the island's most distinguished artist in this medium, and the luminosity and vivid colours of Tenerife comprise the core of his work. In the words of art critic Sebastián Padrón Acosta, "His delicately luminous watercolours are filled with marvellous flowers, with the hidden corners of our country lanes, the geometry of our wineries, the architecture of our patios, the charm of our gardens and hermitages, the magic spell of our old country houses and castles: all are illuminated on his canvasses by a sharp caressing gleam. In the world of island art Francisco Bonnín is the creator of Tenerife light." *Patio* and *Paisaje de La Laguna* are fine examples of his mellow and atmospheric *costumbrista* work.

Another accomplished *costumbrista* artist was Ángel Romero Mateos. The son of a talented sketcher and engraver, he was born in Cádiz in 1875 and died in Santa Cruz de Tenerife in 1963. He and his family moved to Cuba when he was a child and when they returned to Cádiz the now young adult studied art at the city's Academia de Bellas Artes and then went on to further studies at Madrid's San Fernando Academy. But it was subsequent private classes under Joaquín Sorolla that really opened his eyes to the magic of painting. He learned from the Valencian master how to apply light and shade and use warm glowing colours so that the object depicted seemed to reverberate with its own life.

From Madrid he moved to Tenerife, where he took over the lithographic business his father had established, while still continuing with his painting. In 1955 he held an exhibition of his work at the island's Cabildo and became President of the Real Academia de Bellas Artes. He also concentrated on folklore subjects and nature and his intimate and highly atmospheric *Hogar Canario* (now displayed in the Casino de Tenerife) is an affectionate and respectful homage to his native compatriots, while *Lecheras en Tenerife* (Milkmaids in Tenerife) provides a similarly warm example of *costumbrista* work.

The first Impressionists now began to make their mark. Their twentieth-century pioneer Juan Rodríguez Botas y Ghirlanda (1882-1917), after being tutored by fellow islanders Filiberto Lallier and Valentín Sanz, travelled widely in Europe, exploring Italy and spending a season in Naples where he made innumerable attempts to capture the magic of the bay on canvas. He then moved on to Paris where he created *telas*, or large canvas works, in Versailles. While barely in his prime and still finding his way, his life was suddenly and tragically cut short by tuberculosis but many exhibitions of his work have appeared since his death. *El Barranco del Draco*, a typical example of his richly textured landscapes with characteristic strong colours and brush strokes, can be seen alongside many of his other paintings (which total seventy in all in various locations) in Santa Cruz de Tenerife's Museo Municipal.

## INDIGENISMO

*Indigenismo* was, and still is, a movement dedicated to exploring and respecting native culture. The Las Palmas' Escuela Luján Pérez, named after the early neoclassical sculptor (see above), was created in 1918 for this very purpose, signalling a serious intent by a group of local artists and intellectuals to identify the islands again with their "real" (i.e. pre Spanish) culture. Founded by Domingo Doreste and Juan Carló, and following the ideals of Felo Monzón who opposed the standard Spanish *tipismo* favoured by the fascist Franco regime, the institute was inspired by its members' interest in the islanders' cultural place in the world. The group produced a periodical called *La rosa de los vientos* (1927-28) promoting their cause.

The Canary art world had now acquired the maturity and confidence to look even further inwards, savouring its own unique island heritage and natural beauty. What it needed was a hero who epitomized these values. It found one in a young genius called Jorge Oramas (1911-35). An orphan brought up by his aunt and grandmother, he started life as a hairdresser in Alcaravaneras in Gran Canaria where he would spend spare hours painting outside the shop. He then turned fulltime to art, joining the Escuela Luján Pérez and meeting fellow artists such as the above-mentioned Monzón. He created paintings in the style of Cézanne and also developed a style known as *metafísico solar*, which showed the influence of Franz Roh, a German historian and art critic who in the 1920s coined the term "Magic Realism".(This, incidentally, has little to do with the same term later applied to the works of Latin American novelists such as Gabriel García Marquez, but instead describes a way of looking at everyday things until they assume a new appearance or identity, stranger and more magical, in the eyes of the artist.) The art critic Agustín Espinosa saw things more simply: "Owning a work by Jorge Oramas is like opening a window and seeing a living part of our island."

The keynotes of Oramas' work were brilliant colours and luminosity. There is no hint of darkness. Neither is there sadness in spite of the artist's early and ultimately fatal illness. Recurring motifs are *campesino* Canarians, buildings, nature, vegetation, cacti and palms. His images glow in the subtle Atlantic light, their intense colours reflecting human warmth and a will to live. His first exhibition at the Círculo Mercantil de Las Palmas included the celebrated *Aguadoras* (water carriers). Oramas died from tuberculosis at the age of 24, still painting during his last three years while undergoing treatment in Las Palmas' San Martín hospital.

Plácido Fleitas, who was born in Telde, Gran Canaria, in 1915, was another member of the Escuela Luján Pérez. A traditional-cum-realistic modern sculptor who favoured working in the open air, he too based his clay, stone and wood creations on native Canary themes. After working briefly in Fuerteventura he went to Paris in the 1950s and in the course of his studies met Picasso and Oscar Domínguez. Back in the Canaries he formed the modernist LADAC (Los Arqueros del Arte Contemporaneo) Group with Manolo Millares and Felo Monzón and later shifted his focus to mainly abstract work. He died in 1972.

A trio of talented sculptors who also followed the *indigenismo* path appeared in the 1920s. First among them, born in Lanzarote in 1904, was Francisco Lasso, more popularly known as Pancho Lasso. During his formative years as an artist there he befriended the young César Manrique and was commissioned by the Arrecife Town Hall to create two statues honouring doctors: Molino Orosa and Blas Cabrera Felipe. The best of his work can be seen in the Cabildo de Lanzarote. His planned 1933 *Monumento a La Internacional*, a huge outdoor statue, was not displayed to the public until 75 years later—two years after his death in Madrid, where he had been preparing an exhibition on his homeland.

One of Lasso's closest working colleagues was Eduardo Gregorio López Martín (1903-74) who sculpted mainly in wood. He taught art at the Escuela Luján Pérez and also worked in Barcelona, Venezuela and Tangier where he was influenced by the simple Moroccan *esculturas negras*(or "black statues"). He was noted for his imaginative use of colour and creation of original ceramic figures, winning a number of international prizes for his craftsmanship. One of his more sober and enigmatic

Eduardo Gregorio López Martín, *Macla* (Mataparda/Wikimedia Commons)

works, located in a peaceful corner of Santa Cruz de Tenerife, is the block-shaped geometric *Macla* (which signifies a symmetrical group of identical figures, usually made of glass though in this case concrete).

Another particularly colourful and multi faceted sculptor was Las Palmas-born Tony Gallardo (1929-96) who combined his artistic activities with an equally active role in left-wing politics and in his later years cut a flamboyant, white-bearded neo-Messianic figure. After befriending Felo Monzón, Manolo Millares and Martín Chirino, all of whom helped trigger his interest in sculpture, he held his first exhibition in his home town in 1950.

As with many other island artists who looked to broaden their geographical and creative horizons, the other side of the Atlantic beckoned and Gallardo spent several years in Venezuela where he was influenced by another Canary resident, the artist Juan Ismael (see below). His Latin American career quickly soared and he was soon appointed professor in Maracaibo's Escuela Nacional de Artes Plásticas. It was here that his interest in social struggle was born and he joined the Venezuelan Communist Party, encouraging muralists to use their work as "cultural agitators" in deprived areas of Caracas to further the country's class war. He also came in close contact with far-left Spanish exiles who had fled there to escape the ruling Franco dictatorship.

On his return to the Canaries he founded the Latitud 28 group and helped reorganize the banned Communist Party in the islands, also setting up engraving workshops and organizing popular theatre groups whose performances were aimed at reaching all levels of society. After he was caught organizing communist assemblies in the northern Tenerife area of Sardina del Norte the Francoist authorities arrested him and sent him to a prison on the mainland. Undeterred, he continued working on various projects in his cell. One of the key sculptures to appear on his release was his *Homenaje al campesino* in El Hierro though his most original later creations, known as *magmas*, were made from volcanic rock. Towards the end of his life he moderated his political views, producing works such as his *Homenaje a la constitución* in Maspalomas. (See www.tonygallardo.com.)

## PLASTIC ARTS AND METAPHYSICAL PAINTERS
Interest in the plastic arts now took off and one leading exponent, Las Palmas-born Juan Jaén (1909-2008) was influenced in this field from the age of nine by his brothers, though unlike them he was allergic to paint and so concentrated on working with wood. Six years later, at the tender age of fifteen, he joined the Luján Pérez group under the direction of Juan Carló, combining traditional Canary native themes with a contemporary *vanguardista* (avant-garde) style—a strange hybrid of primitive and classical moods. He never used models and worked purely from memory.

After completing further studies in Barcelona he—like Tony Gallardo—emigrated to Venezuela where he taught at Caracas' Escuela de Artes Plásticas Cristóbal Rojas and ultimately settled down in the country. On one of his many return visits to the islands he created busts of historic figures such as the Venezuelan humanist and poet Andrés Bello in the University of La Laguna's campus and the independence leader Francisco de Miranda. He died in Caracas in 2008 at the ripe old age of 99.

Relative youngster Néstor Santana, who was born in 1944 in Garachico, Tenerife, shares with *misticismo* maestro Cristino de Vera (see end of this chapter) the honour of being the greatest Canary painter alive at the time of writing (2014). He was also the islands' first true metaphysical artist. Santana likes to depict "strange eerie places" that demonstrate a bizarre dislocation between the past and present and the subject and space which he, she or it inhabited. In his work there is often a secret magical meaning which conveyed by the arrangement of unrelated objects. He gravitated from using sombre colours (his *pintura negra* period) to more vivid light-filled images and his eclectic blend of old and new themes is highly personal and expressive.

According to the late English philosopher and historian R. G. Collingwood, a former Professor of Metaphysical Philosophy at Oxford University, his form of painting is "an expression of emotional opinion in art form". Néstor Santana himself sees his chosen field of artistry as follows: "There is a metaphysical intention in all my works, an attempt to reveal what's hidden beneath the surface and can only be seen with sensitive eyes." He adds that he paints the sensation an object arouses in him rather than the object itself and sees painting as "a road towards knowledge".

Santana lived and worked in Caracas from 1963 but, unlike Gallardo and Jaén, eventually returned to settle in Tenerife. He held many exhibitions over the years both there and in Gran Canaria and continued to travel from his island base to the United States, Germany and Russia. Half his life has now been spent working abroad. He has tried to incorporate the insights gleaned from those overseas experiences into his work as he feels that living solely in the Canaries tends to make one an overly-detached observer, merely looking at things instead of being involved with them. His most recent Canary Island exhibitions have been *Indagaciones* (Investigations) in 2004 in Tenerife, *Perfil* (Profile) in 2007 in Gran Canaria and *Origines* (Origins) in his home town of Garachico in 2012.

## SURREALISM

Oscar Domínguez (born La Laguna 1906, died Paris 1957) was the islands' first genuine surrealist. As unconventional in his life and work as his Catalan idol Salvador Dalí he was a mischievous child who liked "destructive" toys and who grew up amidst a mishmash of eccentric knick knacks—from insect collections to Canarian folklore items—amassed by his father in their old Tacoronte house where a local woman would tell him colourful island legends and tales of witchcraft. A tormented soul, he suffered from a rare illness known as Acromelagy (swollen parts of body, in his case the head) which severely hampered his talent and drove him to an early death by suicide. His main visit abroad was to Paris where he met, and was influenced by, another idol, André Breton. Though he ultimately failed to evolve a truly personal style he did produce a range of uniquely haunting images ranging from mountainside butterflies to deformed faces and he is warmly regarded and respected in the islands' art circles today.

Rivalling Domínguez for the title of finest Canary surrealist is Juan Ismael (Ismael Ernesto González Mora) who was born in 1908 in Fuerteventura and died in 1981 in Las Palmas. *Indigenismo*, abstract art, magical realism and metaphysical work all came within his eclectic range as did sketches, engravings, ceramic work and photo montages, and he also made various literary forays into poetry and essays. His very first artistic exhibition was held in the Teatro Circo de Marte de Santa Cruz de La Palma and from 1931 he studied at the Real Academia de San Fernando in Madrid and held exhibitions in the capital's main cultural centre, El Ateneo. In the late 1930s he lived and worked in various corners of mainland Spain including Lugo, Santander, Salamanca and Bilbao.

His left-wing views attracted the attention of the repressive Franco government but he managed to return unhampered to the Canaries where in 1947 he founded PIC (Pintores Independientes Canarios) alongside other notable island painters such Carlos Chevilly, Félix Bordes and Jorge Damaso, and in 1950 he co-founded LADAC with Plácido Fleitas. Continuing his travels he worked first in Barcelona and then crossed the Atlantic to Caracas where he met and exchanged ideas with Juan Jaén. A decade later he returned to settle in Spain, first in Madrid and then the Canaries. He finally received full recognition as an artist in 1970 with his oil and canvas masterpiece *La Mina*, which won a major award after being displayed at the 14th Exposición Bieneale de Bellas Artes in Las Palmas.

ABSTRACT ART

Initially a self-taught surrealist, Las Palmas-born Manolo Millares (1926-72) switched his focus to abstract painting when still young and moved to Madrid in 1953 where he founded the El Paso group with artists Antonio Saura and Pablo Serrano. Later he became associated with another group along with Antoni Tàpies and Enrique Tábara. Their joint aim was to eschew concept and theory in art in favour of the all-important "gesture". Like his colleagues he made collages from burlap, sackcloth and other basic materials and applied paint in only the most basic colours: black, white and red. Though he was born in the Canaries his work was intricately individual and had little to do with *costumbrismo, indigenismo* or any other island themes. He eventually became an international figure in the surrealist world and his overseas exhibitions included one at the Matisse Gallery in New York in 1961.

Rafael (Felo) Monzón, in contrast, was almost exclusively involved in Canary culture in both his life and work and a staunch defender of the liberty and rights of his fellow islanders. Like the short-lived Oramas and legendary architect-cum-artist Manrique he was an iconic island figure, unconditionally admired by his compatriots. Born in 1910 in Las Palmas, where a street is now named after him, he became first a student at, then a director of, the Escuela Luján Pérez. Together with Ismael and Plácido Fleitas he then founded the avant-garde LADAC in 1951, and then with Lola Massieu the Espacio group in 1961. He organized the groundbreaking *Murales en la calle* exhibition in the Triana district of Las Palmas featuring adventurous works by many new artists. A dedicated and outspoken socialist, he was imprisoned by the fascists during the Civil War.

After his release Monzón was appointed an academic of the Real Academia Canaria de Bellas Artes San Miguel Arcángel (RACBA) and received the first Fine Arts award from that school. Monzón never rested on his laurels. He was ever enquiring, ever seeking new art forms. His work was energetically eclectic, initially expressionist, then evolving into *indigenismo*. He was also a master of plastic arts, and became a key figure in the abstraction of the 1950s. He even touched on mathematical themes and kinetic art. For him everything was grist to the mill of creation. Mexican-influenced murals and social realism also featured strongly in his vast repertoire, as in later works like *Platanal* and *Risco* (which he described as a "critical image of the marginal city"). He also constantly portrayed the violent physical terrain of the islands, their volcanoes and their primal geology. Yet though he was firmly entrenched in island culture he found time to travel and to hold various exhibitions in locations as far afield as Havana, Munich and São Paolo. By the time he died in 1989 his place of honour in the islands' list of cultural heroes was secure.

Monzón's only female colleague (a lone woman battling among a host of male Canary artists) was the robust, honest and outspoken Lola Massieu, who began her studies in her famous uncle Nicolas' academy.

She was born in Las Palmas in 1921, completed her first oil paintings—portraits, landscapes and still-lifes—nineteen years later, and moved into figurative art in the 1950s often using similar themes. She evolved her own personal style of gesture and expression and held her first exhibition in the Pueblo Canario in 1958. Less than a decade later she was awarded the Premio de Honor for her participation in the Bienales del Gabinete Literario, the first woman to be accorded such a privilege. Over the years she held numerous art exhibitions in the Canaries and Madrid and in 1990 received her final accolade: the Premio Canarias de las Bellas Artes. She died in her native city of Las Palmas in 2007.

The only abstract sculptor in this group, Martín Chirino López, was born in 1925 in Las Palmas. He differed from his earlier *indigenista* sculptor compatriots in that he used iron to create his strange personal works, having first encountered and become attached to this medium in the dockyards of Puerto de la Luz, where his father was a port director. He studied in Madrid and London, where he was influenced by the contemporary works of Henry Moore and Barbara Hepworth, and finished his training in the forges of private workshops back in Gran Canaria. His first exhibition was in Madrid's prestigious Ateneo and he subsequently co-founded the El Paso group in 1957 with Manolo Millares. As his fame grew he had exhibitions in São Paolo in 1959 and the following year in New York's MOMA where his work *El Viento* featured his most recurrent theme, the spiral. Later highly individual works included *Lady Lazarus*, which was dedicated to Sylvia Plath. In the early 1960s he opened his own workshop in San Sebastián de los Reyes in Madrid but the Americas lured him back and he spent much of his later creative years in New York. His many awards included the 1980 Premio Nacional de Artes Plásticas for his work in its entirety, and in 2002 he became the director of the CAAM (Centro Atlántico de Arte Moderno) in Las Palmas.

No list of great Canary artists would be complete without yet another mention of César Manrique. "Before anything I consider myself a painter," said the multifaceted architect, landscaper, urbanist and sculptor, thereby adding yet another string to his bow. In addition to displaying the other earlier-mentioned architectural talents he emerged as one of the leading figures of the islands' abstract art movement. In 1953 he founded the Fernando Fe gallery in Madrid and three years later had his first exhibition in the Spanish capital taking great care in his work to avoid directly copying his role models Picasso and Matisse. As his fame in this area increased he organized numerous worldwide exhibitions in the 1960s.

## WILD AND MYSTICAL

A fellow student, and kindred spirit, of Felo Monzón, Juan Ismael, Nicolas Massieu, Pleito Fleitas and other Escuela Luján Pérez founders was Antonio Padrón, who was born in Galdar, Gran Canaria, in 1920. Unlike them, however, he was an accomplished Cubist and Fauvist. (The latter name is derived from the French *fauve* or wild beast, and the movement's key features were strident colours accompanied by thick lines that sometimes seem at odds with the colours.) Fauvism, which dealt in obtuse ways with landscape and human relations, was arguably disconnected from the real world while Cubism connected with that world by means of geometric forms, with a single object such as a face being seen from several different angles. Padrón held his first exhibition in 1954 in the Museo Canario and died, with years of potential creativity still ahead, just twelve years later at the age of 48.

Last and far from least, in a category that is all his own, comes the eccentric and melancholic Cristino de Vera (described by *El País* journalist Juan Cruz as "the last mystic".) De Vera, who was born in Santa Cruz de Tenerife in 1931, creates his art of *misticismo*, which he reached after progressing from expressionism to abstraction, through the medium of pointillism, a form devised by the French post-Impressionist Georges Seurat, in which dots replace brushstrokes. The overall result is a contemporary take on figurative expressionism. De Vera uses both artificial and natural light and a bevy of seemingly incongruous elements, such as the cranium and dry rose in his *cráneo y flor*, to create his own austere but poetic world.

Although he has spent several decades in Madrid he still sees himself as an essentially Canarian painter. Quietly reclusive by nature, he is widely known as the *pintor del silencio* (painter of silence), a mood exemplified in works like his hauntingly sombre *Bodegón* (wine cellar). He has won a whole spectrum of awards and was the subject of a documentary in 2005. Four years later saw the opening in La Laguna, Tenerife, of the Fundación Cristino Vera which houses the best of his output as well as temporary exhibits of works by contemporary giants such as Miró and Tàpies.

Feria del Libro, Santa Cruz de Tenerife

## Chapter Thirteen
# ARCHIPELAGO OF WORDS

## THE FIRST POETS

The islands' very first written works were primitive transcriptions of the original Libyan-Berber language used by the native Guanches and which appeared, notably, on the tiny island of El Hierro. The most important of these *petroglifos* (petroglyphs, or stone etchings), carved on smooth slabs of local rock and as yet undecipherable—in spite of efforts by many experts over the years to uncover their meaning—are the so-called *Letreros* of El Julán, which were discovered in 1870 by Juan Padrón in the central southern part of the island.

It was not until the arrival of the Spaniards many centuries later that a genuine island literature was born. A profusion of Canary Island writers slowly emerged over the following years, inspired in their work by the islands' chequered history and wild natural setting of sea and mountains. They gained a special niche in the world of Spanish letters, which the modern Gran Canarian poet and translator Andrés Sánchez Robayna christened "una microtradición literaria insular". The Tenerife lecturer and philologist María Rosa Alonso, in her 1977 book on historian Agustín Millares Torres' marathon classic *Historia general de las Islas Canarias* thought that the archipelago's poets and writers were particularly obsessed with the awesome geographical presence of her own native island, with its wild *sierras*, imposing Mount Teide and surrounding ocean to which they attributed symbolic significance.

The Canaries' earliest written work was the short, anonymous fifteenth-century lament *Endechas a Guillén Peraza* (quoted in Chapter 4.) A full century later the Las Palmas-born Bartolomé Cairasco de Figueroa (1538-1610) wrote the islands' very first epic poems, evoking the exploits and legacy of several legendary Guanche heroes in vivid works like *Selva de Doramas*. As a precocious child, at the tender age of thirteen Figueroa took possession of a *canonjia* (sinecure) in Seville where he lived for a while with his family. He next furthered his studies in Portugal before returning to the islands where he held *tertulias* (literary-oriented group conversations) in his home with other humanist writers such as Abreu y Galindo and Antonio de Viana (see below). In his later years he helped defend Gran Canaria from attacks by prominent pirates such as Drake and acted as a negotiator during the great raid by Peter van der Does.

His most important opus, *Templo Militante* (1602-14), was a highly ambitious four-volume poem describing the lives of saints, while his more complex *Esdrujúlea* (whose title refers to the term *esdrújula*, in which the stress of each word is placed on the ante penultimate syllable) was praised by Cervantes, Góngora and Lope de Vega though it must have proved more of a challenge than a pleasure for the common reader of his time. His other works include the more accessible *Comedia de recibimiento* and his translation of the epic *La Gerusalemme liberate* (*Jerusalem Delivered*) by the Italian Torquato Tasso in which he expanded the original work slightly to include some references to the Canaries.

Las Palmas' legendary Cairasco Theatre, designed by the Albacete-born architect Francisco Areño y Alarcón, was a turning-point in Gran Canaria's cultural development and is today the home of the city's Gabinete Literario (Literary Cabinet), a meeting place for cultural events. Built on the site of the poet's former house in an ornate neoclassical style complete with Tuscan columns, balconies and a décor of allegorical art figures, it first opened its doors to the public in 1845, but barely three decades

Teatro Cairasco, 1890 (Luis Ojeda Pérez/Wikimedia Commons)

later was revamped and renamed first the Tirso de Molino and then in 1924 the Pérez Galdós Theatre before assuming its current role as a literary mecca. The Pérez Galdós Theatre subsequently re-opened in a new location and has hosted operas and major theatrical works over the intervening years.

Two Canary-born writers followed this literary pioneer with creations of their own, not in the islands but on the other side of the Atlantic. The first of them was José de Anchieta (1534-97), a La Laguna-born Jesuit missionary who after being sent to Portugal's prestigious Coimbra University travelled to Brazil where he learnt to speak the local Tupi and eventually wrote the country's very first grammar book on that hitherto purely oral native language. He also produced medical books and religious poems. Apart from his writings his main claim to fame is that he co-founded São Paolo in 1554 (then a small settlement bearing little resemblance to today's megacity of fifteen million souls).

The second transatlantic poet, strongly influenced by Cairasco de Figueroa, was Silvestre de Balboa (1563-1647). Originally from Las Palmas, he is thought to have inaugurated Cuban literature with his *Espejo de paciencia*, or "Mirror of Patience" (Havana, 1608), an epic adventure poem describing the kidnapping of a Cuban bishop, Don Juan de las Cabezas Altamirano, by a French pirate Gilbert Girón (who was killed by a Cuban slave in the subsequent rescue attempt).

One of Figueroa's younger colleagues, Antonio de Viana (1578-1650), concentrated more on home-based themes, drawing heavily on the Canaries' colourful past. *Antigüedades de las Islas Afortunadas* (1604), a sixteen-canto work recounting events during the conquest of the islands, was written when the author was still in his twenties, probably in Seville where he studied and practised medicine and where the book was published. The definitive epic Canary poem, it describes in a blend of reality, fiction and legend local heroes and heroines such as the legendary Guanche Princess Dácil (now commemorated by a statue in La Orotava) who was one of the islands' many valiant defenders. It is conventionally myth-reviving and linguistically uninspired in some parts but memorably evocative in its descriptions of the island's rugged topography. The main source for this work was Alonso de Espinosa's *Historia de Nuestra Señora de Candelaria* (see below). María Rosa Alonso, in her introduction to Viana's opus, observes: "What he succeeds in doing is to write a history of the islands in verse, which is one of the principal objectives of epic poetry, but with the desire that its contents are true, although he knows full well that this is not entirely the case here."

## HISTORIANS

Throughout the sixteenth and seventeenth centuries several notable historians produced detailed, mainly accurate—though on occasions fanciful—chronicles of the islands (some of which are already mentioned in Chapter 4). One of the first was Fray Alonso de Espinosa y Paz who was born 1543 in Alcalá de Henares and left Spain to become a Dominican priest in Guatemala where he first learnt of the reported miracles of the Virgin de la Candelaria who had been worshipped by the Guanches long before the Castilian invasion of the Canaries. Tradition has it that in 1392 two goatherds came across a statue of the Virgin on the beach near Güímar in Tenerife and took it to a cave where it was venerated as a Guanche goddess. (Castilian conquerors later identified it as an image of the Virgin Mary which might have been washed ashore from a ship wrecked in a storm.)

Intrigued by this tale, Espinosa y Paz sailed to Tenerife to make further investigations and was inspired to write his famed *Historia de Nuestra Señora de Candelaria*, an ambitious work in four volumes. The first of these covered the geography, customs and burial practices of the pre-conquest islanders, the second the history of the image itself from the time of its original mysterious appearances, the third the various stages of Spanish conquest of the islands, and the fourth the purported cures and miracles performed over the years by the image. First published in Seville in 1594, the book is considered to be one of the best and most accurately detailed accounts of life in the halcyon days of the Guanches.

Another somewhat unexpected account of the islands entitled *Descripción e historia del reino de la Islas Canarias* and written by the Italian engineer Leonardo Torriani appeared just two years before Espinosa y Paz's magnum opus. To gather material for this work Torriani spent five years travelling throughout the archipelago, ostensibly checking fortifications in accordance with his professional brief but—as his interest in his surroundings and the islands' past increased—additionally investigating many other aspects of life. He was particularly captivated by the traditional melancholic Guanche laments that presaged the famed *Endechas a Guillén*

*Peraza*. One such cryptic plea was this timeless Hierran expression of unrequited love:

> What's the point of bringing and carrying
> The water, the milk and the bread,
> When Agaraf won't even look at me?

A more down to earth, though not always reliable, chronicler to appear at this time was Fray Juan de Abreu Galindo (not his real name but the pseudonym of an Andaluz Franciscan priest). He revised and added the finishing touches to his main work *Historia de la conquista de las siete islas de Canaria* (1593-1602), which had originally been started by a Seville-born poet and soldier Gonzalo Argote de Molina. Much of the material used was gleaned from Espinosa y Paz's above mentioned work, especially the descriptions of Tenerife, while other factual details of the islands contradict those of both Torriani and Espinosa y Paz, both of whom are generally judged to be more trustworthy sources. It remains, however, a highly readable account, providing it is taken with a pinch of salt.

The following century saw three other notable historians publish their own individual island chronicles. First of these was Juan Nuñez de la Peña (1641-1721),a humanities scholar from La Laguna, whose *Libro de las antigüedades y la conquista de las Islas de Canaria* (a shorter version of its original unpalatably long title) saw the light of day in 1676 and was enlarged and revised three years later. Viera y Clavijo (see below and in earlier chapters) lamented its lack of criticism, philosophy or particular literary merit but acknowledged the writer's genuine love for his subject, and the work is widely regarded as the first "official" account of the islands' history.

The second historian, Tomás Arias Marín y Cubas (born 1643 in Telde, died 1704 in Las Palmas) started his scholarly life as a student in logic and philosophy at a Franciscan convent in Gran Canaria and then went on to Salamanca University to obtain a degree in medicine, which became his main career. Nevertheless, his interest in the islands' past was such that he found time to write the *Historia de las siete Islas de Canaria* which was published in 1687. He was extremely sociable by nature and much of the information in the book was gleaned first hand from his revealing conversations with both town and country inhabitants.

The third and most renowned historian was the poet, botanist, playwright, picaresque novelist, astronomer and humanist José de Viera y Clavijo, born in 1731 in Los Realejos in Tenerife and by far the most outspoken, eccentric, original and *polígrafo* (wide ranging in his choice of subjects) of all the islands' chroniclers. He was renowned above all for his massive in-depth *Noticias de la historia general de las Islas de Canaria* (literally, "News of the General History of the Islands") in which he glorified the myth of national hero Doramas. First published in 1772, it was expanded to eight volumes in its final revised version. His other works covered a fascinating diversity of fields. As a satirical poet he wrote his epic *Los vasconautas,* which strongly reflected Dante's influence in its depiction of the protagonist descending into hell accompanied by Doramas and also drew comparisons with *Paradise Lost.* In his other role as a botanist he lamented the destruction of the natural landscape in a number of essays and articles. (Today there is a botanical garden and cultural park in Tenerife named after him.)

## BAROQUE, *ILUSTRACIÓN* AND NEOCLASSICAL WRITERS

The seventeenth century also heralded the arrival of Baroque writers, led by Pedro Álvarez de Lugo (1628-1706), an accomplished sculptor, painter and man of letters whose chief prose works were *Vigilios del sueño* (1664) and *Convalescencia del alma* (1689). One of his finest creations was *Ilustración del sueño* (Illustration of the Dream), an account of the life and work of the great Latin American Baroque poet Sor Juana Inés de la Cruz. His style was summed up by Viera y Clavijo as "emphatic, verbose, figurative, dark, sententious and blustering, but... filled with erudition and high morals".

His contemporary Juan Bautista Poggio Monteverde (1632-1707), a La Palma writer of Genoese descent, was a member of the Grupo de La Palma which met regularly to discuss literary matters. Fellow writers who attended these early *tertulias* included Álvarez de Lugo (see above) and Pinto de Guisla (who wrote chronicles of La Palma and was also, more ominously, a "Consultor y Calificador del Santo Oficio de la Inquisición). An elegant stylist, Poggio Monteverde wrote principally about heroism and love in romantic works such as his *Sonetos a los ilustres heroes de Hungría* (1688).He was ordained as a priest in 1688 and also composed the *loas marianas* (hymns of praise with a maritime theme) for various religious processions including Corpus Christi. Another of his loves was the theatre, for which he wrote a number of plays, including *El Prégon* (1690), *El Ciudadano y el pastor* (1696) and *La Nave* (1705), which were of such a high standard that Viera y Clavijo christened him the "Canarian Calderón" (in reference to the prolific playwright Pedro Calderón de la Barca, of *La Vida es sueño* fame).

Probably the greatest religious writer of this time was Fray Andrés de Abreu (La Orotava, 1647-1725). His main works include the *conceptista*-style poem *Vida del Serafín en carne y vera efigie de Cristo, San Francisco de Assis* (1692), which comprised 3,000 verses written in octosyllables and abundant in metaphors. Little is known of his private life apart from the fact that on one occasion he was tried by the Inquisition for having an illicit love affair.

A colourful precursor of the subsequent *Ilustración* movement, which sought to break away from the rigidly ornate and authoritarian Baroque style, was Cristóbal de Hoyo, the Vizconde (Viscount) de Buen Paso (1677, La Palma-1762, La Laguna). This distinguished aristocratic traveller and tireless defender of free expression lived an extraordinary life of action and tumultuous passions. His writings were strongly influenced by those of the Galician monk and educational reformer Benito Jerónimo Feijóo, who was the leader of the Hispanic Enlightenment movement which sought to debunk the myths and superstitions that had blighted the country's thinking for so long, and his *Carta a la Corte de Madrid* vigorously attacked corruption in high places: another key root of Spain's decadence at the time. On the purely literary side his poem *Soneto al Teide* was influenced by Góngora whose adventurous lexical complexities he emulated while still preserving his own individual style. His 1733 *Soledad escrita en la isla de Madera*, meanwhile, showed a more reflective and melancholy mood.

Tómas de Iriarte (born Puerto de la Cruz 1750, died Madrid 1791) was in turn a satirical neoclassical and humanist poet whose work *Fabulistas literarias* was famous for its attacks on literary men and their methods. One of its most incisive pieces was called *El Canario y otros animales* (The Canarian and Other Animals). He also wrote an equally outspoken play, *Hacer que hacemos* (Doing What We Do) which was performed in Madrid under the supposed authorship of Tirso Amarete (an anagram of his real name). Eventually his broad minded views and irreverent sense of humour incurred the wrath of the Catholic authorities, and for a while the Inquisition took an uncomfortably close interest in his sympathies with French philosophers. His early death from gout in Madrid at the age of 41 possibly saved him from serious retribution on the part of those relentless judicial witchhunters.

## ROMANTICS AND REALISTS

The next major writer to emerge was a Romantic poet, historian and musician, Agustín Millares Torres, whose *El Último de los Canarios* (The Last of the Canarians)—a tale of court romance which also examines Guanche values after the Castilian invasion—has a nostalgic Fennimore Cooper ring both in its theme and content. Also ranking high among his works are *Historia de la Gran Canaria* (1860) and *Biografía de Canarios celebres* (1871).In an alternative journalist guise he founded the periodical *El Porvenir* and his many musical compositions included overtures, hymns, marches and waltzes.

It was two eminent realists, both with strong Canary connections, who next dominated the world of Spanish letters. One was Benito Pérez Galdós, born in 1843 in the Las Palmas' working-class *barrio* of Triana and the author of masterpieces such as *Episodios nacionales* and *Fortunata y Jacinta,* which were set, like most of his works, in Madrid, where he lived from the age of nineteen onwards. His models were Dickens, Balzac and Dostoevsky and his aim was to convincingly recreate the atmosphere of nineteenth-century urban social life, a genre he felt had been badly neglected in his own country's literature. His colourful *madrileño* characters equalled in range and scope the London, Paris and Moscow personages conjured up by that giant trio of European contemporaries, and today he is rated by many as the greatest Spanish novelist after Cervantes. He died in1920 and his house at Calle Cano 6 in the Gran Canarian capital is now a small museum dedicated to his life and works.

Miguel de Unamuno (1864-1936), the other major Spanish literary figure of this period, was not of Canary origin yet he wrote more about the islands—and one in particular—than the native islander Pérez Galdós (who in fact published virtually nothing about his homeland). The distinguished Basque writer-philosopher was exiled to Fuerteventura in 1924 by order of Spain's then dictator-prime minister Miguel Primo de Rivera because of his outspoken anti-monarchical views. He was only four

Unamuno, 1925 (Agence de presse Meurisse/Wikimedia Commons)

months on the island, but during that short but fruitful stay he became closely attached to it. He wrote poems and essays expressing his love for the timeless aura of the landscape: "The bare, gaunt island of Fuerteventura, born out of the fiery entrails of the earth, ruins of volcanoes; this russet skeleton tormented by thirst. And what beauty! Yes, beauty!"

By nature a simple, down to earth man, Unamuno enjoyed *tertulias* (sociable discussions) with local people, whose warmth and friendship he welcomed. The island provided the therapeutic boost he so greatly needed after his vain but valiant tussles with the mainland authorities. "For me Fuerteventura was an oasis where my spirit drank reviving waters and from where I left refreshed and fortified to continue my journey across the deserted civilization," he said, even expressing a wish at one stage to be buried on the island's Montaña Quemada.

When Unamuno was informed by his son, after making an arduous two-day crossing to Gran Canaria to meet him, that Primo de Rivera has pardoned him and that he was free to return to return to Madrid he refused and continued his exile in Paris, in the company of fellow creative artists and thinkers, until 1930 when the days of the dictatorship were over. Today the Casa Museo Unamuno created in his honour occupies the old house he stayed at in Fuerteventura's capital Puerto del Rosario.

## Surrealists and Impressionists

Indisputably the islands' greatest surrealist novelist was the *tinerfeño* Agustín Espinosa García, who was born in Puerto de la Cruz in 1897 and died in Los Realejos in 1939. His controversial novel *Crimen* (1934) with its provocative Oscar Domínguez-designed cover showing a naked, possibly abused, female body, scandalized the more conservative sectors of the literary world as did the book's graphic portrayals of sex and violence. It was viewed by many sections of Canary society as "pornográfico, précoz, indecoro and insolente" (pornographic, precocious, salacious and insolent) and was banned until after Franco's death. On publication it rapidly became a cult, breakthrough classic, and its savagely satirical style was compared at the time with the works of Quevedo, Boccaccio, Cervantes and Rabelais. In these less shockable times, however, it has far less impact and in recent years has become somewhat unfairly neglected.

La Gomera-born Pedro García Cabrera (1905-81) was a great impressionist poet whose personal life comes straight from the pages of an adventure novel. A member of the radical Generation of '27, he was arrested at the start of the Civil War, sentenced to thirty years in prison and sent to Sidi Ifni in the African Sahara on a prison ship (ironically named *Viera y Clavijo*). A year later he managed to escape from jail and take a boat to Dakar where he survived undetected for several months before eventually returning to Spain via Marseille to fight in Andalusia in the Civil War. He was arrested again in Granada while the war was still in progress and not released till 1946.

His poems, such as *Líquenes* (1928), were strongly influenced by the sea, as in this simple and understated piece:

Sailing, sailing, sailing.
filling the eyes
with endless marine horizons.

Sailing, Sailing.
gathering a collection
of all the ocean's waves.

Sailing.
Like an inflated sea lichen
adrift in the sea.

Others linked man made structures and the neighbouring ocean seamlessly:

And in the evenings the shadows of the towers,
the chimneys , the houses, all take a stroll
to swim from the beach
and cavort in the waves

And afterwards, in the early morning,
barefooted as always
they creep across the landscape
and climb the mountains
to tell them what things
they have learnt from the waters.

Later he wrote intensely about his personal experiences in prisons and warfare. His *Entre la guerra y tú* (Between the War and You) was written mainly behind bars while his later *La arena y la intimidad* (Sands and Intimacy) also includes rich evocations of the desert. Having suffered like Cervantes (who was himself incarcerated for five years by the Turks) he became an invaluable observer of, and crusading commentator on, life in captivity. Freedom was not totally forthcoming even after his release as he remained under house arrest in Santa Cruz de Tenerife for many years though as a concession he was allowed to hold a small bureaucratic job.

More tragic was the fate of a slightly later writer, Domingo López Torres (1910-37). If Granada has its renowned poetic martyr in Federico García Lorca, the Canaries have their own in this virtually unknown and even younger socialist poet who was murdered by the authorities during Civil War after having been held in particularly sordid conditions in a concentration camp for his political views. With tragic shades of the Count of Monte Cristo's escape from the Chateau d'If, López Torres was thrown into the sea in a sewn-up sack.

During his short tragic life he wrote *Lo Imprevisto* (The Unforeseen) in prison (which remained unpublished until 1981) and *Diarios de un sol de verano* (Diaries of a Summer Sun). The latter, his most important work, adopted the Ultraist style, which directly rejected the self-consciousness of modernism in favour of evocative imagery, elimination of rhyme and references to the modern world. (A distinguished advocate of *ultraismo,* incidentally, was the Argentinian Jorge Luis Borges, who was resident in Madrid at the time and drew up a four point manifesto published in the *Nosotros* magazine in Buenos Aires in 1922: 1. Reduction of lyrical element to metaphor; 2. Deletion of useless middle sentences; 3. Avoidance of ornamental and nebulous artefacts; 4. Synthesis of two elements into one, widening its suggestiveness.)

López Torres was the only island poet to be executed at the hands of the authorities. It is sad that while García Lorca, thanks to recent work by the Madrid-based researcher Ian Gibson and a number of TV programmes and films, is now virtually a household name (as to a lesser extent is the *alicantino* poet Miguel Hernández, who suffered a similar fate), the young murdered Canarian still awaits his epitaph and due recognition.

## MODERNISTS AND TWENTIETH-CENTURY NOVELISTS

A notable early modernist writer was Angel Guerra, who was born in Teguise in 1874 and died in Madrid in 1950.(His real name was José Bethencourt but in homage to his idol Pérez Galdós he adopted this pseudonym taken from a character in one of the Canarian's Madrid sagas.) Guerra was a much travelled journalist and politician who also became a *diputado* (parliamentary delegate) for Lanzarote for over a decade. Passionately concerned with social conditions he obtained the post of Director of Prisons and in this new capacity championed many reforms and improvements one of which involved creation of a new prison in Las Palmas.

He was also an ardent *costumbrista* and regionalist who believed a people should know its history in order to recover its soul, and he based his tales, like *Mar afuera* and *Rincón isleño*, on local island life. His best regarded work, written in an agile naturalistic-expressionist style, was a novella called *La Lapa* (The Limpet) which was published in Paris in 1908 and relates the hardships suffered by an islander, Martín, who loses all his worldly possessions in a shipwreck yet does not give way to despair. It is a symbolic, epic tale of a simple man's destiny in which the ocean—as in so many other Canary works—plays a dominant role.

Guerra's contemporary Tomás Morales (1884-1921), who was born and died in Gran Canaria, was both a qualified doctor and a leading post-modernist lyric poet, influenced by Salvador Rueda and the Nicaraguan Rubén Darío. As a young man he went to Madrid to lecture on writing and study medicine before settling down in the islands to practise in 1911. His masterpiece was the two-part poem *Las Rosas de Hércules* (1919-22) which attracted public attention with its highly evocative cover and vignettes designed by the colourful symbolist painter Néstor Martín-Fernández de la Torre (see Chapter 12). The outstanding section is *Poemas de mar* which, yet again, reflects the Canary Islander's obsession with the sea. The Casa Museo Tómas Morales, converted from his parents' house in the Gran Canarian town of Moya, is a shrine to his life and works.

A companion modernist poet to Morales was Domingo Rivero (Arucas, 1852-Las Palmas, 1929) who lived in London from 1870 to 1873, before moving on to Seville and Madrid, and on his return to the Canaries enrolling in the Gabinete Literario in Las Palmas. Something of a late developer in the writing field, he did not publish any poems until he was 47 and only then was it thanks to Eugenio Padorno that his short, intense works were finally assembled in a 1998 volume entitled *En el dolor humano* (In Human Suffering) which includes key poems like "La Silla" (The Chair), "Piedra Canaria" (Canary Stone) and "El Muelle viejo" (The Old Jetty). In the latter he affectionately evokes memories of changing times in the eyes of the aging dockside regulars:

When the evening sun dims its rays
And its pale reflections leave in shadow
The rough paving stones of the seasoned esplanade
As is their custom at this hour, the old timers arrive.

They would see, in another age, the white sails of ships
Crossing the blue watery plain
Like a modest presage of the city yet to come.

And today from the old, silent and deserted jetty
Their troubled eyes observe, departing from the new port
For Marseille or London, Hamburg or Liverpool,

Instead of those tiny sailing ships of yesteryear
Powerful steamers exporting goods
And staining the blue horizon with black smoke.

Rivero befriended Unamuno during latter's stay in Fuerteventura (see above) and wrote a moving poem about him there: "…and in the parched and melancholy island walking in the shade towards the dawn like Dante in exile". Today he is commemorated by Las Palmas' Museo Poeta Domingo Rivero, which hosts a constantly-changing programme of exhibitions with literary themes.

The final member of this modernist trio was Saulo Torón (Telde, 1885-Las Palmas. 1974). After losing his mother and two sisters to fatal illnesses when he was only two (though his father and a brother survived) he worked in a British-run Las Palmas company for most of his life, but as his interest in literature grew he became a member of the Escuela Lírica de Telde and wrote as often as he could in his spare time (recalling T. S. Eliot in his attempts to follow his muse and alleviate the boredom of his bank clerk job). One of his best loved works, written in a simple, natural tone, is the 1926 "El Caracol encantado" ("The Enchanted Snail")—a tragedy of love with, yet again, the sea as a major theme. He gradually developed a spare, intimate, deliberately non-epic style similar to that of Antonio Machado. Sadness, pessimism and the monotony of daily life are major concerns in his poems and his inward-looking works, which he referred to as *versos humildes* (humble verses), also embraced love themes.

Torón's short poem "Sin rumbo" (Rudderless) expresses beautifully his sense of melancholy and yearning.

Setting sail on the boat of life
I left the serene port
Faithfully searching for an uncertain future
En route towards my unknown ambition.

I left behind my treasured youth
The beautiful land I'll never forget
And found myself in the empty ocean
The charmless, joyless, immeasurable ocean.

Today, worn by the exhausting journey,
I search for calm and rest
From all those countless tribulations.

Another member of the same modernist poetic group as Torón was Alonso Quesada, or Rafael Romero Quesada (Las Palmas 1885-1925), whose major work, *El Lino de los sueños* (The Canvas of Dreams), emulating Juan Ramón Jimenez's simple "pure" style, was published in 1915 in Madrid with a prologue by Unamuno. Its last section of poems, *Poemas áridas,* was dedicated to Unamuno and includes passages similar in mood to the Basque writer's own evocations of Castilian and Fuerteventuran landscapes. He also wrote about Las Palmas' daily life in what the writer Maria del Prado Escobar describes as an "intelligently ironical" way, focusing interestingly at one stage on the English community resident in the Gran Canarian capital in the early 1920s ("Los Ingleses de la colonia"). He also wrote various other prose works including *Crónicos de la ciudad y de la noche* and would assuredly have produced a much larger body of work had not tuberculosis cut his life short at forty.

A further noted creator of the modernist Canary narrative form, journalist and novelist Miguel Sarmiento (1876-1926) was born in Las Palmas, educated in Mallorca and studied law in Barcelona. There he made contact with Catalan modernists and established a particularly close relationship with Santiago Rusiñol whose dual writing and painting interests he shared. His key works include *Muchachita* (1898), *Así* (1909) and the charming, posthumously published *Lo que fui* which nostalgically described his childhood memories in the Canaries.

But by far the most worldly and urbane of all the modernist Canary writers was Claudio de la Torre Millares (1895-1973) who was born in Las Palmas and educated in England where he was the first Reader in Spanish at Cambridge University (1920-21). A member of Gran Canaria's distinguished Millares literary family, he extended his talents in many other artistic directions, from producing radio programmes and collaborating on films for Paramount in Paris to directing theatrical works in Madrid that included an adaptation of a novel by Turgenev called *Primer amor* (1941). Initially a poet, he produced numerous collections including a short modernist work called *El canto diverso* (1918). Subsequently he wrote plays and an eclectic variety of novels, one of which, *En la vida del señor Alegre* (1924), won the Premio Nacional de Literatura.

Another modernist, Isaac de Vega, born in 1920 in Granadilla de la Vega in Tenerife, won the highly valued 1988 Premio Canarias de Literatura along with Rafael Arozarena (see below). His finest book, *Fetasa* (1957), was a blend of dreamlike and symbolic images which inspired him to form a 1950s movement called Los Fetasianos whose priority was investigating the influences of metaphysics and religion in literature. Among his other noted works were *Antes del amanecer* (Before Dawn, 1956) and *Pulsatia* (1988).

De Vega's contemporary and fellow prize winner Rafael Arozarena (1923-2009), a lifelong Tenerife resident, first studied medicine before turning his attention fully to writing. His key books include *Romancero Canario* (1946) and *Mararía* (1973) a highly atmospheric tale of superstition and fate which was made into a successful film in 1998(see below).

A highly gifted non-Canarian twentieth-century novelist who wrote atmospherically about the islands was Carmen Laforet (Barcelona, 1921-Madrid, 2004). Between the ages of two and nineteen she lived with her family in the Gran Canarian capital and her 1952 *La Isla y los demonios* (The Island and the Demons) evocatively described the blossoming world of a young woman growing up in Las Palmas. This work was largely based on personal experience, as was her earlier prize-winning Barcelona-based existentialist work *Nada* which related with cool tautness the search for personal identity by a young woman living with a hostile family in the darkly nightmarish post-Civil War Catalan capital.

Yet another gifted Canary all-rounder was Manuel Podorno, who was born in Santa Cruz de Tenerife in 1933 and died in Madrid in 2002. As well as being a poet, editor and academic he was a highly talented painter who held exhibitions of his works in several European countries. His most notable local cultural achievement was to form an artistic group in Las Palmas known as El Paso while his most memorable book was *A la sombra del mar* (In the Shadow of the Sea, 1963).

Probably the most prestigious Canary writer alive today is Juan Cruz

Ruiz (born 1948 in Puerto de la Cruz). An incisive columnist and commentator with Spain's finest daily newspaper *El País,* he has won several awards as a journalist in addition to writing several books including the satirical *Egos revueltos* (Disturbed Egos).

## THE CANARIES IN CINEMA
Since the 1950s the islands have been a favoured location choice for international filmmakers eager to create their dream worlds somewhere unusual. Many fantasies and (would-be)epics have been filmed amidst wildly surrealist Canary landscapes, enhanced in the earlier days by delightfully clunky special effects—creaking giant tin gods, pterodactyls, brontosauri and the like, which are primitive by today's standards but were highly effective then and helped convert their creator, Ray Harryhausen, into a cult figure among movie nerds.

One of the best-known of these masterworks was the gnomic *One Million Years BC* (in which everyone communicated in grunts) co-starring, frequently against a Teide mountain backdrop, the young Raquel Welsh as a nubile, scantily clad Amazon (or Guanche queen, according to one fanciful local writer, even though no native Canarians existed that long ago). Other similar epic gems have included *The Land That Time Forgot* and *When Dinosaurs Ruled the Earth.* On a more classic literary level John Huston's ambitious 1957 version of Melville's *Moby Dick*, with Orson Welles playing an eccentric priest and Gregory Peck the increasingly crazed Captain Ahab, included several scenes shot on a now unrecognizable Las Canteras beach. Perhaps most bizarre, however, was the one-off 1960s "blaxploitation" western, *Take a Hard Ride*, in which the menacing Lee Van Cleef took on a trio of personable Afro-American actors including stern-jawed Jim Brown and they all rode the Lanzarote moonscape range together, pausing only to water their horses in green volcanic pools.

In recent times an encouraging trend has been for Spanish movie producers to use the islands as authentic locations for relevant Canary-based plots. These include the adaptation of Rafael Arozarena's mesmerizing novel *Mararía* with talented Spanish actors Carmelo Gómez and Goya Toledo in the key roles, and Almodóvar's *Los abrazos rotos* (Broken Embraces) starring Penelope Cruz. A strange suspense movie called *Hierro*, set in that tiny eponymous island, features another Almodóvar actress Elena Anaya who is searching for her lost son amid the haunting landscape. There are slim pickings so far but it is comforting to see at least an acknowledgment from Spain's ailing film industry of the islands' unique cinematic possibilities.

I have my own vivid mental images of other films—mainly with historical themes—that could be made about the archipelago. One, for example, on the great Guanche chief Doramas' last stand against the Spanish invaders at Arucas; another on the guileless Gadifer hunting for seals in the Isla de Lobos while evil Berneval is usurping his role as leader back on Lanzarote; yet another on Columbus' tryst with the formidable Beatriz de Pereza in La Palma (an intriguing sideline premise that Ridley Scott carelessly omitted from his beautiful but turgid *1492*); and a final reflective black and white Bergman-style art film on Unamuno's self-restoring sojourn in the lovely and lonely wastes of Fuerteventura. But maybe such fantasies are best kept to oneself. That way they disappoint neither the imaginer nor the viewer.

# Further Reading

## AUTOBIOGRAPHY

Bouré, Louis, *Contemporary Poetry from the Canary Islands*. London: Forest Books, 1992.

Cawley, Joe, *More Ketchup than Salsa*. Chichester: Summersdale Self Help, 2007.

Crosby, Sheila, *A Breathtaking Window on the Universe*. Santa Cruz de la Palma: Dragontree, 2007.

Gandy, Alan, *Walking the Canary Islands: the Adventures of a Grumpy Middle aged Expat*. Alan Gandy, 2012.

Hirtes, Matthew, *Going Local in Gran Canaria*. Summertime Publishing. WWW.summertimepublishing.com, 2012.

Lenning, Camille, *Notes from the Canary Islands*. Pittsburgh, PA: Dorrance Pub. Co, 1996.

Mahoney, Barrie, *Living the Dream*. Create Space Independent Publishing Platform. https://www.createspace.com, 2011.

Murray, Elizabeth, *Sixteen Years of an Artist's Life in Morocco, Spain and the Canary Islands*. London: Hurst & Blackett, 1859.

Sarmiento, Miguel, *Lo que fui. Recuerdos de mis primeros años*. (1926). Las Palmas de Gran Canaria: Domibari Editores, 2005.

Severin, Tim, *The Brendan Voyage*. (1976). London: Random House, 2010.

Unamuno, Miguel de, *De Fuerteventura a París*. (1925). Bilbao: Ed. El Sitio. 1981. Cabildo Insular de Fuerteventura. 2009. Also article *Unamuno en Fuerteventura* by Roberto Hernández Bautista. www.slideshare.net, 2009.

Walker, Richard. Canary Island Adventure: A Young Family's Quest for the Simple Life. New York: Dutton, 1956.

## FICTION/POETRY/JOURNALISM

Arozarena, Rafael, *Mararía*. Barcelona: Noguer y Caralt, 1978.

Coonts, Stephen, *Deep Black: Death Wave*. New York: St. Martins Press, 2011.

Cronin, A.J., *Grand Canary*. Boston: Little, Brown & Co (1933); London: Lindemann Press, 2009.

Cruz Ruíz, Juan, *Egos revueltos*. Barcelona: Tusquets, 2010.

De la Torre Millares, Claudio *En la vida del Señor Alegre,* Madrid: Ed. Rafael Caro Raggio.1924.

De Vega, Isaac, *Fetasa*. Santa Cruz de Tenerife: Interinsular Canaria,1957.

De Vega, Lope, *La Dragontea*. (1598), Madrid: Cátedra, 2007.

Espinosa García, Agustín, *Crimen*. Barcelona: Ediciones Ga, 1934.

García Cabrera, Pedro, *Liquenes* (1928) Madrid: Editorial Idea, 2005.

Guerra, Angel, *La Lapa*. Madrid: Cátedra, 1978.

Gunn, Robin Jones, *Canary Island Song*. Brentwood, TN: Howard Books, 2011.

Hood, Evelyn, *Destiny in Tenerife*. Sutton, UK: Severn House, 2011
Laforet, Carmen, *La Isla y los demonios*. Las Palmas: Editorial
    AduanaVieja,1952.
Lovelace, J. Timothy, *The Artistry and Tradition of Tennyson's Battle Poetry (in
    poems such as "The Revenge" and "Boudicea.")*. New York: Routledge,
    2003.
Padorno, Manuel, *A la sombra del mar*. Madrid: Ediciones Rialp, 1963
Stewart, Mary, *The Wind off the Small Isles*. London: Hodder & Stoughton,
    1968.
Tejera, Nivaria, *The Ravine*. New York: SUNY Press, 2009.
Thorne, Tony, *Tenerife: Tall Tales*. Pittsburgh, PA: Wortleberry Press, 2009.

GENERAL (HISTORY/TRAVEL)
Abreu Galindo, Juan, *History and Discovery of the Canary Islands*. (1682). New
    York: Elibron Classics, 1999.
Abulafia, David, *The Discovery of Mankind: Atlantic Encounters in the Age of
    Columbus*. London: Yale University Press, 2009.
Arias Marín de Cubas, *Historia de las siete Islas de Canaria*. (1687). Las Palmas
    de Gran Canaria: Real Sociedad Económica de los Amigos del País, 1986.
Berthelot, Sabin, *Histoire naturelle des Îles Canaries*. (1836). Las Palmas de Gran
    Canaria: Fundación Mapfre, 2006.
Berthelot, Sabin, *L'Ethnographie et les annales de la conquête des Iles Canaries*.
    Paris: Béthune, 1842.
Bernstein, William, *A Splendid Exchange: How Trade Shaped the World*. New
    York: Grove Press, 2008.
Bontier, Pierre, *Le Canarien: livre de la conquête et conversion des Canaries 1402-
    22*. Rouen: C. Métérie, 1874. English version: *The Canarian*. Trans.
    Richard Henry Major. Cambridge: Cambridge University Press, 2010.
Cairasco de Figueroa, Bartolomé, *Templo Militante*, (1613). Madrid:
    Universidad de Madrid, 2008.
Cioranescu, Alejandro, *Thomas Nichols, mercader de azúcar, hispanista y hereje*.
    Santa Cruz de Tenerife: Cabildo Insular de Tenerife, 1963.
Cólogan Soriano, Carlos, *Los Cólogan de Irlanda y Tenerife*. Santa Cruz de
    Tenerife: La Isla Libros, 2010.
Darwin, Charles, *Geological Observations on the Volcanic Islands and Parts of
    South America Visited during the Voyage of the H.M.S. Beagle*. London:
    Smith, Elder & Co, 1856.
D'Este, Margaret, *In the Canaries with a Camera*. London: Methuen & Co,
    1909.
De las Torres, Victoriano, *Carnet Guanche*. Las Palmas: Imprenta San Nicolás,
    1962.
Edwardes, Charles, *Rides and Studies in the Canary Islands*. (1888)
    IndyPublish.com, 2008.

Ellerbeck, J. H. T., *Madeira and the Canary Islands: Being Notes written to Illustrate certain Photographs and Lantern Slides taken.*London: Ellerbeck Bros., 1891

Espinosa, Alonso de, *Historia de Nuestra Señora de Candelaria.* (1590). Santa Cruz de Tenerife: Goya Ediciones, 1977.

Glas, George, *A Description of the Canary Islands.* (1682). New York: Elibron Classics, 1999.

González Lemus, Nicolas, "Relative to Visits paid by British Travellers to the Canary Islands." www.nicolasglemus.com, Oct. 2011.

Houellebecq, Michel, *Lanzarote.* London: Heinemann, 2003.

Latimer, Frances, *The English in the Canary Isles.* (1888). Whitefish, MT: Kessinger Legacy Reprint, 2012.

Leclerq, Jules Joseph, *Voyage aux Îles Fortunées, le Pic de Ténériffe et les Canaries.* (1880*).* Whitefish, MT: Kessinger Legacy Reprint, 2010.

Mason, John, *The Canary Islands.* London: B. T. Batsford, 1976.

Norton, John, *The Canary Islands, A Concise Guide for the Visitor.* London: Hale for the Union Castle Mailship Company, 1971.

Panthou, Patrick de, *Îles Canaries.* Paris: Hachette. 1964.

Piazzi Smyth, Charles, Teneriffe: *An Astronomer's Experiment or Specialities of a Residence Above the Clouds.* (1858). Cambridge: Cambridge University Press, 2010.

Schwartz, Stuart B. (ed.), *Tropical Babylons: Sugar and the Makings of the Atlantic World 1450-1680.* Chapel Hill, NC: University of North Carolina Press, 2004.

Thomas, Charles W., *Adventures and Observations on the West Coast of Africa, and its Islands. Historical and descriptive sketches of Madeira, Canary, Biafra and Cape Verde Islands.* (1860). London: Forgotten Books, 2013.

Vieira, Alberto, "The Fortune of the Fortunates: The Islands and the Atlantic System". CEHA (Centro de Estudios de Histórico do Atlantico). Funchal:1999, www.madeira-edu.pt/

Viera y Clavijo, Jose, *Noticias de la historia general de las Islas Canarias.* Santa Cruz de Tenerife: Imprenta y Litografía Isleña J. N. Romero, 1863.

Villanueva Jimenez, Jesús, *El Fuego de Bronce.*Madrid:Libroslibres. 2011.

Violan, Angeles, *Naif Guide to Canary Customs.* Tenerife: Ed. Zech, 2006.

Wendt, Herbert, *It Began in Babel.* New York: Houghton Mifflin, 1963.

Whiting, William B., *Andamana: the first Queen of Canary and her remarkable and successful coup d'etat.* New York: F. O. Jenkins, 1875.

Whitford, John, *The Canary Islands as a Winter Resort.* London: E. Stanford, 1890.

## NATURE AND WILDLIFE

Belcastel, Gabriel de, *Les Iles Canaries et la Vallée d'Orotava.* (1862). Nook Books (online publishers) paperback, 2012.

Clarke, A. G., Prion *Birdwatcher's Guide to the Canary Islands*. London: Prion, 1996.

Harris, Henry E., *Essays and Photographs. Some Birds of the Canary Islands and South Africa*. London: R. H. Porter, 1901.

Holt-White, A. E., *The Butterflies and Moths of Tenerife*. London: L. Reeve. 1894.

WEBSITES:

General Information:

www.gobiernodecanarias.org. Official island government office site (in Spanish)

www.visitcanaryislands.org.

www.canaries.angloinfo.com.

www.grancanaria.com

www.spain-tenerife.com

www.fuerteventura.com.

www.discoverlanzarote.com

www.tenerifeforum.org.es

Canary Island writers:

www.alangandy.com Author of *Walking the Canary Islands*

www.barriemahoney.com Las Palmas-based journalist

www.joecawley.co.uk and www.janetanscombe.com Tenerife-based journalists

# Index of Historical & Literary Figures

# Index of Places & Landmarks